THE LAST LIVING SLUT

THE LAST LIVING

Slüt

BORN IN IRAN

Bred Backstage

by ROXANA SHIRAZI

itbooks
AN IMPRINT OF HARPERCOLLINS PUBLISHERS

IGNITER LITERARY GROUP

*it***books**

A hardcover edition of this book was published in 2010 by It Books/Igniter, imprints of HarperCollins Publishers.

FIRST IT BOOKS/IGNITER PAPERBACK PUBLISHED 2011.

Designed by Meat and Potatoes, Inc. www.meatoes.com
Layout by Bahia Lahoud
Cover by Todd Gallopo
Condoms by Jeremy DiPaolo

The Library of Congress has catalogued the hardcover edition as follows:
Shirazi, Roxana.
The last living slut / Roxana Shirazi.—1st ed.
p.   cm.
1. Shirazi, Roxana.   2. Groupies—Biography.   I. Title.
ISBN 978-0-06-193135-2
ML429.S49A3   2010
781.66092—dc22

2010005842

ISBN 978-0-06-193136-9 (pbk.)

HB 07.28.2022

FOR TIGER. FOREVER.

I AM THE LOVE THAT DARE NOT SPEAK ITS NAME.

LORD ALFRED DOUGLAS, "TWO LOVES"

CONTENTS

INTROCUCTION

She stood there, alone, at the train crossing in San Clemente, California, an explosion of denim and hair extensions, with a battered laptop in her hands.

That was the first time we saw her.

She'd taken the train from Los Angeles to show us her manuscript. We were on deadline for our own books, so we said she had an hour.

Eight hours later, some friends had joined us and we were all sitting drunk in a cabin on the beach, listening rapt as Roxana Shirazi read portions of the tale that follows.

It was the best Saturday night we'd had in a while.

"Do you want me to stop?" she'd ask in her demure English accent.

"What else have you got?" we'd ask.

"There's the one where I got Avenged Sevenfold to pee on me."

"Yes, for God's sake. Read that one!"

At the time, this wasn't a book yet. It was a collection of detailed notes, essays, snapshots, and journal entries of her experiences in hotels, on tour buses, and backstage mingled with childhood reminiscences. And not only was each one riveting, shining a light into the trapdoors of the rock-and-roll circus, but it was told in such a unique voice. The writing was muscular, ornate, and unapologetic. This was a woman who was not a victim, but who made rock bands her victim—and got off on pushing them to extremes that made them uncomfortable. She believed the rock-and-roll myth, and when she was unable to find anyone who lived up to it, she chose to embody it herself. Until she made the mistake of falling in love with a rock star.

All of this, in addition to her disturbing sexual coming of age in Tehran in the midst of the Iranian revolution, gelled into a story we'd never heard before. At least not told like this.

We had to get it published.

We sent a few choice excerpts to several editors and agents. They all said that after reading them, they couldn't get the images out of their head. Yet they refused to put the book into print. Like the rock bands Shirazi had seduced, they said the book was out of their comfort zone. It was too much.

So we decided to put it out ourselves.

The Last Living Slut is a beautiful memoir of growing up in the political turbulence of Tehran; an unflinching portrait of teenage cultural dislocation in London; a backstage romp that makes Pamela Des Barres' *I'm With the Band* read like a nun's diary in comparison; a white-knuckled tale of jilted love and brutal revenge; and the most gripping real-life account of female depravity we've ever read.

The rockers mentioned in this book may still have the Polaroids, but you now have the images. And they are unforgettable. We promise you that.

—*Neil Strauss and Anthony Bozza*
  Igniter Books

A FEW THOUGHTS ON THE WORD "SLUT"

Quite simply[1], slut means an individual (although the word most commonly refers to females) who frequently engages in sexual activity[2] with a lot of partners.

When describing a male who frequently engages in sexual activity with a lot of partners, the words often used are stud, player, horndog, and so on—and sometimes male slut. However male slut is a label that men usually wear with pride; it is a term of approval and envy. A male who frequently has sex with a lot of partners is patted on the back, looked up to with admiration because he is merely carrying out a role that is assigned to him as a man. It is seen as a progressive step toward the development of masculinity. It is celebrated and encouraged. It is the equivalent of childish misbehaviour and being naughty.

With females, however, the disapproval is taken to the realm of stigmatization.

A female's pursuit of sexual pleasure and sexual adventure is still seen as a negative characteristic, somehow making her a bad human being. A female is not defined in terms of her humanity, but in terms of her sex life.

So, logically, does enjoying sex with different partners make someone a bad person? How can an individual's sex life define them wholly as a human being? Surely human beings should be measured by their human qualities and characteristics: kind-hearted, funny, lazy, expressive, determined, shy, mean, boring, bossy, happy-go-lucky, and so on.

Sex, even though it's just a small segment of our existence, is still such a beautiful, sensual experience, and exploring one's sexuality and sexual diversity should be respected and celebrated.

In this book, I am the last living "slut" embodying the negative meaning of the word, and the first living "slut" embodying a new, positive, and celebrated meaning of the word. Some will say that the word slut can never be independent from social and historical meanings attached to it (just like "nigger" or "queer") and will always be bound and steeped in the negative sense of the word, and thus there should be a new word to describe a sexually active and experimental individual to detach it completely from its previous meaning. Well, maybe, but in this book at least I have been conceited enough to give myself the authority to change the meaning of a word. Love your body, love your sexuality, and realize that you are a bad human being *only* if you are unkind and cruel and do harm unto others—and not because of your sex life.

—Roxana Shirazi

---

[1] As much as I would love to write about how gender is socially constructed—and how the concepts of masculine and feminine are merely *performances* that have been produced as truths and taught to us from birth—I have a story to begin.

[2] Please note that the term sex always means consensual sex. Any sexual act that is not consensual is not sex; it is an act of violence.

PROLOGUE

Donington Park, England
June 9

"Roxana wants to do the whole band," Tommy Lee says to Nikki Sixx, pointing at me. I sway between them, dressed in white linen and lace, eyes glistening with liquid warm honey, mouth parted like meat, body needing to be double-penetrated by these two rock legends.

"Mick would die," I murmur, mindful of Mick Mars' degenerative bone condition, yet relishing the headline that would accompany the act: "Death By Sex: Girl Kills Rock Star Mid-Fornication."

Vince Neil's vice for the day is two bone-brittle blondes, the type whose eating disorders are just another accessory. It's afternoon, high summer, and we're indoors under the intestinal-tube fluorescent lights by Mötley Crüe's dressing rooms at Download Festival. The reek of emo emanates from every corner as little boy bands slumber and lounge, all panda-eyed and girlie-haired. They are elfin boys with big ears and crayoned black liner proudly gunked on, who have scrawled *angst* and *pain* and *I hate my parents* on their striped tops. They pretend to be aloof on the steps of their porta-cabin dressing rooms, as if they don't notice the detonating presence of rock royalty—Mötley Crüe.

I drink Earl Grey tea from a frail cup as Tommy Lee offers to feed me Jägermeister. Teenage girls dressed in '50s diner-waitress chic look at him, all doe-eyed Pollyannas. They are fluff, chicken feed. And I shoo them away. Tommy kicks out the girls I brought for him because they look like groupies: all ripped fishnets and synthetic dresses. I speak Greek with him because he's half Greek. He is a hyperactive, kindhearted toddler on speed in a man's lanky, skinny, tattooed shell. He's toothy, and has dimples and a rasping gasoline voice that fucks me in the cunt.

But I want Nikki Sixx, my Elvis, inside me as well.

"I'm a squirter," I tell Sixx.

"We like that, don't we, Tommy?" he says, his voice a gooey slur, marinated in decades of distilled degeneracy.

Tommy takes me to his dressing room and locks the door as his bodyguard assumes the position outside. He cranks up the techno music he's so in love with to gangrene-inducing levels.

"Can't you put Mott the Hoople on instead?" I beg him.

"This is the music to fuck to! Fuck yeah!" Tommy says, bouncing around like a hyper child. "I wanna see you squirt, Miss Wet!"

He is so bossy, ordering me with that gravelly roar of his. I obey, spreading my legs from beneath the lovely puffy cotton dress my mum bought me. I never wear knickers. It's been a habit since girlhood.

Tommy's eyes eager-up like a boy wolf. I spread my pussy wide open and dildo myself so I can ejaculate all over Tommy's lucky floor. "Is Nikki coming too?" I wish it were 1983, when they were rock's most cretinous band.

Tommy, eyes ablaze, plays with me and kisses my flower. I'm so fucking horny. I wanna get double-fucked by Tommy and Nikki. I go to find Sixx.

Nikki tells me to be patient. He wants me to himself when he's back in England.

London, England

Two Months Later

"You sound so angelic," Nikki Sixx says.

"I can be a whore in the bedroom later if you want," I reply.

"So do you and Livia come as a team?"

His voice is nasal and bookish-sounding, and it drags on like syrup. I cannot believe I'm talking to Nikki Sixx on the phone. I am a very lucky girl.

"I'm starving. When are you getting here?" Nikki says.

"Soon ... soon."

"Come to the hotel. I'm waiting. Hurry up!"

My heart is alive, full of the moon. I am going to dinner with Nikki Sixx. Little old me: the Iranian refugee girl with the mustache. The biggest nerd at school, the one who lost her virginity at twenty-four. Suddenly all the others—all the Sunset Strip nobody musicians, the has-beens, the never-wases, the ones who fucked my heart—don't matter. They have no meaning. Nikki Sixx is waiting for me.

In the taxi on the way to his room, I feel like a coronary is coming on. Livia tries to calm me down in her flowery way. She isn't fazed by all this. To her, Nikki Sixx might as well be John Regularsmith from the local chippie.

Livia is a model. She is ravishing. We both look like stars. Not too revealing, not too modest. Gleaming, coiffed, perfumed, and moisturized. She, a blond Marilyn; me, a raven Ava Gardner.

Nikki is waiting in the St. Martins Lane Hotel lobby. His feline, aquamarine eyes slant like a jaguar's; jagged, jet-black hair tumbles and crashes over them. I know a lot of people who would give their kidney or an important finger to be in his presence. I am overwhelmed. I try to be civilized and not spontaneously lactate as my femininity begins to open up like a lotus flower. We hug and kiss and go to dinner.

On the way to the restaurant, my hair flusters and shimmies in the gusty winds and rain of August in London. I listen to Nikki talk about his life and watch him give American hundred-dollar bills to every homeless person we pass. I wonder if he is a lonely spirit, no longer a legend of rock-and-roll excess: Having committed every foul and abominable degenerate and depraved act to man, woman, and self—dying twice in the process from heroin overdoses—what does he have now? Who is he?

"That's just marketing. It's business," he insists adamantly about his image. I am instantly deflated.

"You should have worn flat shoes. Those heels are gonna hurt your feet." He points at my PVC-gleaming, dagger stilettos as we enter the trendy, paparazzi-infested restaurant Nobu.

"Okay," I mutter in disappointment, tottering on with no knickers underneath my miniskirt.

Livia looks at me. She is a dream come true: Innocent Lolita sexuality, natural blond hair toppling over her face, wide blue eyes smiling back at Nikki. I wonder if he even has sex anymore, or if it all died within him like some lost, sodden memory of a past life. I hope he does, and I hope he wants us; that way I'll also get to fuck Livia, whose porcelain body I've been reluctant to touch for fear of shattering it.

I eat oysters and massage Nikki's shoulders. "I want to get into gardening," he says with such pleasure that I imagine him daydreaming such things as he sits in his Malibu mansion, the lonely rock icon. I try to engage in the conversation, but I know jack-shit about gardening. Instead I talk about the residue of '80s hair bands: Ratt, L.A. Guns, Faster Pussycat. But Nikki knows jack-shit about what's going on in the old-school rock world these days.

I tell him about my ultimate teenage sexual fantasy: being double-penetrated by him and Axl Rose.

"Oh really?" His eyes spark. "And what did you move on to after that?"

"Porn, of course," I say.

He nonchalantly tells me that he likes to sit at home and masturbate. "Date rape," he calls it. His voice is a monotone drag. And yet he is somehow interesting, like a good magazine: packed full of information and detail. We talk about his desire to travel to my home country of Iran, spirituality, and the weather—at which point he turns suddenly around to face me. His chin points, inquisitively like a teacher, and he asks: "Why don't you have a boyfriend?"

I swallow a bite of the funny-looking raw fish he ordered.

A dreaded feeling—one I thought had evaporated from my heart—suddenly surges into my head. I don't think. I swallow. I tell the truth.

"Because I fall in love."

PART 1

HOME

ME, MY MOTHER
& GRANDMOTHER

There is the band. Any band. Standing there—three towers of high, acid-blond spikes and two raging, dark manes. Bare chests, eyeliner, leather, sweat, I-wanna-fuck-you-baby attitude. Guitars and bass and drums and twenty-five-year-old testosterone penetrate the air like hard-core porn. They face their adoring audience, which gazes up at them from the black mass.

There are the young: a bubbling cauldron of pasty white necks straining inside midnight clothing. Fashions bought from Camden on a Saturday afternoon, some baggy to hide their youthful chubbiness. They have zebra tights and matted hair in flaccid ponytails, black liner tracing their Red Bull–vodka eyes. The girls' breasts, at least, are firm, all puppy fat and tender skin. The heat sends the aroma of laundry soap off their logoed clothing and into the fetid air, mixing with beer and young sweat. In their emo gear, they will scream the lyrics. And then they will go home to bedrooms tucked safely in suburbia, their walls full of posters and angst, their floors carpeted with crushed cans of Red Bull. They will lie there, in awe of the night.

Then there are the hunters, predators hiding in corners, slim and sleek like cats in heat. Tight corsets and slit skirts, hair tidy-messy and obvious. Sapphire eyes, wolf-shaped and sprinkled with glitter lash from a box. They're seductive but haughty as a pearl necklace, pouting with arched eyebrows. They want the lead guitarist because "he's hot." Their vicious heels and fish-cold faces are emotionless, but their cheekbones could cut glass. Ready to pounce to the rhythm of their night's strategy, discussed, planned, and dissected in hushed tones in the jaundiced light of the chicks' toilets, gazing in mirrors covered in lipstick marks, paper tissue, and longing so intense it burns like lava.

Of course there is always the older groupie mafia, whose compulsory sedate demeanor nevertheless reeks of a still-rabid desire to get them *some rocker meat* for the night. They hang around, defeated and heavier, packed into denim. They have sucked and chewed, fucked and crashed their way through all the other sleaze hair rockers of the '80s that were spawned by Mötley Crüe. They went on actual dates with them before they were married and divorced and married again. They have the original stories of broken hearts, and the hazy bloated memories and scars to prove them. Their sallow bodies are awash in whiskey and sperm. The flickering light catches the hard lines on their faces. At forty-something years old, they're desperate, angry, ready to push these younger girls outta the way. Without this world, they would be nothing. This is their identity.

The older boys are always at the front, with sagging tattoos and hackneyed talk of the good old days. They want to catch the shit hitting them in the face, the head, whatever. It takes them away *that* much from their two-by-fours and kids' packed lunches and PTA meetings. Their once-long hair is now in violent retreat. But they saw it all: the Pistols, Sabbath, the Sweet, the rest. They saw the blood, the shit, the razors and needles, the vomit, the pretty little chickens. This is beautiful, like their morning wood at fourteen and the spotty teenage-boy need for getting laid that came with it. They know all the songs and try to make every gig. The cash they spend on seeing bands is supposed to be milk money for their children, but this is their life, their blood, their every happiness. Just like me. Because rock 'n' roll is my type O.

When all your thoughts and emotions are consumed by rock 'n' roll and all your actions are dependent on the movements of a rock band, then your life becomes like that of a junkie. The blood that rushes through your veins, the breath that catches your throat, your tears, your cash, your enormous love, your brainwaves, your perfume, your orgasms . . . everything. *Everything.* But it's all an illusion: the love you feel so passionately, the bond of friendship, the endless hotel rooms, the emotional support you give and take, the food you eat, your guttural hollers of ecstasy, your jealousy, your thirst. The exhaustion and the cold and the heat, the heels that swat your skin, the condoms you use and don't use, the STD tests, the locked jaw. It is a high, a new realm, a space you can enter without warning or awareness. And it can become your pulse, permeate your genetic makeup. This I know.

When it does, suddenly all the decisions you make are not entirely yours. And you don't know how it happened. You have little control over your emotions and actions. And it's all because of a rock-and-roll band.

This is my life.

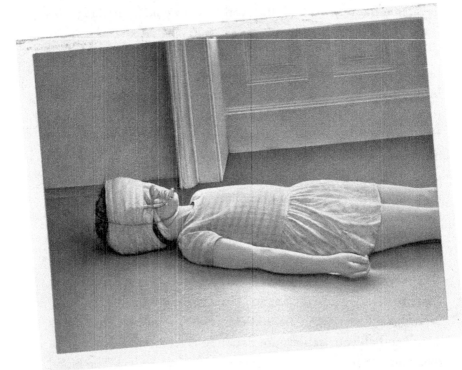

I WAS A CHILD BASKED IN GUNFIRE, ISLAMIC LAW, AND SEXUALITY

was born in a military hospital in Tehran, Iran. My mother was a twenty-four-year-old political activist who'd chosen the Russian-run hospital as a nod to socialism, the political movement she'd aligned herself with in her resistance to Shah Mohammad Reza Pahlavi's regime. I was born into a totalitarian society with little social and political freedom, where only the Shah and the ruling elite benefited from the country's wealth while ordinary people didn't have access to decent health care and education.

As soon as her belly swelled, my mother knew I was going to be a girl. She just didn't know how naughty I was going to be. When her water broke, my eighteen-year-old aunt proudly accompanied her to the hospital. Once inside, my mother learned that the hospital's sanitized and celebrated reputation was a sham: it was an institution of clinical cruelty. My mother was in labor for sixteen hours—my head was so big that I couldn't easily come out—but labor drugs were strictly against hospital policy, regardless of the situation. Instead, the nurses believed in discipline, so they slapped and kicked my mother to make her push harder. They screamed and shouted at her to get on with it. A fine mist of blood rose on the veins of my mum's milk-white neck. At one point during the ordeal, my mum thought about running out of there with me still inside her. But before she could, she passed out on the table.

I was born in the early hours of the morning. The nurses whisked me away to prevent physical contact with my mother, which was also against hospital policy. They left her alone, lying on the operating table in the vacant room without water for three hours. Unable to get up, she resorted to licking droplets of sweat from her face.

Every day for a week, the nurses brought me to my mother for five minutes of breastfeeding, convinced that their military regimen was for the good of the patient.

A few weeks after I was born, my eighteen-year-old aunt and uncle were arrested, tortured, and interrogated for being anti-Shah activists. From that day until the revolution in 1979, various friends and members of my mother's family were constantly getting arrested for their political beliefs and activities. My mother and I made countless trips to Tehran's notorious Evin Prison to catch a glimpse of them behind bars.

My first childhood home belonged to my grandmother, Anneh. It was there, in the middle of Iran's revolution and the subsequent war with Iraq, that I remained, basked in pure love and happiness during the terror of revolutionary gunfire, Islamic law, and my initiation into sexuality.

CHAPTER

3

I was six months old when I went to prison with my mum. It was only for twenty-four hours, but it was enough to affect her for a long time.

My grandmother, my mum, and I were at home one afternoon when the SAVAK, the Shah's secret police, broke down the door. There were four or five of them. I was in my mum's arms as she watched them break and tear everything apart in my grandmother's house, looking for leaflets, literature, books, and any other anti-Shah paraphernalia that would prove my mother was a political activist. My mum's face was sheet-white. I screamed while my grandmother prayed in the corner.

"Get up. You're coming with us," the men barked at my mum.

Though she obeyed, she insisted that she had to bring me, my nappies, and my milk bottle. They marched her, with me in her arms, to a car waiting outside and sat on either side of us as they drove to Komiteh Moshtarak Zed-e-Kharaabkaari Prison, used by the SAVAK for interrogation. Once inside the prison, my mum was blindfolded and led along a hallway, still carrying me. When they took off her blindfold, she saw that she was in a small room. They left her there overnight, where she watched me sleep as she awaited her fate.

The next morning, she was taken to an interrogation room and I was handed to the guards. She was petrified that she'd be raped, tortured, and killed, and there'd be no one left to take care of my grandmother and me. Fortunately, the interrogator was lenient. He questioned my mum about her and her brothers' political activities. She must have convinced him she didn't know anything, because suddenly he snapped at her to get out. She grabbed me from the guards, ran out, and found a taxi to take us to the safety of our home.

❧

I led a fairy-tale existence in the sunshine-soaked dusty back alleys of Narmak, a small, up-and-coming lower-middle-class neighborhood in northeast Tehran. I played day and night in the alley outside my grandmother's ancient two-story house.

The air outside was arid, and smelled of trees and dry clay. In the summer at about five P.M., after their afternoon siestas, the adults would soak the scorched ground of their doorstep with splashes of cold water, and the air would dampen with the smell of just-rained-on ground.

The house had a vast roof. On blazing hot summer nights, like everyone else in the neighborhood, my grandmother, my mother, and I would put our bedding outside and sleep under the stars that crammed the raw Persian sky. We slept in a *pasheh-band*, a white gauze tent that kept the insects away. It was held up by nails in the squat wall surrounding the rooftop. In the night, I'd see chimneys like gap teeth in the blackness, and hear the low hum of the neighbors' murmurs and velvety laughter coming from their rooftops.

In our home, there were four small spaces on the ground floor sectioned off as rooms by a wall in the middle. Just past the front door was a small foyer with nothing except a gold-leafed mirror, a telephone, and a storage cupboard for stacking bedding sheets and duvets—this was our reception area. Just past it was a room with biscuit-fragile windows and a glass door that led into the garden, the window frames all painted in the same chipped lemon-yellow paint. This room was where my mother and I—and sometimes my aunt and cousin—slept on yards and rolls of cotton sheets and puffy rose pillows that my grandmother had kept immaculate for years. On the other side of the wall was a living room with an old clunky black heater that let out foul fumes. The room had sliding doors to create a space for my great-grandmother to sleep at night. With her raven-black braids hanging to her knees, she'd sit in a dark corner of that space, vacant with Alzheimer's, dressed always in a long white gown, a lone figure staring ahead.

Every inch of the downstairs floor was covered in layers of thick Persian carpets, which crashed into one another like watercolor waves. Intricate squiggles, flowers, and curves exploded in a frenzied dance on electric turquoise, deep browns, and shameless reds, hypnotizing me. I'd sit there trying to make sense of their designs but eventually give in, preferring to join them, lie on them, kiss them.

The second floor was unoccupied. It had two rooms, one with its own balcony overlooking the garden, an ancient kitchen, and a decaying bathroom. Gray stone steps led to the ground floor, which was where we lived. The front door was short but thick. It was never locked. Instead, it stayed open to let in the constant stream of relatives and neighbors who ate, slept, gossiped, loved, cried, and laughed with us. Immediately to the left of the main door was a tiny bathroom with a porcelain squat toilet and a shower.

Next to that was the crumbling kitchen where my grandmother sat amid a palace of pots and pans, creating the most intoxicating carnival of dishes: *ash-e reshteh, ghormeh sabzi, zereshk polo, sholeh zard,* and my favorite, *koofteh tabrizi,* from the northern city of Tabriz where my mother's family was from. The dish is a heap of minced meat mixed with crushed walnuts, tarragon, and *zereshk* (tiny dried sour berries) and rolled into a massive, round meatball with a boiled egg planted in its delicious heart after it's cooked.

The kitchen where my grandmother cooked had a dungeon-like cellar. It was a place of dread, accessible only through an iron hatch hidden under a rug. One day curiosity got the better of me and I slipped my fingers through the bars of the hatch and lifted it. I peered into a bottomless black hole. Climbing down the greasy cloth-bound ladder, I could feel the presence of monsters waiting for me. The cold air gripped my head and seeped into my widened eye sockets as I struggled to see in the pitch-black. My feet touched the ground and I stood there, shivering with cold and fear, terror and repulsion swimming through my wrists and throat as I awaited some unspeakable horror.

I knew there must be rats and cockroaches crawling everywhere, but I just stood there like a scarecrow in my thin cotton dress, letting the thrill of fear give me a fantastic rush in my tummy. I didn't dare walk around in case I bumped into something—maybe even my dead grandfather. (An uncle had once told me that his body lay down there among the musty papers from the past.) After a minute or two, when I couldn't stand it any longer, I climbed back up the ladder, to the light and warmth. My soul and heart embraced and fed on the thrill I'd experienced. So whenever I felt the yearning, on silent afternoons, I would tiptoe once again to the kitchen, lift the heavy, cold, iron hatch, and climb down so I could see beyond my world. Sometimes I even felt a sense of holiness elevate me in those confines. My grandmother would always call after me, but in my mind I was far away, ready to be transported to the dark side.

I FOUND SHELTER IN HER LAP AND HEAVEN IN HER PROTECTION.

y grandmother was goddess-like in her aura. Her motherly instinct extended to everyone she encountered. Her nickname, Anneh, means *mother* in northern Persian dialect. Her lungs racked by years of asthma and her heart swollen by unconditional love, she constantly gave her energy and time to the people in her life. She always worked hard to ensure that the banquet of dishes she carefully prepared delighted everyone. Sunny by nature, she relished life, always dancing and laughing. The sheer pleasure she took from the smallest things—like selecting shades and textures of cloth for dress-making—gave her pure joy.

"My home is everybody's home," she'd say, glowing with pride while dishing out dinners to random relatives and neighbors who dropped by. Sadly, though, as her eyesight faded, she sometimes made little mistakes in the kitchen—like adding sugar to the stew when she meant to use salt. And the antiquated horsepills her doctor prescribed for her asthma thinned her skin. Over time, we would see her veins, bulging and blue, swimming beneath the translucent white skin of her frail hands, decorated by a treasured ruby ring her children had given her on Mother's Day. "One day it's going to be yours, my princess," she'd say whenever I tried to play with it.

Still, she remained beautiful, with chestnut brown hair fashioned in a bob and honey eyes glistening with natural seductiveness, just like my mother's. "*Ashraf khanoom*, you're always dressed so chic," I'd hear women tell her at *mehmoonis* (family parties). "Is it from Paris?" They'd sniff around her bags and dresses, and she'd always end up giving away one thing or another.

Even though this was the peak of the Shah's rule, a time when Westernization was being heavily promoted, she still covered her body with a long, flowery *chador*—the Islamic head-and-body covering—when she went out of the house. She didn't do it for religious purposes but strictly because she liked tradition.

TEHRAN, IN GRANDMOTHER'S GARDEN

People gathered at our house at night, and Anneh always started the dancing, getting everyone on their feet to move to the Iranian pop songs blasting from the cassette player. She was happy, always singing, always full of light. She welcomed everyone into our home with such genuine love and warmth that I wondered if anything ever really upset her. I found shelter in her lap and heaven in her protection when I put my head against her fat tummy, hearing the clutter of her insides and sniffing the faint smell of her Western perfume, while my mother went to work every day teaching teenagers at the local school.

My mother had a psychology degree and taught literature, psychology, and Arabic, leaving early in the morning and coming back at dusk. She had gone back to work four weeks after giving birth so she could provide for me and my grandmother. Sometimes her breast milk seeped through her shirt mid-lecture.

In many ways, my mother was the opposite of my grandmother. Even though she was only in her mid-twenties, she was serious, quiet, and pensive—and an active revolutionary. She'd rush home from work and demonstrations to do chores, pay bills, find doctors, and fix the home.

"Don't forget the duck-shaped bread," I would yell after her as she left the house. She never did forget to bring back a piece of duck-shaped brioche. I remember waiting for that bread with uncontrollable joy rushing through my body.

My mother shunned makeup and fancy clothes, embracing simplicity and somber colors as a revolutionary stance. The only beauty routines she adored were ironing her hair fire-poker straight with the household iron and waxing her legs to gleaming marble smoothness with homemade wax.

"Here, help me rip these sheets, my darling," she said one afternoon, looking up from the fraying garments strewn around her on the floor, gooey, yellow, hot wax on her leg and spatula in hand. *Rip, rip, rip*, went the old sheets to become strips for her legs. I watched my mother squeal in pain for the sake of beauty as she applied and then ripped the cotton strips away.

"I wanna do it!" I whined. I wanted to be glamorous, too.

"Not until you're twenty," my mother snapped, tending to her slim white legs. She wanted me to be a child, not to rush into womanhood. But by the age of five I already loved makeup. I was obsessed with dressing up in the latest fashions, and desperately wanted platform shoes and flared trousers.

I screamed and howled, driving my poor mother to tears. As far as I was concerned, it was detrimental to my existence to be denied a pair of platform shoes. And my mother went mad if I touched makeup, so when she was off at work and my grandmother had her afternoon siesta, I would sneak into my grandmother's makeup bag and cream on her neon-pink lipstick and chalk on nightclub-blue eye shadow.

We hardly had any money, but I was a spoiled princess. Everyone in my family doted on me, especially my grandmother, who bought me so many dolls that they overtook the living room and made for quite a lively tea party. Still, I stamped my feet and cried through my whistling snotty nose because it wasn't enough. I wanted her to buy me a bride doll that I'd seen in a shop window.

Even then, I always wanted more than I had.

very morning, after my mother left for work, my grandmother and I began our day. First I'd run to the neighborhood bakery to get *nooneh sangak*—a foot-long triangular bread the man would bake while I watched. They would throw a slab of dough into the clay oven. It was still steaming when they brought it out, with tiny stones from the oven clinging to its underside. As they folded it, they would tell me to watch my fingers, but I didn't care; I let the hot bread sting my mouth as I gobbled it down while running back to the house.

When I got home, we'd have breakfast sitting around the *sofreh*— an oil cloth spread on the floor for serving food—or sit by the fishpond in the garden. On the sofreh, feta cheese, herbs, fresh double cream, honey, and sour cherry jam were laid out with the hot tea. My grandmother brewed tea in the *samovar*, an hourglass-shaped decorative metal container that boiled water as steam escaped from its head, allowing the tea to brew slowly.

After the dawn prayer, an old, toothless lady by the name of Masha Baiim would come by most mornings to help my grandmother around the house. Her face was a brown, weathered map etched with deep lines. She had the patience of a saint and long black hair, which she wore in two braids hanging by her waist like rope. I was generally horrible to her, giving her hell and the occasional bite on the arm when she wouldn't let me do the things I wanted to do.

After breakfast, I would go out to play with my friends in the alley. All the neighbors in the little houses knew one another. Our mud alley was always sunny and orange. Then we would roam the *maidoon*—or square—in the center of the neighborhood. In Tehran, every square had a number and was the social hub of the surrounding area.

By the time the sound of noon prayer wailed from the nearby mosque, the neighborhood buzzed with activity. The first to arrive was the salt seller, an old man who hobbled through the alley croaking "*Namaki! Namaki!*" ("Salt seller! Salt seller!") and selling the raw rock salt he carried in a sack on his bent back. A few women would bring out scraps of dried bread, leftover food, or sometimes unwanted clothes to exchange for a piece of rock salt. I remember feeling lucky that I wasn't as poor as the salt seller, whose skinny face would break into a humble, toothless grin as he collected the goods and sauntered off to the next street.

We played until the traders arrived at noon with their cartfuls of merchandise. In the winter, the beetroot seller wheeled his cart to a stop at the top of the alley. I would run to get coins from my grandmother. Peeling off the dirty outer layer of the cooked beet would expose the steaming hot flesh beneath. My teeth sliced through the chunks and I let the hot juice wash over my gums. The tamarind man was there year-round, selling us lovely sour-salty tamarind. In the spring came a man with *gojeh sabz*—small unripe sour green plums—which we would sprinkle with salt and eat until our stomachs ached.

Sometimes, in the middle of a hopscotch game, the cinema-rama man would appear. He'd wheel in a big box. We'd put coins in, look in a peephole, and be transported to another world. A world of corseted ladies with pink boas, fancy lace, and exotic hairbrushes. When the time ran out, we'd beg the adults for more money so we could exist just a little longer in *Shahreh Farang* (foreign city). I'd peer into it so deeply that my left eye would be bruised. And then my coins would run out.

"You can't have money for this *and* the wheel!" my mother or grandmother would say, looking up from their work cleaning fresh herbs for dinner. I loved the mini Ferris wheel that rolled into the alley once or twice a week. It always drew a massive crowd, even though the top of the wheel rose only ten feet off the ground. It felt grand to sit in those old moldy seats in the sky.

Throughout the day, the sound of mournful prayer from the loudspeaker of a nearby mosque served as a fearful reminder to pray to God. In our home, my grandmother would promptly put on her chador and turn to face Mecca, the holy city. A deep and respectful silence would fall over the neighborhood as the grown-ups gathered their prayer mats and *Mohr*—a small chunk of holy clay that supposedly came directly from Mecca.

Some days, during the siesta that followed, I played alone in my grandmother's garden. I felt like a princess there: the garden was my court, the fruit trees ready to serve me. A pomegranate tree, which opened her baby pink flowers in summer, showed the world she was ready to bear autumn fruit. Next to it stood a sour cherry tree—my favorite. Lifting the hem of my dress, I would pluck the tiny cherries and gather them in my skirts. I was greedy for that fruit, even more than the blackbirds who competed with me to fill their bellies first.

At the end of the garden wall rose the tallest fir tree I had ever seen. Its trunk was so wide and its branches so dense with pines that it provided a shield for me and my cousins' childhood games.

On the left side of the garden were the roses—pink, yellow, and white. Puffy roses. Scarlet buds pursing their lips to the sky in a kiss. Right in the middle of the yard was a small round pond filled with goldfish and green slimy moss. Often I would undress and float naked under the water, holding my breath as long as I could to feel the slither of the fish and slippery moss against my chest and tummy. My cinnamon ringlets were soaked but, soon enough, the crisp Persian sun would toast them dry as I sunbathed naked on the concrete.

"Put some panties on! Bad girl!" my grandmother or mum would scold in a loud whisper if they caught me. But I loved the feeling of my body exposed in the water and the sun. I wanted to be free.

When the adults awoke from the siesta, it was time for early evening tea, which was exactly like breakfast. In the summer we enjoyed tea in the garden. Then, in the evening, everyone put on fancy clothes to go mehmooni, visiting relatives' houses to eat, dance, and have a good time. My mother usually took me to see her sister and my cousins in Foozieh, a seedy part of town that smelled like sewage. We stood by the road and shouted our destination at the orange taxis speeding by—the customary way to flag down a cab—until one stopped and we climbed in, sharing a ride with others headed that way.

Most of the men in my mother's family were political prisoners, leaving the women alone with their children and forced to stay with their parents or in-laws. My aunt's husband was a political prisoner along with my uncle and my mother's cousins. Day and night, the adults would sit talking about the political situation. In the 1970s, Iran emerged as one of the oil giants of the Middle East and the Shah established himself as a monarch, with a plan to Westernize our society. By 1973, Tehran was considered one of the world's most innovative capital cities, with religion operating on the fringes. Scores of villagers and farmers filtered into Tehran to take advantage of the prosperity promised to them by the Shah. But government corruption ensured that the promised trickle-down of wealth only pooled around government officials and friends of the Shah. The gap between rich and poor rapidly grew wider.

Soon, due to a lack of jobs and housing, an abundance of shantytowns, teeming with disenfranchised villagers and farmers, sprouted up around Tehran. As unrest spread through the citizenry, the ruling body hardened into an even more stringent military dictatorship. The Shah imprisoned anyone with opposing views, and stripped away civil liberties and the right to strike. Freedom of speech and the press were eliminated, and anti-Shah activity was punishable by torture, imprisonment, and even execution. The Shah activated his own secret police—the SAVAK—who ramped up terror by raiding homes believed to house anti-Shah literature and arresting all suspects encountered on the way.

In this turbulent political state, dozens of resistance groups sprang up, many of them with multiple branches. Their ideologies may have differed in their particulars, but they were united in one objective: to overthrow the Shah's military dictatorship and bring freedom and social equality to the people of Iran.

As public unrest and anti-Shah demonstrations increased, so did the gunfire in the streets. My grandmother's house began to turn into a base for intensifying political activity. The SAVAK raided houses in our neighborhood daily. And life became more hazardous.

MY MUM

I SOON REALIZED THAT IT WAS OPIUM THAT WAS THE LOVE OF MY FATHER'S LIFE, AND THAT HE'D GRADUALLY BECOME BORED OF ME.

 wasn't aware of what a father was until I began to notice that other children had a man as another parent and I did not. There was a tall, thin, quiet man with tinted glasses and a mustache who came to visit me once in a while. He was nice to me, but I didn't know how he fit into the tightly woven pattern of my family. He stuck out in my family like a salted pretzel stick in a candy store. He was unlike anyone I had ever met.

Whenever my father visited our house, I'd grow shy and hide from him. My grandmother was nice to him, but I noticed that he and my mum hardly spoke. It didn't cross my mind to wonder why he didn't live with us the way other Daddies lived with Mummies. I figured he must have liked me since he made an effort to talk to me. But my childhood instinct told me that he did it out of obligation, not because he wanted to. So I scowled and didn't say much back to him.

He was good-looking and distant, like a film star. And he was quiet and always seemed unhappy. So I put on my best dresses hoping he would notice and want to spend more time with me. As I became aware that he was my father—my daddy, someone who should love me—I acted coy and dressed prettily because that's how girls got the things they wanted. He would pick me up for scheduled visits and take me to the nearby park, *Haft Hoz* (Seven Lakes), to buy cooked liver from the street vendors and go on the mini Ferris wheel. Once, when my stomach was upset and I had diarrhea, he took me to the bathroom; I was very embarrassed that he should see me in such odious circumstances.

Often, my father took me to his sister's house nearby, where he lived with his mother and younger brother. I remember thinking that my three cousins were noisy and naughty children, not refined at all. But I loved playing with my girl cousin, dressing up in chic ladies' dresses and heels. Still, I never smiled in the photos we took on those visits. "Who's this girl here scowling like a donkey?" my father would drawl, pointing at me in the pictures. It was the only time I saw him express anything close to emotion.

I adored my father's family: my aunts and uncles and cousins. They were lovely, kind, and fun to be around. But I just didn't feel like smiling. I was a bad child, like my dad said. My father's family enjoyed simple things, like watching movies and eating food together. It was an alien Disneyland. Simple pleasures and laid-back indulgences constituted the family foundation, unlike my mother's home where everyone was a political activist.

Though my father's visits came less and less frequently with time, I still waited for him at the door, ready in my best flowery cotton dress, my tight ringlets freshly shampooed and clipped out of my face. When he didn't show up, I would chastise myself. "I'm not pretty enough," I'd think. "I'm too boring for him." Eventually, my grandmother would shout at me to give up and come in.

"He probably got ill or something," she'd say. "Maybe there was an accident."

"But when he telephoned, he said he was coming. He *will* come." I believed in him, because surely my daddy was a nice man. He had to be. I never cried at the huge wall of hurt and disappointment that secretly overwhelmed my heart when this man who was supposed to be my father didn't show up or call when he promised. And on those rare occasions when he did, he was grouchy and silent.

I soon began overhearing the adults talking about opium, and how it was something that men did—especially older men, like taxi drivers. I soon realized that opium was the love of my father's life and that he'd gradually become bored of me, because I was a nerdy girl who was not fun.

But my father wasn't the only adult in my life, and I found comfort in other adults, who often told me I was a pretty girl. I began to seek attention from other males—boys my own age or older relatives. I grew determined to make them like me by becoming the most beautiful girl they had ever seen. This soon formed the backbone of my sense of self. It became my armor and made me happy.

The less I saw of my father, though, the more I longed for him. I closed my eyes and fantasized that he would pick me up and smile, take me to interesting places and laugh. He became a fantasy figure, like the seasoned movie star he resembled. Eventually, though, I grew tired of waiting for him, and my fantasies turned to the soldiers on television.

he first time I masturbated was winter, just before the revolution. I was about five years old, and there was a constant stream of men in uniforms invading my daily life. The spectacle of the SAVAK, who terrified me, gave me a delicious dark thrill that hit me in my gut in a way it wasn't supposed to. I found myself attracted to the soldiers on the streets and on TV, parading with authority, with power.

One afternoon, it came exploding out of me. I was watching the news. The marching troops were so awesome, so powerful, that I gave in. Crawling under the *korsi* (a low table covered in blankets with a heater attached), I squeezed my eyes really tight and pictured soldiers walking up to me one by one as I lay naked on a dirt road. They each leaned over and looked at my body, admiring it and wanting me. I got a funny feeling in my tummy when I thought of that. A dangerous, powerful explosion washed over my little body and made me feel like a queen. A feeling of urgency overwhelmed me. So I put my hands in my panties and touched myself where it throbbed. I had found a secret and it would take me to a place of ethereal and majestic beauty—my beautiful secret world. I felt higher than anyone else. I felt invincible.

All my first cousins were boys. They teased and chased me constantly, and I began to love it more and more. They were the first people I'd found whom I could actually seek out to receive male attention. I began dressing deliberately in my best girlie clothes, swaying my hips and flirting as I walked out on the street to play. I had a huge crush on the slightly older twin boys who lived next door. In my attempts to get them to like me and want me, I did what worked: I acted coy and needy, even though I was really quite a tomboy.

One summer afternoon, while all the adults slept, I asked the twins to teach me to tie my shoelaces. I sat at the bottom of the stone steps leading to the second floor of our house, and slid up my skirt to reveal my bare legs. As they stood over me, I lifted one leg up to them so they would see all the way up to the top of my thigh. Then, slowly, they taught me to tie my laces. Their skin felt hot on mine. And I felt loved.

CHAPTER

8

HE SHOWS ME CARTOONS AND TAKES ME PLACES. MY DAD NEVER DOES THAT AND SO I GAVE HIM SEX IN RETURN.

 walked up the massive jaw of stone gray steps. Up, up, to the second floor. Looking down, I saw my candy-pink nail-varnished toenails poking through my plastic slippers. Still I carried on, my heart beating with excitement and the dirty shame of the duty I had to perform. I was a bad girl. I would go to hell. Definitely. I was five years old.

The man was renting the apartment from my grandmother. He was single and full of energy. He had thick black-rug hair and was playful with me. His name was Mr. Karimi. I played with him all the time. In the afternoons, he let me ride in his white Peykan car, which shook and prattled, the engine's wet purring guzzling greedily around the sunny, sleeping neighborhood.

My grandmother was sleeping downstairs. My mummy was at work at the university. I couldn't wait till she came back with the duck bread. I wanted to go outside. I was dying to steal some fruit from the neighbor's persimmon tree. The fat bellies of the pregnant fruit were ready to burst. I wanted to pick monkey flowers with the other girls and chase the twin boys next door.

I didn't know why I liked Mr. Karimi. His room was dark and he prayed all the time. I didn't understand why. He always said I should pray with him, and sometimes I did. I loved the smell of the Mohr. It smelled like the heavenly damp clay of the rain-soaked ground. I loved the safe feeling of throwing the slippery chador around my head and body, and I loved praying to God. It was peaceful. I'd learned all the prayers by heart, but only the shorter children's versions.

Karimi finished praying and smiled at me. Then he called me into the room. A golliwog sat on the shelf with a big head full of tight, black curls. Its puffed-up lips were like two sausages, and it had a pair of bulging eyes inside a nodding head. Karimi turned the wall projector on. It was Bugs Bunny. He drew the curtains shut and closed the door, then locked it with a key. In the silence I heard only the warm humming of the projector and the thumping of my heart.

Karimi sat me on his lap facing the wall. On the screen, Bugs Bunny jumped up and down like a demented yo-yo. *I love cartoons. Karimi must like me.* He let me watch them because he liked the special place between my legs, the soft, squishy place where I weed from. His fingers felt too thick and there were too many of them. He was so unhygienic—didn't he know that place was germy? His fingers were going to smell.

I heard a *zip*. The cartoon was so colorful. So full of crazy characters. I wished it had a princess in it. Karimi's breath was hot as he whispered things against my neck that I didn't understand. There was something between my legs. It was what boys like my cousin had. I thought Karimi must love me. We were doing something bad. I would go to hell. I would definitely go to hell.

Karimi finally stood up and unlocked the door. He went to the bathroom, washed his hands, came back, and put some socks on. The cartoon was over. I could go now. The room smelled like holy rose water.

I don't know which came first anymore, my childhood sense of sexuality or the lodger upstairs.

Karimi had moved in because my mother wasn't earning enough to take care of us. One day I heard her telling my grandmother that my father had taken the money she had hidden under the carpet to pay for his opium.

Karimi had a black mustache just like my father. But he was tall and wore crisp white shirts. He smelled like sweat, but I liked him. He was kind to me. When I sat in the passenger seat of his car, I felt like a spoiled rich girl.

Karimi did many things for me, and I started to spend a lot of time with him. When I went in search of his companionship every afternoon, I knew what was going to happen—and yet I did it, again and again: Facing Mecca, he taught me how to recite the Qur'an and say the afternoon prayer, kneeling on the mat, pressing our foreheads against the Mohr, and muttering it under our breaths. Afterward he'd take me to his bedroom. He'd always lock the door. The projector hummed warmly. I was scared. Frightened. Never had cartoons triggered such adrenaline in me. The bedroom of this man was where I belonged and it would be unnatural for me to leave it. No one was ever going to help me. When he put me on his lap, however, my place was confirmed in the flames of hell—and I knew that too. I was a bad girl. Tainted. I knew then that this was my destiny. *I must love it. I must love this. This—it is who I am. He loves me; he takes care of me; he shows me cartoons and takes me places. My dad doesn't do these things.* His fingers would slip into my panties. I wanted to vomit from fear, but I gave him love instead.

I sat still afterward until he washed his hands and told me to go downstairs. He didn't even have the courtesy to show me girlie cartoons like *Cinderella*, only Pink Panther and Bugs Bunny—and I hated him for that.

hough a sliver of me got off on the sexual contact with Mr. Karimi, I knew what he did was disgusting and unnatural. What made me happy was playing sexual games with the boys and girls my own age.

During afternoon siestas, the nightly gunfire, and whenever panic erupted in the neighborhood, I got together with my cousins and neighbors, male and female, and played our games—*mummy and daddy* or *doctor and nurse*. Skirts would be lifted, tiny trousers would be unzipped, and we would show each other our downthere, each of us examining, touching.

I began to feel more sexually aware of my body, and because of this, whenever my grandmother took me to the local public bathhouse, I became rigidly shy and self-conscious of my nakedness. Our shower was nice enough, but going to the public bathhouse was like being reborn in body and soul. It was a ritual event, where everyone went for hours to luxuriously scrub and steam themselves as they exchanged gossip, drank ice-cold Coca-Cola, and exfoliated until their skin sparkled.

After collecting our fluffy white towels from the clothesline, my grandmother would fold the family's freshly washed underwear into a cloth sack. I would take my baby doll, get her dressed, wrap her up, and then we'd walk through our alley and down the hill. When the wailing of *azan* (prayer) from the mosque opened up, my heart would burst quietly with peaceful happiness. At that moment, as my grandmother held my hand in the Persian dusk, I felt a divine euphoria.

The bathhouse sat crumbling like a giant cookie. Past lives and weary bones still lingered in its doorway. Inside, distant voices and muffled splashes echoed in its hollow belly and ricocheted against the high glass-domed ceiling. There were private cubicles with a shower and bath, and a communal area where women washed together. Once the clanky metal door of the changing room banged shut, we peeled every layer. With towels wrapped around us, we were ready to dish the dirt.

The bathing hall always hummed. Child brides scrubbed until they squeaked. Skinny, old, long-haired, fat, young, gold-toothed, saggy, hennaed, jeweled, haughty—giggling women of every variety—waddled, lounged, and shared secrets. Rolls of flesh gorged on lather, the foam wallowing in the water.

As I grudgingly let the towel slip from my skin, my grandmother would spot neighbors and relatives, and soon the chatter would start. It seemed to last forever, the steam melting into my pores, the street dirt oozing out. If I opted for a private cubicle, I could open the door and shout "Pepsi!" or "Canada Dry!" and within minutes the ice-cold drink would arrive. It was heaven. Hours later, my grandmother and I would emerge scrubbed red-raw like beetroot, our gleaming faces peeking out from snug, plump head covers to protect us from catching a cold.

One evening while I was walking home from the bathhouse, the SAVAK raided the house at the end of our street. It was the grandest house on the block, with blue iron gates and sinuous trees that veiled the decadence inside. It was my friend Parya's house. She was my age, and very tall and slender with doll hair swinging down her back and cat-green eyes. Unmarked cars pulled up outside the house while the sky gurgled with a thunderstorm. Terrified, I ran home. And, from Mr. Karimi's upstairs window, I watched while they marched out Parya's parents and carried out stacks of books. Her mother was a glamorous woman who wore big tinted glasses and jewels, and had big hair like the women in American films. Her dad, like mine, loved opium.

He was always gray-skinned and sleepy looking. I heard from people on the street that they had been keeping rifles, guns, and anti-Shah literature in their house.

Parya was the first girl to show me her private parts. She had sat on our doorstep one afternoon and opened her legs. She wasn't wearing underpants. I looked closely, examining her flower, red and swollen like a rosebud. It shined, slick and glossy, yet packed in so tight and lovely. Now her parents were being taken away. I never saw any of them again.

In the midst of all this, I still felt loved. Even Mr. Karimi—I knew he loved me. As much as she could, my grandmother would take me to the shops and buy me anything I wanted. My mother continued working as a teacher, though her political activities had accelerated. From what I'd heard, I knew the Shah was a bad man, taking money away from poor people and giving it to his friends and family. This was why people hated him so much and why my mother went into the streets, braving gunfire, to demonstrate. It was the reason we went to Evin Prison in the north of Tehran to visit my uncles.

There I would hear stories of the way the guards tortured the prisoners: flogging their feet with electric cables, depriving them of sleep, hanging them upside down until the prisoners thought their brains would explode. I'd wonder if my uncles were okay whenever we visited them either there or in Ghasr Prison in central Tehran.

I no longer saw my father, and by the time 1978 drew to a close, my mother began to disappear as well, devoting her time to political rallies. My grandmother, miraculously, was still a ray of sunshine in my world. Regardless of the chaos all around, our alley and neighborhood remained a place of happiness. We still slept on the roof on summer nights, giggling with my cousin in the pasheh-band. I worshipped the stars that decorated the Persian sky like hot buttons. I still chased the boys in the alley. And the mosque still grieved with its sound of prayer each day and night. The rich, thick Persian carpets that adorned our house and garden still spread themselves open to me. The pomegranate and cherry trees still nourished me.

THE RUSH OF HOT BURNING SENSATION SWOOSHES IN MY TUMMY AND I FEEL LIKE A BAD GIRL. I AM A BAD GIRL.

It's dusk in the neighborhood, and the sound of gunfire blitzes the sky while frost coats the chimneys. There are people on their rooftops chanting revolutionary anthems, barking and shouting anti-Shah slogans: *"Marg bar Shah! Marg bar Shah!"* Death to the Shah! Rage fills the air more than gunfire.

I love the air at this time of day—the dusk, when shadows hide what people do. The adrenaline, from fear of a possible SAVAK raid, is thick in the air. I stand in the middle of our alley—in the midst of panic but close to our house. My grandmother is inside, worrying about me; my mother is out there somewhere, caught in the brawl and tussle of a demonstration in the streets.

All around, my friends scatter, running into their homes. Only the older boys stay. I hear my grandmother calling me: *"Dokhtaram, biya too digeh, Aash dorost kardam."* (My girl, come inside, I've made some broth.) But I don't go in. I want to stay outside, so I don't make a sound, don't let her know where I am. I like the panic, the rush of danger, the smell of burned wood.

The beauty of the sky and stars at dusk frees my soul. I pick up a small stick from the ground and hide in the shadows where no one can see me. I lift the hem of my flowery dress, slide the small stick inside my panties, and rub the stick all along my crotch. Rub it. Rub it until it feels so good that the rush of hot burning sensation swooshes in my tummy and I feel like a bad girl. I *am* a bad girl. There is no hope for me. I can't turn back.

CHAPTER

11

n one of our visits to see my uncles in Ghasr Prison, my mother took me to a different section of the prison and introduced me to a man I'd never seen before. He was rake-thin, hollow-cheeked, and as dark as tea. He was smaller than my father, but he too wore tinted glasses and had a black mustache.

We shook hands through the silver metal bars. He had scars all along his wrists and frowned at me when I stared at them. I heard him whisper to my mum that he had tried to kill himself in the public baths one day when he'd heard the SAVAK were coming to take him to prison. It was a bleak winter and people were being killed all the time. I was constantly frightened, but I joined in the revolutionary anthems with my mum and uncles' friends. I knew each song word for word. And even though I hadn't started school yet and couldn't really read, I was given children's books on the evils of capitalism and how socialism was the only way human beings could live in equality and harmony.

Just before the Shah fled Iran in January 1979, the man from Ghasr Prison came to our house. We switched off all our lights and sat in the dark while hollers and shrieks on the street outside twisted into a riotous roar as men and women, their hearts filled with anger and fear and resistance, clashed with the Shah's army.

The man had come to stay. It was late, and I larked about as usual. We ate dinner by a gas lamp around the sofreh with my uncles, who had also been released from prison. Suddenly the new man stood up and began barking orders at me as he pushed me into the adjacent room. "You're not allowed food until you shut up," he shouted. My mother said nothing. I didn't know this man; I had no idea who he was or why he was screaming at me. I clasped my hands to my ears to block out his yelling. Tears flooded my face.

"Come on, soldiers! Come and take this bad man back to prison," I yelled through my sobs until my voice splintered. "He's a bad man. He's hurting me." I kept sobbing and yelling, hoping the SAVAK would come take him away. But they never did; I was forced to put up with him and his ways for years to come.

Shortly after that night, the man became my new father. He came with grisly relics of torture, hacked and carved into his body by the prison guards who tried to force him to snitch on his friends. I touched the dents and deep cavities on his wrists and ran my fingers along the zigzag scars on his back, fascinated by the tunnels etched on his flesh.

"Darling, leave your father alone!" my grandmother would scold as she prepared delicious dishes for the new head of the house.

"And stop calling him by his name," she whispered to me later that night, after hearing me use his first name, Saeed. "You must call him Dad now."

Dad, Dad, Dad. As I went to sleep that night, I rolled the word over in my brain as if I were learning some new language. I felt like a normal girl now that I had a proper dad at home. We were a real family. My mother had finally found someone who was just as politically motivated as she was. I was happy for her—even though he scared me with his sudden mood swings and chilling cries at night, when flashbacks of prison torture invaded his dreams.

Soon, he and my mother were leaving regularly to march in the streets with thousands of others to fight the Shah's terrible regime and start a new Iran. I found myself nestling constantly in my grandmother's vast warm lap or laying on the lush carpets by the clunky heater, praying they would return alive.

With my new dad came a whole new set of cousins, aunties, and a sea of ready-made faces who were now my family. One of these was a silver-haired granddaddy who taught me the Qur'an and the ritual of *Namaz* (prayer) so thoroughly that I felt a new holiness and purity take over my soul. I prayed three times a day without fail, reading from the Qur'an loudly and lovingly. Fasting during Ramadan became a holy sweet experience. Arising at dawn to pray, I felt closer to God and all beautiful things. I knew God loved me even though I did naughty things in private.

My new granddaddy was wonderful and kind. He was my first real experience with a father figure, and I loved listening to his wise tales and guidance. When he instructed me to recite passages from the Qur'an, my whole being felt complete.

I would also sit and watch him smoke opium. He'd hold a square metal container. Inside were hot coals and little black bits that looked like buttons, which he would melt on the coals. He'd bring a ceramic pipe to his lips. The sweet, pungent perfume hissed at my nose and smooched my lips as the luscious aroma enveloped me. I'd feel hypnotized, as if I were floating through a thick, smoky curtain into an Arabian fairy tale.

Finally, on a dull winter day in January 1979, the moment everyone was waiting for arrived. I stood on the doorstep and listened to the cars honking, the people singing jubilantly in the streets. Slushy snow capped the pavements like moldering cake, but the air was spiked with euphoria. I walked the streets with my mum and stepdad's friends and jubilantly belted victory songs about working-class people united against a dictator who bled the poor dry. I worried about the state of the world and whether our new leader, this kind-looking, bearded old man called Khomeini, would make people happier.

CHAPTER

12

After the fall of the Shah, our little family moved to a block of apartments that was a ten-minute walk from my grandmother's house. There was a fig tree in the garden, and many new friends nearby for me to play with. The apartment block was in a small alley with a maidoon at the end.

When I found out that the new regime forbade mixing boys and girls in school, I was peeved about not getting to go with my boy cousins and threw one of my spoiled brat tantrums.

The new leader of the country, Khomeini, was the supreme spiritual leader whose word overruled everything. The people of Iran had just started to breathe a sigh of relief after ridding the country of one tyrannical regime when Khomeini announced a system of governance called *Velayat-e faqih* based on the rules of Islam formulated by himself and other clerics.

Anyone opposing this was considered to be against Islam and was punished accordingly. It became compulsory for women to cover their hair and bodies. Makeup, nail varnish, perfume, ties, and cologne were seen as Western symbols, and wearing them was considered counterrevolutionary and subject to severe punishment. Denying Islam was punishable by death. Adulterers were stoned. Those who had sex outside of marriage incurred lashes. Thieves, if caught, would likely lose their right hand and left foot. Women were required to get permission from either their father or husband for almost every activity. And since the sexes were not allowed to mix, all public spaces, including buses and offices, were segregated. Even dancing was forbidden.

This climate of fear continued to accelerate quickly. *Pasdar*, the armed revolutionary guards, and the *Komiteh* (the morality police patrolling the streets) punished anyone they wanted. Violence toward women who flashed just a strand of hair or a speck of makeup became common. I had to wear a *roosarie* (head scarf) and a somber *montoe* (a long black robe) over my clothes. I was lost in heaps of fabric; apart from my face, every inch of my skin drowned in thick cloth.

"We've gone from bad to worse," I'd hear my mum tell my grandmother in a somber whisper, as if there might be covert spies for Khomeini among our neighbors. "God, when is our country going to be free?"

Every morning at school, we lined up to display our fingernails to the head teachers, then bowed our heads and recited from the Qur'an in rhythmic unison. I found the prayer hypnotic and soothing. In the afternoons, I devoured my class work: math, science, and literature. The hard work paid off and I achieved straight As in every subject at school. The head teacher gave me flowers and my family fawned over me. "She has a unique beauty, and so intelligent, too," my aunts would nudge my mother, gathering around to observe me like some rare plant. "She will definitely find a nice husband."

I spent my free time in the alley, reading fairy tales and talking about boys with Soraya and Zari, my dearest friends in the world, who were like sisters to me. Together, we ruled the neighborhood. The other girls followed us, hanging on our every word. When they gushed, "You are a princess, like Cinderella," my heart swelled full of love.

My new dad ditched his job as a cab driver and started a construction company, where he made much more money. Soon he took us to gorgeous uptown restaurants and bought me prettier clothes, which I enjoyed showing off.

I lusted after the boys who lived nearby—many of them street-wise, bad-boy types. I would strut down the street in my platform shoes, ambling around the corner where they hung out. Though I acted innocent and unaware of their gaze, I'd slide my head scarf back just so, revealing my pearl hair clips. And I'd unbutton my montoe slightly, sauntering right past the Pasdar stationed at the end of our street. My friends watched from the windows, giggling nervously at what was either my extreme bravery or stupidity.

My uncles grew increasingly frantic. The new Islamic regime was torturing and executing everyone caught criticizing the government in any way, along with anyone thought to harbor left-wing, anti-government views—the pro-monarchists, the liberals, the intellectuals, anyone who did not actively follow Islamic practices. Even teenage girls who resisted religious teaching at school were considered potential threats and imprisoned, tortured, and executed.

My family began burning left-wing literature in the house. Late at night, I'd sit with my parents and relatives as they drove to the edge of town to dump boxes and boxes full of dangerous papers in the secret black waters of the river. All the freedom fighting, the turmoil, the blood spilled to liberate us from the Shah's dictatorship had only put us in a far more dire situation.

AT SCHOOL IN IRAN, SECOND ROW FROM THE BACK

I DECIDED THAT I WOULD TRY IT WITH TWO BOYS WHILE IN THE NEXT ROOM WAR SONGS BLARED OUT FROM THE TELEVISION.

My baby brother came along, chubby and dribbly, smiling a fat, toothless smile, on March 21, 1980. It was *Eideh Norooz*, the non-Islamic holiday that also marks the first day of spring and the New Year.

My stepfather rushed my mum to the hospital that day, leaving my grandmother, aunts, uncles, and me waiting for news. We sat around the *Haft Sin* table. Haft Sin, meaning seven Ss, refers to seven specific items beginning with the letter S in the Persian alphabet that must be placed on the table during Norooz. Each of the items symbolizes a different concept: *Sib* are apples symbolizing beauty, *senjed* is a dried fruit that symbolizes love, *sir* is garlic, *sabzeh* are wheat sprouts grown in a dish for the occasion, *somagh* is the cooking spice sumac, *sonbol* is the plant hyacinth, and *sekkeh* are coins symbolizing prosperity. Decorated eggs, a mirror, lit candles, and a goldfish also crowned the table.

In all the excitement surrounding the new baby, I forgot about the holiday gifts. I didn't need any—my brother, that chubby little bundle of sunshine, was the best present in the world. That day, I wrote my new brother a letter telling him how much I loved him and that he was a natural-born beauty.

Six months later, war erupted between Iran and Iraq. Air-raid sirens began shrieking like caged beasts. The sirens screamed every day. They scared the shit out of me, making me think we were about to get bombed, slaughtered.

All day, every day, military songs blared from our TV. The government wanted each male citizen—even old men and teenage boys—to fight the Iraqis. They promised martyrdom, an automatic free pass to heaven. We could not turn away from the broadcast images of families waving good-bye to their sons. A few boys from our street left to fight Saddam. Their mothers wailed hysterically from the pain of the sacrifice their sons were making for Islam.

During this time I took frequent walks to my grandmother's house, either after school or in the early evening, as the grieving dusk prayers boomed from the mosque's loudspeakers. Doom and fear hung thick and stagnant in the air as more and more men were called to war. The dusty nights were bleak, the street vendors increasingly desperate.

Walking beyond the main street, with cars violently whizzing past, angry drivers screaming, and armed men in Jeeps looking at me funny I'd smell the aromas of cooked liver and freshly baked nooneh sangak. I passed the pastry shops with strawberry-glazed cream puffs and crumbly confections in the windows. Dolls with spider-leg eyelashes and exotic animal toys with drum sets slept in shops, closed for the night. Teenage boys, likely just days away from war's brutality, pedaled bicycles along the sooty streets. The rich little girls held tight to their daddies' hands by florist shops crammed full of funeral wreaths and bridal bouquets.

I would run to my grandmother's house, pressing my head against her heaving bosom and big belly. I breathed deeply, inhaling her love. It was a small, safe place in the world. I no longer missed my real father: My new dad taught me how to ride a bike, holding on to the back and running behind and letting go only when I told him to. He taught me how to dine like a lady, but he also slapped me when I was bad.

One day, as I played with my bike in the yard with my mum and dad, my first daddy appeared, tall and slim with his film-star-tinted glasses and lovely lips. Avoiding eye contact with me, he walked right up to my new father. His whisper was dry and straight to the point: "I don't want to have any more responsibility for her. I won't be seeing her again. You can officially be the dad." Then he turned and left as hurriedly as he'd come. I looked down at my bike, at the Pink Panther stickers on the plastic between the handlebars, at the glitter-sprinkled dancing dolls in the basket, and I felt like nothing. I knew that I was damaged goods.

It was around this time that my stepfather first beat me. I remember standing in the shower where a bright, fresh pool of blood gushed from my nose and stained the water. My face was all puffed up and ugly and I fucking hated looking ugly. I thought I deserved it because I'd been a smart-ass, and getting smacked in the face was part of the deal for a cheeky kid who answered back. No one stood up for me, not even my mother; after all, he was her husband now, and Iranians don't discuss such things. It brings shame on the family.

By now my brother was a toddler. He would wiggle his wobbly jelly bottom whenever a war anthem played on TV, which seemed to be every five minutes. There was practically a funeral a day in the neighborhood. Shrines dedicated to the local martyrs sprouted up all over town; gorgeous colored lights bathed the dead soldiers' photos. At night, while the lizards slithered near the lamps in our yard, bombs destroyed the smaller southern cities, and even Tehran endured the occasional blast. When the sirens sounded, we swarmed into our block's underground parking garage for shelter.

Despite the terror, I thought life was still grand. I loved my friends and was the top student at school. I studied the Qur'an and devoured my textbooks, hungrily lapping up lessons in science and history. Religion was different, however, because religion made me feel peaceful and at one with God—especially since it was everywhere: on TV, blaring from the mosque's loudspeakers, and at school, where heaven and hell were constantly drummed into our brains. If I was a good girl and said my prayers every day and loved God, I would go to heaven. If I was a naughty girl, flaunting my sexuality and flirting with boys, I was destined for hell.

God, I tried to be virtuous and pure. I tried so hard. But I was tainted by my dirty thoughts. I just couldn't help myself. They became real every day when I played with my boy cousins and neighbors in private, hidden from the eyes of adults. I would get naked and rub my eight-year-old chest against my cousin's bare torso. Then in the afternoon I'd find my nine-year-old neighbor, a boy named Hamid, and get him to play doctor-and-patient with me. I would undress, climb in bed, make him examine me down there, and lie silently, letting him explore. I would bring Soraya and Zari to my room and ask them to look at my body and touch my private parts, relishing every sigh, every touch, every finger. In the midst of it, I could still feel God looking down upon me with loathing.

One night I decided to try it with two boys. I had exploding feelings in my tummy but no logic in my head. While my parents and family friends gathered in the living room to talk politics and war songs blared from the TV calling everyone to sacrifice their sons, I brought my younger boy cousin, Kian, to my room and asked Hamid to join us.

"We're playing servants and housekeepers," Hamid told Kian, somehow reading my mind. "She's going to lie down on the bed like she's asleep. You have to pretend you are a servant and do as you are told."

Hamid's imagination is just like mine, I thought gleefully.

I lay down on the bed and closed my eyes. Hamid ordered Kian to touch me. I pretended to doze like Sleeping Beauty. Hamid was harsh with Kian, commanding him to kiss my feet and thighs. I felt like I was floating. I felt like a queen. The game made my tummy tumble with frenzy. I worried that we were too cruel to my cousin, who, bewildered and meek, went along with whatever we told him to do.

I knew I had power—a real power—over boys. And I exercised it whenever the fancy took me. One afternoon, I finished school early after a grueling day of listening to sermons about heaven and hell and where we might end up if we got on the wrong side of God. Clutching my books, with thoughts of fires and snakes running through my mind, I walked home. There I found our neighbor's eight-year-old brother hanging around out in front. Knowing no one was home, I took the wide-eyed boy into my room and forced him to kiss me. I fondled under my panties and straddled him as I removed my *hejab* (head scarf). He panted hard, fingered me, and blushed crimson. I was in ecstasy, a pack of wild wolves in my belly. There. Now I was definitely going to hell.

y family made frequent trips to *Shomal* (the north of Iran), where crystal waters and powder-soft sand welcomed us. On the drive there, we passed majestic blue mountains. The Persian wilderness, the forests, the lakes, and the ancient hills looked like a fairy-tale painting. There were small cafés and restaurants tucked into the belly of the mountain. We rested on their sofas and beds, atop intricately patterned cushions, while being served little plates of feta cheese, Persian dips with freshly baked bread, and hot tea in dainty glasses. Sometimes we shared our hotel room with a harmless snake; the damp weather invited many wiggling creatures.

By 1982, the beach had been segregated: a makeshift wall divided the men from the women, despite the fact that all females still had to adhere to the Islamic dress code, even in the sea. One afternoon, as I scampered around the beach, a male Pasdar screamed obscenities at me for not covering my arms and legs. I felt like a criminal.

Another day, as we were driving home from Shomal, I gently held my new baby sister—less than a year old—in my arms, wondering how long it would be until she had to cover her body, too. Suddenly we were pulled over by the Pasdar. They screamed at my parents to get out of the car. We had no idea what we could have done wrong.

The Pasdar threatened to prosecute my parents, all because a bit of my leg was showing beneath my montoe. My parents turned white with panic, realizing that they could be dragged in and tortured, or worse, for my infraction. It took twenty minutes for my dad to negotiate a cash bribe with the Pasdar. Finally, they let us go. That was a good day.

A few weeks later, after a long night's drive to Shomal, I woke to find we'd arrived at a farm. The farmer greeted us with breakfast—fresh eggs, feta, fresh bread, double cream, and honey—on his sofreh. My uncle and aunt were traveling with us, and I could see sadness in their eyes. That morning, my uncle and aunt told us they too were planning to leave Iran. Having been blacklisted by the government for their activism, they planned to escape to Turkey on horseback.

By 1983, missing people were very much a part of daily life. Torture and mass graves of prisoners dominated every adult conversation. I'd often overhear horror stories about the torture methods used in Evin Prison; too often these tales involved yet another relative who had been executed. Most of my family and their friends had plans to escape Iran or were trying to get out.

By this time I was nine years old, but I still didn't completely understand the panic. I was too busy playing with my friends and cousins. However, I was fed up with covering my hair and skin. So I rebelled by paying more attention to the dresses and accessories I wore beneath my montoe. I watched Hollywood films, which were sold under the counter at the grocery store and smuggled into our home by my stepdad. I watched Scarlett O'Hara—her lips and her hips and how she moved. I put on shows for my relatives, imitating famous Persian singers and copying their every dance move.

One man, who moved into our apartment building, started to take a special interest in me. Remembering my grandmother's lodger, I hesitated to go to this new neighbor's apartment alone. But I convinced myself that this time would be different. This man was a doctor, after all, and he got on well with my parents.

One day, he promised me chocolate if I would come visit him. I skipped up the stairs, jubilant. *Chocolate, chocolate, chocolate,* was all I thought.

When I entered his apartment, it seemed too dingy and dark for a doctor. Unkempt plants, dirty clothes, and stacks of magazines cluttered the room. He shut the door and took me to his bedroom. Where was my chocolate?

Without a word, he pulled my panties down and then took his pants off. Was this normal? Was it my destiny? Why did men do this? Was it my fault? "No," I said, and tried to wriggle out of his grip. But he forced my legs open. Mr. Karimi had been much gentler. This neighbor's down-there was hard against my thigh and it hurt. I was scared. I hated it. It made me feel sick.

I was afraid and disgusted. It felt wrong, the way it had with Mr. Karimi. But I let the man do what he had to, just so he would let me go. I never told anyone, not even God when I prayed to him during Namaz.

CHAPTER

15

PLEASE, DON'T SEND ME TO ENGLAND. I WANT TO STAY HERE AT HOME, WITH MY FRIENDS.

It is an Iranian tradition to spend nights at mehmoonis, the family parties that brightened our evenings. These were more than just casual visits uptown to exchange pleasantries and have a drink; they were lavish and colorful affairs, full of dancing and affectionate banter, with the women in immaculate makeup and the host serving a banquet of dishes. There was always some excuse for a mehmooni—a cousin's birthday, for instance—and I loved dressing up for them, scrubbing my face with harsh soap and scraping my hair into a severe ponytail. My stepdad would drive my mum, my little brother and sister, and me through the dark and busy streets of Tehran, past pickled-walnut sellers standing lit by gas lamps on the curb and panicked chador-clad women toward the north of the city, where the rich and the grand lived. I would sit in the backseat like a lady, scrubbed and grateful for my life.

At one of those mehmoonis, I met him. He was the son of a family friend. At thirteen, he was already a street-smart rebel with pale skin and green eyes. My first bad boy. When he invited me to his birthday party a few days later, I knew he liked me. There were no other girls invited—all boys and only me. It was going to be heaven. My mother took me shopping for a new dress to wear to heaven.

The electricity was out in the city that night. I waited in the dark by our house gates, watching the lizards scratch their warm bellies on the rough wall. An uncle and a cousin picked me up to take me to the party. The neighborhood was quiet. It was nights like these when the hush would often be destroyed by bombs and sirens and carnage. But I didn't care: I was fucking euphoric.

At the party, about twenty boys buzzed around. Since there were no other girls there, I got to dance with all of them. But my heart was sweaty for the boy. Finally, he winked at me and took me by his side. For the rest of the evening, we sat next to one another, arm against arm, our bodies sizzling.

I adored him, but I knew I'd never see him again. In two months, I was being sent to England with my grandmother, and I really didn't want to go.

"Please, don't make me go to England. I want to stay here at home, with my friends," I cried to my mother a few days after the party.

"You'll get a better education."

"But I don't want to be sent away from here. I don't want to leave you!"

"It's for your own good, my dear," my grandmother chimed in. "This regime is so bad. Everyone is escaping."

"Can I still do sociology if I go to school there?" It was my favorite subject.

My mum laughed. "Yes. They have it there, too."

"But I don't speak English!"

"You don't have to go to school until you've learned it."

Part of me thought it was all a bit of a lark. England—a glamorous new world with shiny things, chic clothes, fancy hairdos, and lots of clever books I could read to become educated and ladylike. And so I agreed to go to England with Anneh accompanying me. I never would have done it if I had known what would happen next.

MY PASSPORT PHOTO FOR ENGLAND

pART 2

LOST

THE ENGLISH AIR POISONED MY GRANDMOTHER'S LUNGS. SHE STOPPED AND CLUTCHED HER CHEST RIGHT THERE.

t was the summer of 1984, and the whole neighborhood came out to wish me well on my trip.

"You're coming back, aren't you?" Zari and Soraya sobbed, crying into my back.

"I'll bring back lots of presents for you," I promised.

"Here's a photo of me," Zari said. "So that you'll never forget me."

My mother's eyes were puffed up, raw and pink. It was for the best. Her mother and oldest daughter were getting away from this government, heading to a new world of freedom. It was a shame we couldn't all go as a family. They wouldn't allow that: It would be too obvious that we were emigrating and not coming back.

My stepfather proudly posed for pictures. Two days earlier he'd taught me that English people did not put their elbows on the table during meals and always spoke in a genteel manner. He saw England through the romantic haze of Jane Austen books.

The night before we left, the whole neighborhood came to see my grandmother and me—aunts, uncles, cousins, and a sea of unknowns. I was lost in a watercolor of lipstick kisses and distant perfumes, snug hugs and constant photographs. Before my baby sister had gone to bed, I'd sweetly kissed her chubby mouth. My little brother, four years old, giggled shyly at all the attention I was getting.

By early morning, everyone had filtered out of our house, leaving my grandmother and me with our suitcases. In preparation for the trip, I removed my red nail polish in case the authorities noticed it and interrogated me. I was too excited to sleep. I thought this would be a short adventure and then I'd come home.

At three A.M., my stepfather drove us to the airport. A frenzied air-raid siren pierced the sky, and in the car, the dry heat retched over us. Sitting there mutely, I bubbled with unspeakable emotion as we glided past sleeping neighborhoods. I was going to miss playing with my friends and stealing fruit from the splitting persimmon tree.

At the airport, of course, we were interrogated. The Pasdar took my grandmother and me into separate cubicles for a physical search. His touching tickled my ribs, but a black-chador-clad woman carried out the body investigation silently and hostilely. Finally, I slid through the plastic curtains to find my grandmother sitting on a chair in her cubicle. A couple female officials were slicing out the inner sole of her shoes.

On the plane, sitting beside one of the huge exit doors, my grandmother joked about whether the ginger man behind us was also ginger down there as well. She always joked like that.

I was ten years old and I was on my way to England, a symbol of freedom and abandon, where I could walk around in public without an Islamic head scarf and its matching somber montoe and have no fear of being stopped by the morality police. I was filled with excitement at the thought of the sophisticated education I would receive and the blond, blue-eyed English boys I would be seeing. In my mind, England was a wholesome, orderly place, where everything gleamed as if brand new, where every woman had the demeanor of Mary Poppins, and every man had the quaintness of a gentleman. I was trusting and optimistic. These were the last moments of the real me—grounded, unfragmented, uncomplicated.

The instant we entered British airspace, I unwrapped my tent-like Islamic uniform, peeling it off my head and body. I had grand plans to apply the right shade of polish to my nails to fit in with the glamour of England. I chose the color from the previous night's party, because I liked the instant brazenness of its unforgiving red. The light cotton, spaghetti-strapped dress my mother bought me for the trip bloomed when I removed the massive cloak. Cocky little me, spunky street-smart spoiled girl: I was finally going to feel the breeze of freedom on my skin. With my bright red fingernails, no one could stop me.

As the plane landed and we shuffled into the terminal, the air slapped against my bare arms, chest, back, neck, and legs, shocking me. I felt naked. Not since the age of seven had I walked outside without my Islamic cover. It was cloudy, nearly three P.M., and all was hushed. I was used to loud people all around me—talking, kissing, shouting, laughing, and gossiping—and to being surrounded by color. Now, I saw only gray. I was used to sunshine and warm flowery greetings from everyone in the street, fruit trees and mountains, and orange taxis. This new land was so bland, unfriendly, and alien.

My grandmother and I were supposed to find a connecting flight to our new home in Manchester, where an uncle and aunt lived. But as we walked through the airport, we had no idea what to do or where to go. My heart beat super-fast and I shivered in the cold. All around me, people stiffened their jaws and whizzed past, going somewhere, seeing somebody. I couldn't understand why none of my relatives had come to meet us at the airport.

Standing in the middle of the terminal in my sexy summer dress—my grandmother still in her Islamic hejab—I held out my ticket to a lady walking past. "Gate three," she mouthed slowly. I didn't know what it meant, but I knew that if I kept repeating it to strangers they'd show us the direction for the plane to Manchester.

Finally, on our way to the proper terminal, we emerged outside, shuffling along with our suitcases into the cold August air. I looked at my grandmother—and saw she was struggling to breathe.

Anneh was determined to be at my side in this strange country. At the age of sixty, she had left behind her home and security, left behind her family and her life, and even risked her health. She suffered from acute asthma, and had flown away from the sun to embrace England's damp, cold climate.

The English air had made its premiere on my exposure-hungry skin and poisoned my grandmother's lungs. Anneh stopped and

clutched her chest right there. I dug her inhaler from the bottom of her leather handbag and watched as she pumped four neat puffs into her tightened lungs. "She'll be fine now," I tried to convince myself, all the while repeating "gate three, gate three, gate three" in my mind.

We sat on the curb so Anneh could rest and catch her breath.

"You stay here while I go find the plane." My voice sounded oddly grown up to me, even though I was terrified. I didn't know what to do. Her face was ashen. I dashed back into the terminal. Inside, I desperately tried to find a friendly face to ask about this wonderful place called "gate three." No luck.

I ran back outside. Anneh looked even worse. Dread froze my throat. Her cushioned cheeks were purple. A choking whistle mixed with a wet crackling sound came out of her mouth. She fought to breathe. Her wide eyes pleaded with me to help her. I was desperate and unable to communicate with anyone. At that moment, I deeply regretted skipping all those private English classes my parents had arranged. My grandmother couldn't breathe. She was dying right before my eyes and no one else could see it.

Again I ran into the terminal to get help. Again, my frantic jabbering drew only blank stares. When I ran back outside, an ambulance was parked by my grandmother, and a policewoman was helping her to her feet. I loved that policewoman so much at that moment.

I remember climbing into the ambulance, and then . . . nothingness.

CHAPTER

17

ven now, no matter how much I stretch my brain, I cannot remember what happened from the moment I climbed into the ambulance until I woke up the next morning in the hospital. It's as if those few hours have been wiped from my memory forever. The next thing I knew, I was awake in a hospital room and my uncles were at my grandmother's bedside.

A few days later, my uncles drove my grandmother and me to Manchester. The August weather was cloudy and drab—always gray, still, and vacuous. The thick syrup smell of the local brewery seeped into the city each afternoon when my aunt took me to the laundromat and into town to buy strawberries, which had been a rare treat in Iran during the war.

We moved in with my uncle and aunt into Cooper House, a concrete tower of public housing that still sits red and stubborn on the curve of Boundary Lane in Hulme, Manchester, its stairways full of bloodied sanitary towels, full of story. That tower will probably always be there, no matter what happens in the world. It is the cockroach of apartment buildings. To me it will always also be full of my grandmother: her history, her brilliant light, her soul, her hair the color of honey, her bad eyesight I once made fun of.

I will never forget dancing around the grounds in my red rah-rah skirt, the one I wore to make me feel more alive. I'd put it on and skip through the stairwells in Cooper House, all the way from number twenty-eight, where we lived, to my friend's place at number eighteen. And all the while, in the marble of my eye, I saw the beautiful patterns of the carpets in our house in Iran. The rich tapestry of maroons and purples by the doorway in the main front room, in the courtyard by the fishpond, and in our garden of pomegranate tree and roses. And every day, my grandmother was slowly dying.

⚬

My uncle and aunt had escaped to England via Turkey. Since they had just started to make a life for themselves in this new world—with a new baby—there was no money and very little food. The flat was tiny. I felt imprisoned, so far from the existence I had left behind. I wanted my family and my dolls. But my main concern was finding something to eat. Every day, my grandmother and I were starving.

"If you look on the ground as you walk around town, you're bound to find a penny here and there," my uncle suggested. "Those pennies will add up and you can buy yourself a chocolate bar."

So I began watching the ground meticulously whenever I walked outside.

In the afternoons while my aunt and uncle rested, my grandmother and I snuck into the kitchen to look for white bread or rice to fill us up. One glorious night, when Anneh returned from one of her many visits to the hospital, she brought back a handful of pears. That night, after the lights were switched off, we lay in our tiny room in the dark, me on the floor, my grandmother on the bed, eating our pears and laughing with joy, as if we were drunk. I felt like a princess that night.

Still, the ghostly pock-hollowed soul of this new world surrounded me, and I had no idea where to go or what to do. Every night I dreamed of Iran. The dreams were so vivid that, when I woke up, I was shocked to find myself on a strange floor looking out at the same tall gray buildings. One night I dreamed about all my friends playing by a sunny lake. We picked fruit from the trees, and I flirted with Babak, a boy from my Iranian school whom I'd had a major crush on. He had a smooth, tanned body. He flirted back. It was nice to see his face; I felt like I was there, until I woke up suddenly. When I realized I was actually in England, I felt sick and terrifyingly alone.

Every morning when I awoke, I would hear the *khut khut khut* of the sewing machine on which my aunt and uncle made their illegal bread and butter. A short Pakistani man named Ismail, with a head as hairy as a boar, brought denim pieces in all shapes and sizes to the house each day. The two of them would cut, sew, stitch, trim, and iron zippers, buttons, and pockets by a yellow lamp well into the night. The more jeans they made, the more cash they received. Sometimes I would help. I had to be a good girl so the grownups would be happy with me.

Not long after landing in Manchester, I was sent to a local school in Hulme to learn English. I really wanted to be able to talk to other kids, but the first English words I learned, naturally, were swear words. "Fuck" was the first one, "hell" the second. Every day after classes I went to the big library in the town center to listen to language cassettes and read phrase books. I started writing poetry and songs about my time in England and keeping a diary about my experiences.

All this time, my grandmother was dispatched to the hospital every few days with asthma attacks that choked her throat. Eventually, my uncles tired of looking after her, and dumped her in a Cooper House flat to live by herself. I don't know how she remained so sunny and optimistic. She had come to England for me and she wasn't going to let her granddaughter down, even if it meant she could barely breathe.

I wrote letter after letter begging my mother to let me come back home, telling her how much I missed my family and friends, explaining how scary it was to walk by the kids in gangs every time I went to shop for bread. I wondered why my mother had sent me here. In Iran, at least, we had enjoyed the luxury of food.

FUCKIN' PAKI, SHE AIN'T NO BRIT! SKIN IS BROWN AND SHE SMELLS LIKE SHIT.

 turned to books and writing to escape my life in England. I had brought over all my favorites in their Persian translation. *Huckleberry Finn* kept me full of passion, and I devoured stacks of novels by Iranian writers: political fairy tales about the inequalities of the rich and poor, stories of wild women with unfathomable beauty, unrequited love, wicked stepparents, and one about a princess who fell in love with a bald, penniless pigeon keeper.

After a few months, my uncle decided to send me away from the squalor of our public housing to a more refined environment deep in the southern countryside to begin the process of Anglifying me. Somehow they'd discovered a charitable English family willing to provide me with food and shelter. So off I went to live with the Carsons in their little stone cottage and attend Long Acre School. The Carsons were old-school hippies who found the idea of an Iranian girl fresh from the ravages of war gorgeously exotic and über-trendy. They took me off my uncle's hands without hesitation.

Their cottage had a massive garden with beautiful flowers and tall trees, and the Carsons had given me my own room. This is it, I thought.

I'm finally in the quaint and peaceful place I imagined—a place where the food and the people will both be nice. Proper England!

Long Acre School sat in a tiny, postcard-English village with perfectly trimmed hedgerows and white fences—a place where people ate politely and said how-do-you-do. The school was in a white building with ivy crawling up its craggy skin. Finicky daisies lazed around its skirts. It had children inside it, well-fed gingers and blondes and blackberry brunettes. They were bread-and-butter-for-tea, rosy-cheeked sorts, destined for Swiss finishing schools and vacations in the south of France. They had not seen many dark-skinned people, let alone an Iranian girl with a mustache.

The Carsons' friends came to gawk at me one by one. Me: sweaty, with the aroma of exotic spices from the bazaars just like they had seen in Marrakech once while traveling in North Africa. How marvelous to have this quietly withdrawn creature from war-torn Iran in their midst, with her fabulous olive skin and traumatized soul.

The Carsons had a three-legged dog named Pickle and a three-legged cat called Flowerpot. The Carsons liked to rescue things from wretched lives. I loved those two animals so much and ended up taking care of them. They had a seven-year-old son named Billy who had long hair and cocoa-buttered skin. I hated that little fucker. I hated that stone cottage as well, because it had such a low ceiling. I hated that I couldn't speak English very well. And I hated being alone without my family and friends. Jacket potatoes and silence gagged me.

At school I was known as the silent, smelly Paki and bullied with much glee and fanfare. "Fuckin' Paki, she ain't no Brit! Skin is brown and she smells like shit," sang a gang of girls. My cheeks flamed with embarrassment.

The constant taunts and bullying made me so anxious that I started involuntarily peeing myself as I entered the school doors. Droplets of pee trickled down into my underpants, and I would tighten my muscles to block the flow. Then I became the pathetic sheep-girl with the pain lodged in her throat, eyes buried deep in the ground as I entered the classroom of two dozen eleven-year-olds.

The first few weeks of class weren't too bad because I didn't understand all the words flung at me. But because of that, it turned physical. The three main girls who hacked at me with their venom-sopped words were named Sally, Michelle, and Jessica. Their eyes, slick and quick, would twinkle as they'd walk toward me, chanting racist slurs, cricket bats at the ready.

I responded by burying myself deeper in my favorite books, like *Tom Sawyer* and *The Prince and the Pauper*, which I read in Iranian. I lost myself in their adventures and fantasized about running away with Huckleberry Finn, whom I felt would make a wild and exciting boyfriend. Oh, how I longed to be naughty—to play games with my cousins and knock on neighbors' doors and run away. I wanted to eat ash-e reshteh and see my mummy and friends and family. I just wanted to be home and be myself, the naughty show-off who had many friends and was adored.

One day I opened my desk to find steamy chunks of dog shit next to my beloved *Tom Sawyer*. My book was ruined; my desk stank. All because I was different.

I learned a lot of English very quickly in those first few months at Long Acre—because I had to. Dairy Milk quickly became my favorite chocolate bar, Wham! my favorite pop group. Between lessons I wrote letters to my mum on red paper, enclosing little trinkets from England: hair clips for my little sister and cartoon stickers for my brother.

18 August 1984

Dear Ma,
Hello. I hope you are completely well and my brother and sister also. How is dad? I am really missing you. I wish you were here. Mum, you don't know how many different types of toys there are here and what beautiful toys they are. Everywhere you go there are toys

and clothes. Clothes that a person wouldn't even dream of. There is a doll here called Barbie and she has everything, lots of shoes, clothes, makeup table, lipstick, eye shadow, kitchen, car, wardrobe, a husband. I wish you were here so you could buy me things that I want. The clothes are very, very beautiful here. The shoes shimmer with beauty. There are lots of beautiful things here but only the rich can buy them. The rich areas are really nice but the rest of the areas are so bad. For example, there are gangs of children who go around stealing and smashing car windows and no one says anything. I live in a really poor area. But at school I am learning the piano. I see mums holding their kids' hands and I wish you were here. I am really upset that you're not here.

Some of the men here have tattoos on their arms and wear earrings and their hair is long and messy. It looks horrible.

Write Back Soon,
Your daughter

In the five months I attended Long Acre, I was allowed to visit Manchester only twice. What I saw darkened my spirit further: My grandmother's life now consisted of sitting alone in her flat between frequent hospital visits. From a sunny laughter-filled home brimming with loved ones where she tended to the fruit trees in her garden, to sitting in a high-rise flat watching the clouds—it was too much to bear. I didn't understand why we had come to England. The bullying at school made me miserable, and my grandmother's life was killing her. Had we given up love for this? What did freedom mean? Surely not this.

My grandmother survived England for nine months. During one of her hospital trips, she caught a bug. That evening, while washing the dishes at my uncle's place, my aunt told me the news. "Anneh died this morning at four A.M.," she said simply. I looked at her for a moment, then carried on wordlessly with my work. I would always remember my grandmother as she was in Iran: joyful, laughing, loving. I felt an overpowering relief soothe my spiky insides because my grandmother wouldn't suffer anymore.

My aunt winced with unease as she watched me quietly bury myself in my schoolbooks. I was determined that my grandmother's sacrifice for me would not be in vain. When I achieved the best marks in my class in French, my teacher rewarded me with a Dairy Milk chocolate bar. This achievement had dire consequences: That day at lunch break, Sally and her gang circled me, gripping sticks and cricket bats.

"Paki, Paki, Paki," they chanted, doing impressions of freaks with screwed-up eyes, distorted limbs, and tongues hanging out of their mouths. "Go back to your own country, Paki!"

I didn't speak. I just carried on reading—lovely, lovely reading. Bad boy Huckleberry Finn, being wild and rebellious.

I was also teased for the things I ate and drank. "It's piss she's drinking," the boys taunted when I opened a bottle of apple juice at lunch. I blushed, embarrassed.

I knew I wasn't completely dark, but I knew I wasn't completely white either. My skin was olive, but secretly I wanted it to be very white—luminous, pure, snow white. One day, I decided to try to bleach it. In the Carsons' bathroom, I slathered thick creamy hair-lightening paste all over my face, avoiding my eyebrows and eyes. I laughed at the snowman in the mirror! Beneath the layers, my face tingled and sizzled like bacon and my eyes burned. When I couldn't take it anymore, I scrubbed the paste off. But instead of turning white, I had only become red and raw.

My mother knit clothes and sent them to me. They were invariably thick wool, soft and so warm because she was afraid I'd catch cold. In one package was a traditional Persian folk skirt and a head scarf. Although she must have spent hours knitting the intricate pink-and-blue designs, I looked at the two items with horror. I knew the consequences would be grim if the gang of girls at school saw me wearing them.

Instead, I hid the clothes in my room. And, for the first time, I began wearing my skirt short. I also shaved my legs within an inch of their lives and left the top buttons of my shirt undone. The day I showed up at school looking that way was the day the girls no longer teased me. I was a Western girl now.

One Friday afternoon in June, I found a bit of blood on my underwear. I looked for a cut and didn't see anything. But there was a screaming pain in my tummy, like an angry alarm clock. The Carsons' toilet was a minuscule room with a frosted window facing their garden. I could hear birds chirping and smell jasmine from the garden. But the scent made me want to retch. The only way I could think to stop it was to dab at the blood from where it was coming with clumps of tissue and hope it would close and dry up.

That weekend, I walked around thinking I was bleeding to death. I didn't dare tell anyone. It was only when I started leaking onto my jeans that Mrs. Carson noticed and pulled me aside. She promptly issued me little diaper things and explained that bleeding happens to all females every month. In the bathroom, I peeled off the plastic strip and mistakenly stuck the sticky side of the diaper thing all along my pubic hair.

In July, my mother managed to leave Iran with my brother and sister. My stepdad couldn't make it; he would remain stuck there throughout the war, sitting on the roof watching bombs hit Tehran night after night.

My mother arrived at the Carsons' doorstep heavy with gifts and my darling brother and sister, bundled up against the chill she was worried they'd get. My mummy was here! Nothing bad would ever happen again.

We moved to student residences on a campus in Manchester that were cheap but clean. My mother, an academic, was forced to clean rich people's homes for money.

Around this time I also got into pop music. I started back-combing my hair and dressing up in short skirts, lace gloves, and tiny tops. Then I'd rush off to care for my cute little siblings. I loved play-ing mummy to my baby brother and sister, two naughty kittens run-ning around bewildered in this new world in which they had landed.

My brother was now five, and had clearly not shaken the life he was born into. He was stuck in war mode: all of his drawings fea-tured airplanes dropping bombs on the people below. I watched as he made explosion sounds and pretended he was in the middle of battle with the Iraqis. It was all innocent fun to him, but I was wor-ried by how much he'd been affected by the war.

My mum rushed around day and night trying to keep us fed. I don't think I've ever seen my mother do anything for herself. One day after breakfast, she brought out a box full of photos. From underneath the pile she removed a twin-set of pearls, given to her as a wedding present. She quietly told us she'd be back soon. When she came back, there was no necklace, just bags full of food.

MY BROTHER AND I, REFUGEE KIDS IN ENGLAND

I WAS THIRTEEN AND SLIPPED MY WHITE PANTIES DOWN, SPREAD MY LEGS OPEN, AND WATCHED AXL ROSE IN THIS BAND GUNS N' ROSES.

I was eleven years old when I had my first orgasm. It was to a porno magazine I'd stolen from a convenience store. I didn't know the facts of life then. Two years later, I had my first gushing-out ejaculation, to Axl Rose.

Most of what I did was in secret. At school, I was a nerd who loved reading and writing poetry. At home, I was the big sister looking after my siblings. But alone, in my room, I was Axl Rose's teenage slut. Guns N' Roses screeched from my Walkman under my blanket. Dressed in fishnet stockings, lacy gloves, and black stilettos like the girls in music videos, I strutted around the room.

One summer afternoon, I was watching TV at my aunt's house. I didn't even know what the word orgasm meant, yet this boy on the screen with the bandana and long hair falling over his shoulders made me fall in love with what my body could do.

Watching him sway his snake hips onstage, howling a loud American rock song—a bad, nasty, trashy boy with strawberry-blond, lank hair; upturned, flared nostrils; and arms with tattoos like a prisoner—suddenly I felt that familiar, crude clench in my belly. The panic-filled urgency conquered me, a gigantic, detonating love-hunger making my vulva throb like a frenzied animal. I had to find a long, hard object, so I grabbed the closest thing: my cousin's bicycle pump. It was my savior, a delicious secret tool. I wanted to be a nasty girl. There was no one around, which made me hornier. I was being naughty.

I slipped my white cotton panties down, spread my legs open, and watched Axl in this band called Guns N' Roses. He was sweating on stage, snarling, and I spread my legs wider for him. Taking the bicycle pump, I slid it between my legs, my vulva dripping wet. I rubbed the bicycle pump all along my wetness until something gushed out of me. It sprayed all over the floor, giving the carpet a clammy smell. I lay on my back, knees trembling. Relief and peace glowed inside me. My body felt warm and grown up. I looked at Axl and smiled. Who was this beautiful boy and what was this exploding feeling that had gushed out of me?

CHAPTER

20

By the time my stepfather arrived in England a few years later, we were living in Bristol in a ground-floor flat. My stepdad needed work; he was a proud and accomplished man, a trained architect with his own successful construction company in his homeland, but here he knew no one.

I took my stepfather to all the restaurants I knew, asking if he could get a job as a dishwasher. He stood sheepishly behind me as I pleaded in English. Inside I cringed in embarrassment for him, but I put on a casual act, as if it were all just a laugh and oh-so-normal. I knew he must have felt a cavernous nothingness being in this situation, but working as a dishwasher was better than not having a job at all. Slowly, he learned to speak English and found better jobs, but I think he harboured some resentment toward me because my fluency in English had somehow given me a higher rank in the family than him.

The five of us slept in one room, lent to us for free by a kindly lady who'd befriended us. There was a kitchen and a bathroom where umbrellas of dry rot mushroomed on the walls and under the side of the bathtub. I'd lived in England for five years and still it didn't feel like home. English culture was not warm and family-oriented like Persian culture. People were cold and stilted, and didn't hug and kiss and laugh as much as Iranians did. They shared no banquet of colorful foods, as Iranian people did every day and night, gathering around, dancing and gossiping. My family was cut off from the sense of community and quality of life they'd once known. My brother and sister, tiny and unaware of poverty, thought it was all a big adventure and that any day now we'd pack up and head back to Iran—back home.

Though she spent her days cleaning for the rich, my mother's spirit stayed strong. But my stepfather, defeated, slowly began to fade away. He was a nothing in this land far away from his family and the business he'd built—lost in a country where he was a nobody, where his friends, achievements, status, and identity were incinerated as if they had never existed. He became silent, sometimes sitting on a chair in our room for hours and staring into space.

At my new school, I became known as the silent Iranian girl. My shyness and dorkiness, along with my early development, which ballooned my mortified chest into two giant blubbers, made my social life even more wretched. Shy to the point of freaky I munched on lunch alone in the playground and wrote poetry about the aches of love, the boys I longed for, and the kisses I craved.

One Saturday afternoon, I decided to write my first book. It was about the street kids of São Paulo, Brazil. I wrote by hand—page after page—about a brother and sister surviving life on the streets. By Monday night, they had escaped their city and ended up on a train bound for Peru. I didn't ever think of the logistics of this; I just loved their journey to find family and a real home. By Thursday night, my hands were sore, but the characters had found their parents. By the time I was through, I'd written thirteen chapters; I called it *The Secret Garden*. It went into the pile where I collected my writings.

ONCE HE'D KNOCKED ME TO THE GROUND, I'D END UP WAILING THERE LIKE A BABY.

 s I became a teenager, the smacks in the face my stepfather gave me turned more creative. He had a deep reservoir of rage—and would aim it at my back, stomach, and legs, dumping his seething resentment of his worthless status onto me.

We were now living on the top floor of a public apartment building and had been given an old piano by a neighbor. I practiced constantly, letting the plinky-plonk of the notes wiggle and tremble under my fingers. My uncles and aunts visited often, and they'd all sit around the piano to take in my recital. Behind our fancy, sugary banter, none of them knew I was getting punched and kicked. A couple of other relatives knew, but no one ever said a thing. I told my teachers at school, but, again, nothing happened. I guess they didn't want to interfere.

I was a difficult teenager, and stubborn with him, refusing to change the channel when my favorite programs were on. My brother and sister looked on as he raised his fists to wallop me on the head and threatened to kick me in the stomach. I tried with all my strength to fight back, but it was hopeless. My waist-length hair would tangle like angel-hair spaghetti in my face, blinding me as I tried to bite his arm and scratch his face. But he was stronger than me, and my arms were just jelly. Once he'd knocked me to the ground, I'd surrender and end up wailing there like a baby.

In a frenzy one night, he grabbed my new kitten and dangled it from our balcony. The kitten hissed and spit, wriggling in his grip. I was afraid he would crush her. My mother screamed at him. I begged him to stop; the kitten was so innocent and lovely. But he wanted to piss me off because he knew how much I hated animal cruelty. In the end, though, he put the kitten back safely on the ground.

That night, I ran away from home. As my family watched TV, I ran out—out into the streets, toward the home of my mother's friend, who never asked any questions.

"Comin' round for a cuppa, are you?" she asked when I burst in. Her family's molded smiles set in stone ignored my tear-stained face and bruises. No one asked questions. They just chose to disregard what my stepfather was doing to me. It was a taboo subject, and we all had to shut the fuck up about it.

ANOTHER ONE OF MY TEENAGE CRUSHES...LITTLE DID I KNOW

CHAPTER

22

 soon returned home, but I was getting tired of home life. The beatings came less frequently, but the fact that no one ever tried to help made me angry.

"You've always been a difficult child," my mother said, trying to be diplomatic. "You're not the easiest person to live with sometimes, and of course that makes people angry."

Coming from my own mother, those words stung like a punch to the gut. I had nowhere to go; I had reached a dead end. At school, I lost interest in everything. My love of books and poetry branded me a nerd; being a rebel and talking back to the teachers was much more cool.

Desperate to fit in with the other kids, I stopped playing the piano, put away my books, and started wearing tiny skirts with see-through tops. I plastered my walls with pictures of Marlene Dietrich, Marilyn Monroe, and Greta Garbo, and I started taking acting and dancing lessons.

At sixteen, I entered my first talent competition, which was held at a nearby church. For days before the event, I practiced my dance moves and sang lyrics over an instrumental backing track. On the evening of the competition, I wore a white, lacy see-through top with a leather mini-skirt and fishnet tights. Then I covered my head and body in a traditional Islamic hejab so the audience would assume I was going to perform a sweet Iranian folk song. Just before going onstage, I removed the hejab to reveal my slutty outfit and did my number. The audience sat frozen, unsure how to react. When the song and dance routine ended, the stunned vicar managed to choke out, "Thank you for that." I left the stage, happy that I'd managed to sing and dance so well without losing my breath.

After that, I practiced nonstop in my room. "She sounds like an animal when she sings," my stepfather joked to my cousins. I didn't give a fuck about him throwing shitty remarks my way. Nothing could hurt me now—I was made of iron.

One Saturday afternoon, when no one else was around, I dared to defy him. When he told me to stop singing, I ignored him. *Wallop!* Down I went. Reeling in anger, I screamed and flailed and struck him back. Big mistake. He punched me until I hit the ground, then he began kicking my body. I lay still, weeping, until he stopped, breathless and pale. He left and went downstairs to put on the kettle. The pain meant nothing; my pride hurt more. I couldn't stand the humiliation. I was the loser in the fight, angry that he'd won only because he had more strength. Downstairs, I heard my uncle and aunt arrive.

"Having a catnap, are we?" my uncle said, peering into my room.

<hr/>

With everyone I knew turning a blind eye to what went on in our home, I took my life into my own hands. At school that year, I decided I needed to make some money to help me escape my home. My stepfather and I didn't speak anymore, and my mother was always tired from working all day at a children's home. The only thing I had was the raging sexual energy inside me that made my pussy throb like a wild animal.

Whenever I was alone in my room I had to ferociously release this feeling all on my own. I loved it. Out it gushed like a hot fountain. I'd rub faster and faster, stifling my moans so no one would hear. Lying in the middle of a puddle on the linoleum floor, limp with euphoria, I thought not of boys, but of being free.

In search of that freedom, I started making secret weekend trips to London to dance in a sleazy strip joint in Soho. The place was a tiny orifice in the wall of a tight alley. Its rusty peach walls and burnt coral curtains drew me into its razzmatazz.

"Changing room is there, luv," the woman who managed the club told me on my first day. She didn't even ask for my ID. I was seventeen. "The DJ will announce when you're on, so get ready."

In the dressing room, I mumbled hello to the other dancers. They all looked about ten years older than me. Feather boas and bangles were flung on chipped mirrors lit by anemic fluorescent tubes. Everywhere glitter glue oozed and dribbled on honey limbs and jelly titties. Talk of bad boyfriends, ill kids, and rent swirled into a whirlpool of words. I was nervous as hell but thrilled to be showing off my body to a bunch of men waiting for me on the other side of the flimsy curtain. I put on my school uniform, did up my hair in pigtails, and stole a peek at the magazine photo of Axl Rose I'd brought, which never failed to give me a wetness in my pussy.

Then I heard my name. I strolled out and calmly slid off my shirt and tie to expose my breasts to the warmth coming from the crowd of cheering, sweaty men. It hit me all at once. I finally felt good about myself—turned on, fueled by the sexiness of my own swelling tits, my curves, and that picture of Axl.

At that point, my existence splintered into two different ditches. At home I lived in a curdled mess comprised of a rabid stepfather and an overworked mother. Our flat, sweaty with my mother's home-made food, was a place of ever-brewing anger and bitterness, sugared over by her attempt to exude love from her steaming rice and stews.

Outside my room, my father argued with my mother in the relentless orange light. "She's a worthless, unemployed waste of space," I heard my stepfather tell my mother one night. "Why is she still living at home? Tell her to get out."

"Sshhhh!" my mother whispered. "She's not worthless. She just needs time to get things done. You have no right to say things like that."

My mummy was my hero for standing up to a bully. But inside I felt he was right. I was nothing—until I put on my Walkman and dissolved into the Doors or Guns N' Roses. Until I was limp and euphoric on the floor once again.

No one knew about my secret life—of the dancing, the nakedness, the jubilation I felt in front of the crowds of men. I didn't dare think what would happen if my family ever found out. To my family, to the kids at school, and even to myself, I was a total dork who read every book in the library and volunteered with animal rights groups. I was a shy virgin with no friends. To my stepfather, I was a useless waste of space. But when I was dancing, relishing the love I felt in front of the crowd, I felt wanted.

⊰⊱

I didn't want to lose my virginity until I was fully in love and issued the promise of a forever relationship. I wanted my first to be my last, and never to let my eyes stray in another direction. I wanted a man who'd love me back and always be there for me.

So I waited. And waited. I had this craving for a male body to entwine with mine, but I was too frightened even to let a man kiss me. The thought of a penis going in my vagina disgusted me. And so I held out for the one, and believed that it would happen one day.

In the meantime, I got myself off with girls—younger girls in particular. I didn't fancy the ones in caked makeup and garish shoes. I liked them simple and unvarnished. One who caught my eye was a fifteen-year-old schoolgirl who lived in the neighborhood. Chubby and chirpy, she reminded me of a chipmunk with her happy-go-lucky demeanor and sharp, shiny teeth. Her name was Leila and she looked up to me. So I invited her over to our house and took her into my room, where we sat up all night watching a program called *Carnal Knowledge* on TV.

"Have you ever done it with a boy?" Leila giggled as we sat on my bed in the flickering dark. In the early hours of the morning, my room hummed with the glow of the radiator and the television's silver lights.

"No, but I wonder what it feels like," I said matter-of-factly. "Let's practice and see how a boy would do it," I continued, laying her down on my bed and climbing on top.

I spread her legs and took off her panties. She was still giggling. Then I took off my panties and rubbed my pussy along hers.

"That feels good." She laughed that chipmunk laugh.

I was close to coming. I rubbed our pussies harder and harder together until I orgasmed, letting out a moan that I was sure would wake my parents. I left a nice gush of cum on her.

"Don't stop now," Leila pleaded in a low groan.

But I was done. Climbing off her, I wondered what sex with a boy my own age would be like.

CHILD OF THE '80S, ME AT AGE 13

I HAD NEVER DONE IT WITH A BOY — JUST A FIFTEEN-YEAR-OLD SCHOOLGIRL.

At the age of twenty-one, I rolled off the edge of the rusting tin lid that was my home and fell into London life full-time. There I discovered a hidden world of Middle Eastern and Pakistani men's social clubs—sweaty, hard-boiled candy drops of privacy stitched into niches of East London—where a multitude of Arab men poured a flurry of cash notes over the dancing girls like flying feathers as they performed the dances of *One Thousand and One Nights*, either belly dancing or Bollywood-style.

Work began at midnight in a neighborhood full of dimly lit curry houses and Indian textile shops, all gold-threaded and shuttered for the night. My Pakistani flatmate, Nasreen, and I would arrive at the club lugging bags fat with costumes. We often worked at a grimy-carpeted cesspit of a place called Sholeh, where we performed barefoot because after dancing all night, high heels killed our feet. The manager, Surinder, a short tubby Indian guy with his shirt half untucked, welcomed us with syrupy greetings and ushered us to the toilets or his cluttered office to change. There we would find a couple other girls already squeezing into heavily embroidered chiffons and mouthwatering silks, gold bangles, arabesque tunics, and thick eyeliner. I jangled in my weighty metal hip belt loaded with coins and a heavily jeweled bra dripping with tassels. I put on a head scarf fringed with gold coins to tantalize and give a promise of what was underneath.

Surinder would start chattering to Nasreen in their language, but all I could make out was *chicken korma* this or *lamb bhuna* that. The deafening thud of Hindi-Punjabi music signaled us to enter the hall. A harem of women danced in the middle of the room. Nasreen and I were instructed to go to the tables, to dance where the men were allowed to touch us, grab our hips, and grill us with persistent, sticky questions.

"Do you do anything else?" They'd raise their eyebrows as their heads bobbed from side to side with leery grins.

"No." We had to say it with a smile and hold back the urge to hit them. When the Arabic music came on, mesmerizing through the thick smoky air, I'd make my way to the middle of the floor to dance. Slinking along to the music of my childhood, I shimmied, snaked, and rolled my body, sometimes putting the sequined veil on my head to get further nods and full-toothed grins of appreciation. The dance was pure temptation, wrapped in crushed vermillion saris, or belly-dancing costumes tasseled with sticky sequins and heavy beading with a promising veil drawn over the eye. It was more about the suggestion of flesh than the actual thing itself—a single raised brow, the lingering sweep of an eye, the shimmy of a hip.

So I shimmied for money, with every curve, every snake-hip move, every quiver of the breast, belly dancing to perfection. In the corner, over by the decaying snooker table, dark-skinned and skinny as a sprig, Nasreen threw Bollywood moves at the ogling men around her.

"Very skinny," the men in turbans would say, shaking their heads sadly.

"And a dark one," others would murmur, as Nasreen forced her mouth to keep stretching for the smile she had to freeze on her face to pay the rent.

The combination of me peering from behind the veil and my tits heaving out of my sequined top always caused a horny stir among the Arab men.

One night, the disgusting, salivating oily men, with their faux Muslim beliefs and thick turbans, finally got to me, and I actually started feeling horny. I grabbed my heaviest head scarf, draped it over my head and mouth, went out into the middle of the dance floor, and removed my heavily tassled bra to go topless in front of the men. My tits jiggled, my nipples stiff as cherry pits as I played with them. But it was my covered hair and face, seen in this context, that was the most erotic to them: The symbol of Islam wronged with the taboo of a naked pair of breasts.

If they had known I was still a virgin at age twenty-three, the men would have been even more infatuated with me. But I didn't tell anyone that I had never done it with a boy—just a fifteen-year-old schoolgirl.

I was concentrating on saving money for university and finding a nice boy who would love me. In time, the graduating-from-university bit happened, and so did the losing of my virginity. The love thing never did though. Instead, I fell hard for rock 'n' roll.

HER CUNT GRIPPED HIM LIKE A WARM FRIENDLY HAND.

t all started when I became homeless.

It was August 2004 and I was forced to leave a beautiful flat in London I'd been sharing with a Finnish girl because she decided she wanted to be near her family and her two lovers. Unable to find anyone to share the rent, I couldn't afford to stay there by myself. It was a Wednesday night as I stood in front of the gold-leafed and cherub-decorated hallway mirror and took one last look. My belongings were in storage and all I had was my handbag, stuffed with cosmetics and pajamas. That night I was going to stay with my friend Karen and her boyfriend, Tom, who worked as a record producer.

I had graduated from university and had given a few speeches on gender and identity at conferences in Europe, which in turn started a battle in me: my inner dork was satisfied, but my urge to be wild was not. I had lost a little more innocence in that time, but I still felt I had to make up for my chaste and bullied teen-age years. I don't remember why I got so dressed up that night, but in the mirror I saw how high my hair was with extensions and how heavy my lids were with charcoal liner and lashes. With my fuchsia top and skinny trousers, I looked like some other girl. It was a balmy evening, the night before the rock magazine *Kerrang!*'s annual awards, when I rode the taxi to Karen and Tom's house, my head full with curious thoughts of Thai food and my nose stuffed full of white lines. Karen wouldn't be around until later, so Tom had booked a table at a Thai restaurant for us and his friend, Stuart Cable, the ex-drummer of the band Stereophonics.

I was bored by the time I got to the restaurant. I hated Thai food and didn't have the patience for chitchat with some former rock star. I associated the rock music scene with the smell of out-of-date piss in a rancid workingman's pub. Though I liked the music itself, I thought of rock clubs as unnecessarily loud, dirty, smelly, and full of stupid people. So I wasn't really that excited about meeting someone from that world. I felt free to be relaxed and completely myself.

When I first saw Stuart, he was standing by the bar and roaring with laughter—the kind of laughter I'd only ever seen exhibited by men who were either really confident or really mad. He was Welsh. He wore a purple shirt and clichéd leather pants. There was a billowing, frizzy mane of hair underneath the black trilby hat he wore. It looked wild and unkempt, but it entertained me. When Tom introduced us, I couldn't help but notice that the rock star had incredibly bright blue eyes; even in the inky shadows of the rainforest-themed restaurant they stood out, ready to fuck or fight. He immediately struck me as confident, but also down-to-earth—funny and a nice guy all in one. He was charisma bottled, like perfume and wine.

We soon found ourselves at a table in a setting that was some-how both a rainforest and a Bangkok whorehouse. Within the brew of luscious greenery and foliage, taped bird squalls echoed and red lights swelled around us. So I ate things that I was not used to, all too spicy and hostile. I wanted my feta cheese salad and lamb grill, but I was starting to like this guy so I swallowed the cardboard Thai food with gusto and relish.

I had never met anyone like him. He was like puréed sunlight, fizzy sherbet, enormous love. I found myself caught up in the sexual chemistry between us, which hooked me in a fresh, new way. When he spoke, his words were drenched in candy. He fucked my eyes with sharp rock-star attitude. And the whole time I felt so beautiful.

After dinner, back at Tom's place, more white lines were laid out on glass. I called my occasional fuck buddy, Lizzie, a well-bred girl fresh from private school. She was tall and blond—very English and dry like toast in her look and manner. But Lizzie was dirty as hell. She may have seemed like reserved royalty, but in the bedroom she became a porn star. Her sexual appetite was insatiable and she was the only girl I had ever met who could match my openness. I thought she would add a bit of spice to the tender meat of Stuart and I.

Stuart was in town to host the *Kerrang!* awards the next day, and he was wired. We looked at his script and I helped him rehearse a few acerbic quips. Afterward, he sat on a stool by the huge French windows that overlooked the Thames. On the cream sofa, Lizzie and I undressed and started making out—licking and biting each other's necks and nipples. Then I sat her down and straddled her, rubbing my sore premenstrual breasts over hers and grinding myself on her lap.

Looking back, I wish she hadn't been there. I ate her like vanilla ice cream, and she helped me have sex by shoving a piece of bath sponge inside me to conceal the fact that my period had started to trickle down. But by then I was cursing myself: All I really wanted was to be alone with Stuart.

When Stuart and I finally escaped to the bedroom about an hour later, my heart was jitterbugging in delirium. We were alone in the peach-colored spare bedroom on a single bed and we devoured one another like savage lions. The square, tidy room with its tall, rose-patterned pink curtains, Catholic in its simplicity, was ready to witness our carnality.

Stuart climbed on top and held me down. He pulled my freshly extensioned hair, and it hurt like a motherfucker. I remember looking at his face, his eyes blazing, his bulky, tattooed drummer's arms pressing over me. It was a new experience, and I felt myself become Harlequin-weak and wide open for him. His fucking was fast and furious, and in that bright room, he looked right into my eyes and his lust and beauty poured down onto my body. As soon as I said, "I want you to cum on me," he decorated my tummy.

I didn't understand how Stuart found the energy and ability to fuck me so masterfully all night, nor how his testicles were able to produce such a huge amount of sperm. By sunlight, I was exhausted but also on a natural high. I remember thinking as dawn crept into the room that I'd never felt so alive or so pure, like an eagle flying over the mountains. And I wanted more. A Jim Morrison lyric lodged in my brain: "Her cunt gripped him like a warm friendly hand."

In the morning, Stuart seemed pained and sheepish, with a look of guilt and inner turmoil about his girlfriend. But we departed as sweetly as we had met.

The experience left an imprint on my existence and stained my flesh carnival-crimson. I was now hooked on the adrenaline rush of that euphoric feeling. The answer to everything I wanted in life was born out of that experience, so I followed it like Sleeping Beauty to the top of the tower. I started tearing through the pages of rock magazines as if in search of the Holy Grail. These rockers, I thought, would fulfill my hunger for a free-spirited life, for breaking the rules, for laughing, for knowing the meaning of *it*.

CHAPTER

25

By 2004, I hardly saw my family anymore, and it was better that way. Going back to my parents' house in Bristol made me feel ill. It was permeated with the musty residue of past memories, reminding me of the silent bullied dork I once was. In London, I had a new flat in Camden and a new family in rock 'n' roll. I was determined to annihilate the past and save my life. The past as I'd known it was closer to extinction every day: back in Iran, the government had remained a strict dictatorship and free speech had become a crime punishable by death. My family was still a hotbed of political activity; none of them could ever go back to Iran.

It was in December of that year that I officially entered the inner sanctum of rock bands. It was my mother's birthday, and my present to myself was an all-night *Kerrang!* party where four new bands played—my first real rock-and-roll event. It was cold, and I didn't know the meaning of too many white lines, so like an aardvark I vacuumed up fat lines of potent powder to help me deal with the cold and the pain of wearing eight-inch heels of shiny metal. Dolora—a schoolgirl friend of mine I called Lori—watched me like a curious kitten as I searched for slutty, attention-seeking clothes, each outfit begging me to pick it for this night, for this adventure. All the while James Douglas Morrison's voice poured from the speakers as the Doors' music filled the tiny room.

Lori had never known her parents, and I didn't ask her much about them because I could see a ring of pain darken the doorway of her eyes whenever I did. All I knew was that she was now staying with a distant relative and made a very long trek to her high school each day. Her seventeen-year-old buxom body was peach-soft, and so devoted to raging white that there were no tones or shadows on her skin. Just miles and miles of Antarctic snow. She had dyed jet-black hair fashioned like Bettie Page and a sunny giggle, eager to please. Though her sexual appetite was sky-high and she fucked with the ferocity of a wild animal, she'd never had an orgasm. Many girls of all ages in our social circle had tried and repeatedly failed to make her cum. I wanted to take her under my wing and look after her. She was becoming my dearest and most loved confidante—and, besides, I really liked fucking her.

Outside, the winds and ice of December did not deter me as we searched for a cab. Inside the taxi, my head whirled like a cuckoo clock and my heart couldn't wait any longer as we snaked through Hyde Park toward Kings Cross, the part of London spawned from vomit and cruelty, a nauseating zigzag of pollution and orphaned construction work.

When we found the venue amid the bowels of this industrial shit hole, it added a taste of bitterness to my cocaine-numbed tongue. A cobbled pathway led to the tiny door of the club—a pathetic attempt to whisper, "I am surrounded by warehouses, but I have character." So my ankles battled with my fucking high heels to balance my wobbly body on the little stones as I lagged behind Lori.

Passing through the club's tiny door, we entered a black hollow gut where strangers walked around, their eyelashes spitting neon-blue mascara, their clothes aggressive to the common man's eye. In one lonely corner, over by the toilets, a Mötley Crüe tribute band conducted auditions. Vince Neils of every shape and size took turns at the mic: skinny and fat Vince Neils, pre-op and post-op Vince Neils came forward to "Kickstart My Heart" and "Shout at the Devil." My ambition for the night had been to stand in front of the Crüe auditions and see if I could spot any potential for wild adventure. But my objective evaporated into the black night as, fueled by cocaine, decomposed by vodka and whiskey, I charged around the two-story club like a mule, looking, looking, with Lori at my heels.

A band called Poison the Well was onstage. It was basically a guy standing still and shouting with a demon-horror-movie voice while four guys clanged and banged instruments behind him. Even in my obscure state, I couldn't stand the sound.

I tumbled downstairs to the female toilets, and I could see the line was a foot long. If I joined the end of it, I knew my bladder would putrefy with all the toxins I'd put into it. On the other hand, there were only a few guys in the men's toilets. So I squatted down in the urinals and took a much-needed piss with the guys. I'd been brought up with manners, so naturally I apologized to the men staggering in. Their double-takes jerked them awake from their drunken stupor. I looked up to see a row of limp penises dangling above me. The stench of stale urine wafted through my hair. The obliterated boys woozily nodded their approval of my vagina and my brazenness. Only when an old man with a battered leather jacket and no teeth looked at me like I was Satan did I suddenly feel ashamed. Still, I recommend that all females fuck the queue and take advantage of the gents' washrooms.

Walking around the club that night—with all the freaks with their illogical haircuts, the wrinkly punk men, the child goths, and the vibe of illicit chemicals—I felt at home. I was Cinderella at the ball flying like an eagle: eyes observant, sharp, marinating in the scene. My tits were Jelly Cones on show, firm and huge, my legs dying to spread open for a rocker. It was the same freedom of soul I'd felt running around in my cherry-print dress in the mud alleys of Tehran at dusk.

Upstairs, I stood and watched a little emo band, InMe, all Essex energy and Bambi eyes lined with kohl, whining loudly as young Japanese girls with Hello Kitty backpacks went ballistic. Soon, it was two A.M. and time to go downstairs, where the headliners, a boy metal band called Bullet For My Valentine, were taking the stage.

Their name seemed interesting, so I bulldozed my way to the front to see what the deal was. Next to me stood a girl with watermelon tits that would've whacked my eyes black and blue if she'd swung around. She was determined to make eye contact with the lead singer, a good-looking son of a bitch. I watched her technique and copied it. I hated the music, but I was looking for an adventure to water color my night. I held a condom in my hand and took off my lucky crotchless panties. While dancing, I threw my underwear at the lead singer's feet.

Then I realized: those panties were expensive. So when the band finished their set, I climbed onstage to retrieve them. He was standing there, the beautiful singer. The cocaine was swimming toward the pit of my belly, and grazing and gnawing at my crotch. So I asked him if he wanted to have a threesome with Lori and me.

And that's when I first went backstage. Backstage—that magical place where your dreams come true. *Backstage*. The word sounded like a delicious secret code, where decadent, exotic stories effortlessly domino into one another. Where there is only happiness and laughter, luscious lips and orgasms, loving friendships and chocolate cake. So I headed backstage.

The security guy was a cliché: big and hostile.

"I want to go backstage, please," I announced, matter-of-fact, like I'd just arrived at a tea party.

He looked us up and down as if we were on drugs, which we were. "You don't have wristbands, so you can't go," he snapped, looking away as if watching a ball game in the distance.

"What do you want me to do?" I said.

A guy walking past stopped in his tracks and smiled. "If you suck my cock, I'll give you a pass," he said, as if this were a business transaction.

I reveled in sleaze, and this seemed like the most typical of all rock clichés and I so wanted to do it. But I decided to take it one step further.

"No. We'll *both* suck your cock at the same time," I said, motioning to Lori, who looked at me with a naughty glint in her china-doll blue eyes. I was a bad influence on her, but she was like a curious kitten, eager to devour any new sexual experience.

The guy with the passes led us both through the doors. Just past them was a tiny room. He took us in there and unzipped his trousers. Getting down on my knees, I started the most perfect deep throat I could. Feeling bad, I decided to push Lori away, not wanting her to get involved. After thirty seconds, I stopped.

"There you go," I said.

"Is that it?" he looked at me, his eyes pleading like Oliver Twist for more.

"I'm shy," I said, grabbing Lori and running out in search of the rockers.

There were a lot of corridors and little rooms back there, all lit up with rows and rows of fluorescent lights, as if there should be no dark corners in which to do dark deeds. Instead, everything should be done in the open fields of this landscape, on these phlegm-soiled carpets under the eyes of surgical lights. We opened door after door until we found a tiny room where InMe was hanging out with photographers and friends. They were so vanilla and milky that I wanted to clap my hands in approval like an auntie after a school play. And then I saw the Bullet For My Valentine boys, all Welsh attitude and emo hair.

I didn't even know his name, the singer. But he was very pretty. I walked straight up and kissed him as if it were the most normal thing in the world. I felt like a teenage fan.

"I'm Matt," he said with those adorable lips, which made me kiss him again. While we were talking about Wales, a wild-eyed cavewoman marched up to me screaming obscenities. She grabbed my hair, pulling me toward the door.

"I don't want any groupie sluts near my band. FUCK. OFF."

Shocked by the pain of having my hair pulled, I held back tears. "I have hair extensions," I mumbled. "They're new." I couldn't understand her demonic rage.

"I'm the band's manager. And I'm Matt's girlfriend," she hissed in my ear. "Get the fuck out of here."

I managed to squirm away and cowered in the corner as if in detention. A few minutes later, Cavewoman, with her Lego haircut and butch clothing, bounced down the corridor as I drifted back to the boys. This time I kissed another boy, Padge. We were talking about threesomes when I felt my hair being yanked again—this time with such force that I let out a guttural scream. She was back.

"I thought I told you to leave my band alone. Fuck off!" Then she grabbed Lori by the hair with the other hand, holding us like two plots of grass. As everyone tried to scrape her off us, I leaned forward to bite her ear. Unfortunately, they managed to pull us apart before I could reach her, and Lori and I were ushered into another room. We could still hear her screaming. "I want those bitches out of here."

So I decided to go out there and head-butt her.

"Please," one of the roadies begged me, "she's one of the most powerful women in London. Don't mess with her."

I pushed past the roadie to look for the bitch. It took half a dozen roadies to staple me to the ground: a few of them fatty, a few muscular. Men are so strong, and I've never had the strength to overcome that power when they hit me.

"Just wait here," they said as they left Lori and me.

Then I heard a voice with an American accent ask, "So did they kick her out?" We turned around to see two biker-type guys I recognized from that awful band Poison the Well kicking back on lounge chairs, swigging beer and smirking at us. Their arms were thick and heavily tattooed, and they wore leather trousers. I got hard just looking at them.

"I'm Derek. I like your tits," the shorter one introduced himself, looking at my chest, which was packed in and displayed from behind four horizontal spaghetti straps.

"Thanks," I said. "I like your American-ness."

"These tits are real. You should feel them. They feel so fucking good," Lori purred from behind me.

Derek opened the door and shouted into the hall to the lead guitarist. "Hey, Ryan, you gotta come and see these tits!" Ryan appeared and immediately announced that he was into auto-erotic asphyxiation.

I took off my top to let my tits swing free and Derek took us out to the bar to do tequila shots and down triple vodkas. After all I'd consumed that night, by my fifth shot, I felt as if my lips had disappeared.

"We're staying at the Columbia Hotel—wanna come?" Derek said, kissing us both. He took the lead, and gave us sexual compliments, which was such a fucking change from the emotionally constipated Englishmen we were used to dealing with. He took each of us on an arm and began to march us toward the exit doors. Before leaving the building, I frantically asked around for a pen. Eventually, some girl found a Magic Marker. On my right arm, in big letters, I wrote:

GROUPIE.

he Columbia Hotel's squiggly staircase reminded me of an old-fashioned carousel, fragile and thin like English biscuits.

"Give us a minute and then come up. Ryan and I are in Room 316." Derek handed me a room key and got in the lift.

"If we do girl-on-girl, I need to shower first," Lori said, panicking a little.

We got in the lift five minutes later. I plonked myself down on the floor, took off my black stilettos, and rolled on a pair of deep lace-top stockings. No matter how drunk I was, I always put on sexy lingerie when I knew I was going to have a wild ride.

We stumbled into the room and saw Ryan playing guitar while Eric scribbled lyrics. I threw my stuff down on the bed and straddled Ryan, the neck of his guitar pushing into the fleshy overspill of my exposed-stocking thigh.

"Are you gonna fuck me?" I whispered in his ear. He looked up and pushed the hair out of my face. Putting his instrument down, he began to gently stroke my ass.

I moved away and went for Lori, who had stripped down to her French-cut purple lace panties and matching bra and spread herself like dairy butter on the bed. She was so young, tender like lamb.

"You have a Miami ass," Derek said, pointing to Lori, "and you"—pointing to me—"have porn star tits."

"Thank you!" I grinned and started peeling off my clothes while sucking on Lori's mouth. I licked her navel and bit her little tummy. Kissing her marble-white inner thighs, I made my way toward her flower. Derek immediately took position behind me, rubbing his crotch against my ass. The stiffness of the bulging denim pressed against me.

I kept eating Lori, even though we hadn't showered.

"I wanna see you girls sixty-nine," Ryan said from the corner of the room as he continued playing guitar.

Lori tasted peachy as always. I hoped I tasted of strawberries and cream and Chanel No. 5, not of fish fingers or feta cheese.

"I can only watch because I have a girlfriend," Ryan said quietly. I had a feeling he'd be like that. He had a certain Amish quality about him.

"But I need to look into your eyes while you're being fucked," he continued, like a scientist. He positioned himself in front of my face so he could study it as I got fucked from behind.

Ryan sighed in quiet happiness as he explained his strangling fetish. I had a feeling his hang-ups stemmed from a Bible-belt mentality, which gave his eyes a quiet, psychopathic look. "I gotta suffocate myself so I can cum," he said. "I use one hand to jerk off and with the other I choke my throat."

"Right on, man!" I laughed as he scurried off to the toilet. This seemed to be a significant moment for him, which we had to respect. I wasn't sure if he was joking or not, but when he returned a few minutes later, his face was purple and his eyes bulged. He couldn't breathe well, so I wondered if he'd finally been able to shoot his load.

It was about eight in the morning by the time Derek, Lori, and I stopped fucking. I was a bit sore as I put on my clothes. The band had to leave and check out of the hotel. The staircase spun before me like candy floss as I walked down. I couldn't sleep for days because of the fairy-tale adrenaline rush I was on.

ROADIES. I LOST MY HEAD. IN THEIR LAPS.

ori and I stuck to each other like glue. Rock bands became our talk, food, and song. I think we were both on a quest to find love and reassurance. I worked like a donkey at my belly-dancing job to make money to travel to gigs. And at the shows, I danced and kissed like I was Cinderella at the ball. Then Velvet Revolver came to London in January. And I became the village idiot.

I loved their songs. I was there for the music, not to get laid. Slash had never been my type, and Scott Weiland looked to me like an anorexic gay junkie who gyrated his hips better than I ever could. Only Duff was remotely interesting to me. He was much more "fuck-me" looking now than in his Guns N' Roses days, when he was essentially a subservient drunk. It was still winter, and I didn't want to put any clothes on, so I decided to see every Velvet Revolver show in London that January.

The line outside the Hammersmith Apollo stretched down the street. Scores of little boys in Guns N' Roses T-shirts waited with their dads, who were in leather jackets and middle-aged euphoria. Fat couples in denim with frizzy mops of hair stood side by side, dutiful and obedient. I was in a crushed velvet corset and a skirt of flimsy tussore. The freezing wind slapped my bare skin. I looked around for groupie-type girls and didn't see any.

Lori and I stood at the front of the line for what seemed like hours before the doors opened. Unknown faces in flannel hoodies handed out flyers for Adler's Appetite, former Guns N' Roses drummer Steven Adler's new band.

The support bands were crap, and I was bored but determined to maintain my stilettoed position behind the barrier, even though I was getting crushed by the heaving crowd and drenched by kids throwing beer. Velvet Revolver blew me away. I lost my voice screaming along with every song.

Someone in the crowd behind me untied my corset and it fell off. That was when the roadies noticed me. "Here's a pass. Come to the aftershow party."' A big bulldog of a guy, who said his name was Anthony, pressed stickers into Lori's hand and mine. They said, "Guest Pass."

In the gutted pit of the mauve-rinsed toilets, we looked into the cracked mirrors. The clunky white sinks hosted squelched toilet paper and broken plastic cups. A group of girls, in blurred lipstick and razored fishnet tights worn under knee-high black leather boots, compared levels of drunkenness and gossiped about the band.

"Slash has definitely got his wife with him," said one with purple hair extensions.

"Yeah, but she's really fat—very trailer trash," said a stick-skinny girl in a baby-doll nightie as she smeared on gloops of lipstick. "Slash is totally pussy-whipped."

"All their wives are here," a voice from the toilet shouted. "Matt Sorum's girlfriend is really young. Did you see her? She's that little blonde with the short fringe who was standing sidestage. She's really pretty."

"How are we gonna get near them then? Fuck!" screamed another, sitting on the wet floor with a plastic beer cup looking genuinely bewildered.

I remember noticing, as I walked out the door, how hard their faces all looked—broken, with a desperate, defeated look in their eyes. They wore far too much makeup, trying to prop up their slouched features. I felt happy I wasn't like them.

Upstairs at the party, I was quickly surrounded by roadies. The bulldog, Anthony, turned out to be the tour manager or something. Carl, another roadie, looked like Robert Redford. Various camera and guitar-tech guys, tired and haggard, sniffed around me like I was birthday cake. I got a bit scared.

Anthony darted over to me in a shot. "Do you wanna come upstairs to the dressing rooms?" he asked. I looked over at Lori, who was wasted, leaning back in the midst of all the crew guys. One of the guys, named Tom, was pulling her up by the arms as she giggled, falling back to collect her belongings.

"C'mon, it'll be fun." Anthony put his arm around my waist. He reminded me of a truck driver, and I felt a bit disgusted, but I still followed him. Lori and Tom trailed behind.

The four of us walked into a catacomb of narrow corridors and up tiny stone steps to the very top of the venue, where empty, compact rooms with lightbulbed mirrors were parceled into hidden corners. It seemed like a forbidden tower, desolate and out of reach to anyone else. Even in my cloudy state, I wasn't surprised that no one else was around. I knew what Anthony and Tom wanted from us in those tiny silent rooms. They switched off the lights, and Lori and I knelt down, as if in prayer, and did what we did in pitch blackness.

I was in full sleaze mode that night, so when we went back to the crew's hotel in Kensington I was delighted to find a party going on in one of the rooms, with beautiful girls sprawled across deep cushions and guys lounging with guitars and beer. Someone put some Mötorhead on full blast and Lori started to tongue a girl who looked like Demi Moore. "You're so beautiful," these model-type girls kept whispering above us—seducing us with a candy swirl of compliments until we were drunk with feathery sighs and kisses. As random people ran in and out of neighboring rooms, half naked and drunk, Anthony pulled me aside and poured thick, brown liquor down my throat.

"Can you come outside with me?" he said. "I wanna talk to you."

Once we were in the corridor, he looked at me hard. I got worried.

"You know the guy who was doing the sound stuff tonight?" he whispered.

"Yeah, what about him?"

"Look, he's an old guy. He's tired and he hasn't gotten laid in months. Please."

"What do you want me to do?"

Anthony knelt down in front of me, hands clasped, begging. "Go see him."

Roadies. I lost my head in their laps. They were waiting for me at the hotel bar. By morning my jaw ached and my lips were swollen. And I hadn't even gotten laid.

got so bored after the Velvet Revolver experience—not just because of the comedown from the Tony Montana portions of white powder, but because the whole experience felt less like reckless, sleazy rock debauchery than like a corporate event. Lori and I were craving another high. So we said, "Fuck it, let's go see Steven Adler's band." They were playing Guns N' Roses songs at Camden Underworld a few nights later.

The club was packed with bandana-wearing long hairs, flailing and swinging their arms as if anticipating salvation. Two goth girls I'd seen stageside at Velvet Revolver stood patient as snakes, peeping at Steven onstage. So many people who had been in the mosh pit at Velvet Revolver were here, too, ramming their young bull horns forward to the very front.

"Steven Adler, man, he's a fuckin' legend," said a boy with a fluffy beard. Two other excited grinning boys, one with a big mane of blond hair like Adler's, were doing donkey drop-kicks with merriment.

We bored our way to the lip of the stage, where we stood firmly, compressed from all sides and baptized with beer, as we watched Adler's skintight-trousered singer, Jizzy Pearl, shriek my favorite songs. The guitarist, Keri Kelli, was the sexiest in the band, but small-boned. And the bassist, Robbie Crane, was cute and raven-haired, but kind of big-boned.

Steven reminded me of a cross between a California surfer dude and a Labrador puppy, with his wild blond mane and constant cheery enthusiasm. Lori and I slid our hands between Kelli's leather-clad legs to make him desire us. "You're so beautiful," Steven mouthed from behind his drums.

Our crotch-stroking was successful. When the band came out to sign merchandise on a table next to the bar after the gig, a voice whispered in my ear: "We're staying at the Holiday Inn in Camden. My room number is 210."

I started hurling chunks as soon as we got to the band's hotel—especially when I saw the two buck-toothed, cross-eyed chicks Jizzy had brought back. There was a shaggy-permed German biker chick of hefty proportions who'd been following the band all over Europe. She was swigging from beer cans enthusiastically, so delirious to be there. There was a short, silent Swedish girl who followed Steven around like a bulldozer. She wouldn't even look at anyone else in the hotel room. Instead, she just stood quietly next to Steven as he ordered everyone around like a toddler tyrant. I had to look up to Steven: He'd been part of a legendary record, *Appetite for Destruction*, by a band whose lyrical and musical weight I really respected. But he had a weird, whiny voice, and talked out of the side of his mouth, lopsided due to a drug-related stroke. I soon passed out, as Lori gnawed away at Jizzy's cock.

The next night, I stashed a fat baggie of coke in my blood-red silk purse, along with condoms, makeup, and mints, and headed out to meet the band at the Hard Rock Café. The place was jammed with Euro-tourist teenage types eating hamburgers with joy in their hearts as they sat worshipping huge posters of Jimi Hendrix. Steven was serene at the center of the action. He sat glowing like an angelic little child, smiling sweetly and bouncing his blond waves around his face.

I was bored, so I stood up to do an erotic dance for the whole place when Robbie and Keri came over.

"Man, she's loaded!" Keri said to Lori.

They decided it would be better for my general disposition if I packed more drugs up my nose to cancel out the drunkenness. I followed the guys' orders and staggered to the bathroom for medicinal purposes. My gums and throat went numb. It felt like there were too many teeth in my mouth, which was bitter and dry. But I was turned on and fucking happy. Minutes after the first escalating rush to my head, the fuck-me-hard passion followed and ignited. I wanted to fuck now, like an endangered species moments from extinction. I hurtled out of the bathroom, with what I was sure were red flames flaring out of my nostrils, and headed straight for Keri Kelli, poor little skinny guy.

"So are you gonna just flirt with me or are you gonna actually fuck the shit out of me?" I hissed in his ear.

He looked scared. In fact, I'm sure he was shaking. I just wanted him to do me right there—to hold my head down and feed me his cock in every hole. His Adam's apple bobbed as he swallowed.

"Umm . . . yeah, I will. Later."

What a fucking wuss.

⚫

A few days later, Lori and I were at the Bristol show when we saw the silent Swede slink out like a vole from a back lair. Jizzy was pissed off that night, but then Jizzy was always pissed off. His face always looked angry. That was the night I met Ostara. She had a cherubic face, child-like and devoid of makeup, with naturally golden ringlets tumbling around her face. She was dressed starkly plain for a groupie, and I wondered why. But then she explained: the dorky, homely look was part of her game plan.

"It always works with rockers," she said in a genteel accent. She reminded me of a porcelain doll, freshly packaged and sealed, complete with quaint mannerisms.

"I'm going to have Steven Adler. He's my idol," she declared delicately.

"Good luck with that," I said. "There's a Swedish girl who's gripped on to him like a koala bear."

"Oh, I really hope I get him," she sighed, dreamily. "I've wanted him for so long."

In her fairy voice, she told us how much she liked pain when having sex. Incredible, orgasmic, jaw-breaking, passing out, sweet darling pain. Then, courteous as a lady, she asked whether Lori or I was with any of the band members: she didn't want to be stepping on anyone's territory.

After the show, the three of us girls got in the band's van. I noticed that Jizzy was digging Ostara, while Adler was cuddling the silent Swede on the front seat.

We drove to the edge of Bristol and pulled in at a rundown motel, where truckers took breaks on their long night drives. When this bunch of half-naked, thigh-high-booted chicks nuzzling on the ears of dirty rockers fell through the doors around two A.M., the elderly woman nodding off behind reception looked as if an electric rod had shot up her anal tract. She watched in silence as fifteen of us stumbled up to the rooms.

I thought Jizzy liked pain, so it made sense that he and Ostara took off together. A few girls left a confetti trail of lost-puppy looks after Steven as he stumbled off to his room with the Swede. So I left Lori and Keri in his room and launched a voyeuristic spree down the corridors.

Peeking into Jizzy's room, I saw Ostara naked and straddling him. She had a big red mark on the side of her arm and he had red raw cuts on his chest, so I figured they'd already consummated their pain. Ostara grinned wide as a canoe as she climbed off to nestle in his arms.

"You gonna come join us?" Jizzy asked.

I ran off.

<hr/>

Though we were exhausted and broke, a few days later Lori and I bought dirt-cheap flights to Belfast to see the band again. We missed them all so much—even their tour manager, Tommy, a big hulk with a handlebar mustache who worked his fucking ass off for the band.

Belfast played host to a gray February sky. The band was performing at the Rosetta Bar, a smashed-up biker's joint. We were merciless in our dress and makeup. Our dagger stilettos were a motherfucker to walk in on the shards of broken bottles and debris strewn on the floor. Planted on benches inside was a sweaty smorgasbord of pissed-off, middle-aged bikers, animated milky white kids, and pouting teenage girls.

In the back, Steven sat on a couch surrounded by his adoring fans, who dangled on every dribbling word. He was smiling and lovely but seemed to be tipping on the edge of violence.

"Here are my girls!" He beamed when he saw Lori and me. "Come sit here!" he said, motioning to his lap. We kissed his cheeks and positioned ourselves lightly on each thigh. As usual, he ordered everyone to fetch stuff and bring him more alcohol. He was also getting ravishingly stoned. Considering that he was a recovering heroin addict, I asked him whether he really ought to be consuming any mind-altering substances. But he ignored the advice, basking in the adoration oozing from his young boy fans, while Lori and I took off our tops to let our tits sway in the stale dressing-room breeze. That was the most fun these little northern Irish boys were going to get in this town.

"Can you help me take a piss?" Steven mumbled to me, stumbling toward a big sink piled with dishes in the corner. "Honey, can you help me out here?"

I didn't know exactly what he meant by "help," but I walked over. He was holding a joint in one hand and a can of beer in the other. Then I understood what he wanted. *Everybody's got something to hide except for me and my monkey.* The lyrics rang in my head as I held his dick for him and aimed it at the sink. When he finished peeing, I shook it and put it back in his pants.

By the time we left for the hotel, Steven was a wreck. A broken-looking skinny blond girl followed us, waiting for anyone who would do her. As soon as we all got to Steven's room, it became clear that it was an utter urgency for him to have *Family Guy* play at full volume on Tommy's portable DVD player. Steven then proceeded to get fully naked, which served as a signal for Lori to go down on her knees and start sucking.

"I said suck it, not lick it!" Steven whined in his baby voice. Lori looked crestfallen.

Stung by his whining, I instinctively jumped into my mommy role.

"It's okay. Let me take over." I stepped in to relieve Lori from her heinous duty. I did my very fucking best, teasing and blowing him like my very sanity depended on it, to stop him from whining like a baby. It hushed him up for a bit, so he must have liked it. I didn't. I wasn't even attracted to him, but I kept going to shut him up.

However I wouldn't have sex with Steven, and that pissed him off big time. Snarling, he moved on to the skinny blonde, just as she came out of the bathroom, all happy and shiny with one of the band members' sperm on her face. I hopped over to the other bed and Lori and I snuggled like babies, listening to Steven fucking as *Family Guy* blared in the background.

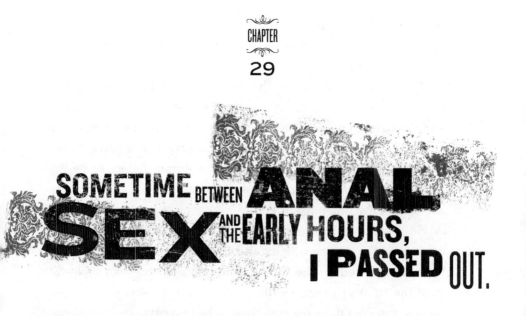

SOMETIME BETWEEN ANAL SEX AND THE EARLY HOURS, I PASSED OUT.

Although I went on occasional binges, I was never really that into drugs. When I did coke from time to time, it was only to feel glamorous. One trip to Cardiff, Wales, though, ended everything.

It was March 3, 2005, and I was weary and full of stale vomit. All I wanted was to dig a hole in the fresh ground and sleep with the moles. My mind felt like a crumbling building, vacant and dumb with Colombian powder, sleepless nights, and bed-hopping. I was like a doll: fully made up, huge breasts, tiny corseted waist, cherry-plump lips, and vacant eyes. Though I'd had another fuck-feast with Stuart Cable, formerly of the Stereophonics, it hadn't moved me like the first time back in August. It had been a night of black hair against black hair. My womb was fed from his rock-starriness, but my mind and body were like a flour mill, and ill with cocaine and exercise. Still, I began planning to write a letter to *FHM* magazine, telling them that since Marilyn Manson had already claimed the title of God of Fuck, then Stuart should be the King of it.

I hadn't even been thinking of going to see a band that night, let alone the Towers of London. But Lori was pulling at my apron like the whining child she could be. To me it sounded like,

"Mommy, Mommy, please can we go and see those bad punk-rock boys we saw last week? We might have some fun this time, since it's not a home show."

We had seen the Towers the previous week in London at the Camden Underworld, and it had been a disaster. It was winter, it was cold, and I was too tired to fight the sugar-rushing hyperactive child that Lori had turned into. Hanging around bands had become like food for her. Ever since our detachment from Adler's Appetite, she'd been like a wounded animal. She needed a pack, a family, as she didn't have one herself.

We were used to American bands. They knew the game, and carried out the routine with natural choreographed precision. Girls were handpicked by the crew or the band: during sound check, from the front of the stage during the show, or afterward if they hung around to talk to the crew. It was the tour manager's responsibility to make sure there was sufficient transportation to carry the girls to the hotel and that enough rooms would be available to handle the band's desires—whether they wanted an orgy, threesomes, or just one-on-ones. That was the etiquette, and it was understood.

The Towers of London were the first English band we'd been with, and even though they looked cock-rock and Mötley Crüe, they didn't seem to know the game. Englishmen never fail to disappoint me with their all-talk, no-cock act. But we'd been lonely since Adler's Appetite had gone back to America, so Lori and I had scoured the rock magazines to find somebody new. In our fragile state, the small color photo of the Towers on page seven of *NME* brought a bit of hope and color into our lives. The one called The Rev looked like Nikki Sixx; therefore, he was going to be mine.

The Towers were a hair band, but their sound was punky, which isn't exactly a leg spreader. Still, I stuck myself to the front of the stage, displaying myself to the band, waiting patiently until the end so I could get The Rev and give him some fun.

After the gig, a bunch of music industry types and *Kerrang!* staffers were milling around the Underworld. Suddenly, The Rev tapped me on the shoulder and handed me a piece of paper with his hotel and phone number written on it in red marker.

But things didn't turn out so rosy. There was no gathering of the chosen girls, no taxis or buses waiting outside to take us to a hotel, no planned action. And so Lori and I had no choice but to follow The Rev and his hangers-on along Camden High Street, past the market and past late-night garages and dealers. My shoes, of the eight-inch, needle-thin variety, gave my calves a workout hard enough to produce blood blisters. But that was all right: I was gonna have fun with The Rev.

By the time we finally reached the Camden Lock Hotel in Chalk Farm, the initial small crowd had become The Rev Army and I was not even sure that I'd get penetrated that night. And I didn't give a fuck anymore. I was used to being looked after, to being made to feel special. But this just made me feel like a hobo, a Camden tramp trailing behind people just to get a sniff of The Rev.

He was beautiful, though, and that was the only reason I stuck around. Upstairs in the hotel, the singer, Donny Tourette, had smashed his fist through the window for some reason when he was alone in his room; people were lined up outside his door, banging to get in. I walked into another room, where a Lemmy lookalike was sitting on a bed talking about squirrels while around fifteen people lay about listening intently. A really young girl in a knitted bauble hat was making a cup of tea and putting biscuits around a saucer.

"Hello, I'm the band's dealer," the Lemmy guy said, extending his hand and smiling at me. The Rev laughed as I sneered my hello, pissed off that there were so many people around. I looked at The Rev, lying back on the bed with little blond girls scattered around him like sheep. And I knew I didn't want to be there.

"C'mon, we're going. This is boring." I tugged on Lori's arm moodily.

"No, I wanna stay!" she whimpered and stamped her foot. What a baby. I left her there and went to wait in the foyer.

That's when I took proper note of Dirk Tourette. He was sitting at the end of the corridor on a window ledge, talking to a stressed-out fat girl. He wasn't really my type: too short and boyish and blond. As I approached him, the fat girl scurried off upstairs. He was grinny like Top Cat and cool, draped over the ledge with his skin-tight bleached jeans, snaked torso, no shirt, and an inferno of peroxide-blond spikes. He reminded me of someone in a sixties film: an arty boy kitten mixed with Jack Nicholson cool.

"Do you want to know why they call me Dirk Diggler?" The words toppled down his lips.

He unzipped his skin-tight jeans and, I swear, this thing rolled out of his pants the length and width of a well-fed baby's arm. I got scared. I stood silently in front of him as he laughed a low throaty giggle. Then he turned and kissed me softly, never taking his gaze off me. He had very light blue eyes, just like Stuart. I liked his quirkiness; it fit in with my own weirdness. He wasn't manly, but he had such raw street-urchin energy that I could smell his free spirit. So when Lori finally came to find me, I left that night with at least a glimmer of hope in my eyes.

———

Now we were on our way to Cardiff to see them again. I had left home with my huge lead-heavy bubblegum pink bag. Inside were a few of my corsets, my black leather and lace bodysuit, and a lico-rice medley of shoes: some of them movie starlet, jewel-encrusted, baby pink styles; others angry, rock-chick, PVC types.

On the train, I worked on my letter to *FHM* about Stuart as Lori painted her face. I'd chosen the same outfit I'd worn to the *Kerrang!* all-nighter. Though I usually considered all-black outfits bad luck, this time I thought it might bring me luck. I wore a black halter top with an open front and four rows of thin horizontal straps that reined in my breasts, and I finished the look with a short black skirt cinched by a pink-bowed trousseau at the back. Lori had on her shaggy Afghan coat.

The venue was near an old castle about a fifteen-minute walk from the station. The March wind was cut-glass sharp, ripping my thin skin. The gig was over by the time we arrived, and people milled around like black and red ants. As usual, each member of the band was followed by bunches of ecstatic and grateful girls—beads of perspiration on their apple cheeks, bursting with euphoric pride. The band's reputation must have seeped into all the dark pockets of the country, into every village and every groupie's bedroom, gnawing at their *NME*-moist panties and making them go find and conquer this band that gave cock so easily and fed on cocaine. It was still early days for the band, so many offers of free pussy from every corner of the land must have been mind-blowing for five twentysomething-year-old boys.

The Rev was signing autographs as we approached. He seemed shy, unlike Dirk. Afterward, we talked with him for a bit. Then Lori and I decided to go join the others in the band's tiny dressing room.

"I'm gonna take you with me and fuck your brains out. You're fucking hot," Dirk whispered discreetly into the back of my hair as he walked past. It made me feel ecstatic and at peace and validated. He had his guitar out, and started playing some song as giggling girls and boy fans watched adoringly. I sat on a white square table across from him. A Marilyn Monroe–esque blonde cozied up to Dirk, but even as she did, he refused to take his gaze off me. He had effortless charisma, raw street spunk, and cunt-wetting sexuality, and I was hooked.

That night became a blurry blare. I was exhausted from days of drinking, drugging, and fucking, but I still carried on drinking and drugging like a traffic jam.

The band wanted to ravage the town. Dirk wanted me to go with him on the tour bus, but I was being pulled from the other side by Donny, Dirk's brother. As lead singer, Donny had to have first go with a girl before anyone else in the band. That was the rule.

Eventually, I wriggled free and ended up with Dirk, Snell the drummer, Tommy the bassist, and Stoksie the tour manager. The

Marilyn Monroe girl looked close to tears; she gave me looks of venom for taking Dirk's attention away from her. She walked with Donny, The Rev, and Lori, followed by a couple strippers and hangers-on, to a club called Metros.

I was felt up by everyone on the band's bus, but only Dirk interested my head and sexual organs. Even in my drunken state I saw him for the beauty he was: charismatic, arty, and free-spirited. My friends thought he was effeminate and looked like a goat.

Exhausted, I downed triple vodkas one after the other to take the edge off. As hordes of hangers-on clung to each band member, I danced in the middle of the floor, making sure everyone noticed me. The Rev danced with one of the stripper girls—a cute, petite brunette. Grabbing her away from him, I stuck my tongue down her throat. Then I grabbed The Rev and stuck my tongue down his throat as well. I brought the two of them together, and the three of us kissed. Just to make sure I was getting enough attention, I took off my top to a Franz Ferdinand song. From the corner of my eye, I spotted a guy who was so hot I decided to blow him right there. By now my head was underwater and slow, and I felt myself being grabbed by someone.

"You're comin' wiv me!" It was Donny, lead singer and appointed brat.

"No, I'm looking for Dirk. Where is he?"

"He's over in the corner."

"I'm going outside," I said to Donny. "Just stay here and I'll be back."

"Put your top on," he said.

I'd left my bag downstairs, even though I had £100 in it from my belly-dancing tips. A vaguely okay-looking policeman walked past; I tried to kiss him because I'd never kissed a policeman, and I liked uniforms.

"Oh, there you are." Donny came running up the stairs into the cold of the night. "Come on, let's go," he said, grabbing my arm hard, digging his nails into my alcohol-soaked flesh.

TOWERS OF LONDON U.S. TOUR 2005

SPECIAL GUEST the Strays

ON TOUR WITH THE TOWERS OF LONDON

"But my bag is inside. And what about Dirk? At least let me get my bag and coat."

I ran downstairs and found my bag and my long brown coat right where I had put them. People had been kind not to steal them.

By the time I left the club, I was falling apart. I had never felt so close to complete obliteration before. I just wanted to lay down and die. But Donny was waiting for me outside. He hailed a taxi. After giving the name of the hotel to the cab driver, he turned to me and started eating my face. I was his catch for the night, and I was too out of it to protest, even though he didn't interest me in the slightest. He was like a hyena, salivating all over me without a hint of a smile or a flicker of warmth. It was a ritual of the beast: do drugs, catch meat, and feast. So I shut the fuck up, lay still, and let him tuck in.

We reached our destination and I saw yolk-yellow lights through the window. The place was big and glamorous, not what I expected after the Camden Lock Hotel. Donny paid the driver and dragged me into the lobby. By this time, my head was so fucked I was ready for a lobotomy. After lugging my sodden corpse upstairs, we walked through mazes and mazes of corridors that reminded me of *The Shining*. These were bright corridors, and I wanted bleakness. Suddenly, Donny stopped pulling me and turned to me. Undoing his skin-tight jeans, he brought out his huge erection and pressed into me.

I guess they really are brothers, I thought.

"Lie down, lie down here," he panted hurriedly, as if his life depended on fucking me right there in those sunshine-bright corridors.

Looking at the bacon-and-egg-colored patterned carpet made me gag. I'd had no dinner, so there was nothing to bring up except the vodkas I had gulped down earlier. "Donny, no, please, I can't. Not here. I feel sick. Please."

"Okay, I'll lie down and you can sit on my cock. Just c'mon here." Donny lay down as if positioning himself for an operation, and I hitched my mini-skirt up and pulled my panties aside. I didn't want to be fucking in the blinding lights in the corridor of a hotel; I wanted to run and hide, to find some dark room and pass out. But I climbed on top and let him fuck me the way he wanted anyway. All I kept thinking was that someone was going to open a room door and see us, and that I was blowing my chances with Dirk by having sex with his brother.

Then, as Donny thrust into me, I threw up beige-brown chunks all over his chest and down my leg. I wondered what it was—soup, maybe? It dripped all over my chin as Donny carried on fucking me. He was going to ravage my body, no matter what.

The next thing I remember, I was lying down in a dark room with two double beds. I didn't know how I got there, but I knew we were still in a hotel.

"I'm gonna fuck you in every hole," Donny whispered to my face, his peroxided hair falling over his eyes.

I stood groggily, trying to leave. I really didn't want to be in his company, but he was wild-eyed, relentless, sticking his hand up my skirt and fingering me even as I walked away. Starting to snap out of my drunken haze, I fumbled my way through some sort of sexual activity, so he could just cum and leave me alone. I took him so deep in my throat, I thought his cock was going to reach my heart. There was no reaction from him, just silence. I got the strongest feeling that this was a ritual he had to fulfill solely because his image compelled him to do so. I wondered if he was even truly enjoying it.

Sometime between anal sex and the early hours of the morning, I passed out. At some later point, I heard Lori come into the room. She was merry drunk and had energy to play. And so it started all over again. Donny took turns devouring every inch of our skin, every drop of energy, every bodily fluid like juicing the life out of a battery. His cocaine must have been nuclear-powered; even after Lori and I became carcasses, he was still buzzing raw like a werewolf.

The three of us were in the middle of copulating when I heard someone come into the room. It was Snell, the band's tiny drummer, wearing their uniform of bleached tight jeans and spiked blond hair.

"Oi Snell, come on. Come over 'ere!" Donny shouted.

"O'right, what's goin' on 'ere then?" He was so sweet and cute, with a little boy's smile.

"Come and join in. Go on, get in on the action." At this moment, Donny reminded me of Dickens' Artful Dodger. He was nimble-footed and naughty, positioning all our bodies into a ménage-à-quatre, with Snell inside me, Lori sucking my tits, and himself in my mouth.

An hour later, at around eight A.M., Donny decided he wanted to film us so he could send the footage to his buddy back home, someone he called the Kid. So Donny shook me awake and directed me and Lori to fuck each other. The room was airless, and stank of unwashed genitalia. I willed myself to climb onto Lori and cooperate so Donny would leave me alone. I went through the motions like a pornographic robot. Afterward, Donny sent the video to various friends of his and had us speak to the Kid on the phone. Then, finally, we were allowed to rest.

The next time I looked at my watch, it was 9:10 A.M. and I had to get the train back to London for work. I'd just started an afternoon job in an animal rescue shelter, and I didn't want to let the abused cats and dogs down. I stood up, brushed my teeth, and gathered my belongings. Still in last night's clothes, I felt groggy and worried about missing work. I kissed Lori and Donny on the mouth, told them good-bye, walked toward the door to open it—and it all went black.

I remember waking up and wondering why I was on the floor. My feet were pointed toward the bathroom and there was a man in an ambulance uniform above me, shouting my name.

"What happened?" I asked no one in particular.

"You had a seizure," the ambulance guy said.

I had never had one of those before. I turned my head to see Lori and Donny in the far corner of the room talking animatedly. The ambulance man gave me an oxygen mask. He asked some routine questions and helped me to my feet. Then he gently laid me back on the bed, on which I'd tried so desperately to get some sleep the night before.

I rested, holding tight to the oxygen mask. It was lovely and made me happy. I loved the ambulance man for being so nice to me and taking care of me. I felt like I needed him. As I drifted off to sleep, I realized I'd been right about wearing all-black clothes: they were bad luck.

pArT 3

FOUND

I STRADDLED HIM RIGHT THERE AND THEN, IN THE MIDDLE OF NIGHT, AMID THE THICKET AND THE FLOWERS.

fter my seizure I felt like a zombie, as if my head were under water and my senses were blocked. I felt disconnected from reality, as if in a dream. During the convulsions, I had bitten my tongue so badly that for a couple weeks I had to suck liquid food through a straw. This was what cocaine had done to me, and I was terrified it would get worse. I was convinced I had a brain tumor or a hemorrhage. Even though my brain scan and EEG revealed nothing abnormal, a Nurse Ratched–like neurologist I saw a week later in Bristol, near my mother's house, confirmed that I'd had an epileptic seizure, which scared the fucking shit out of me. How had I done this to myself? Was I being punished by God for living the way I did?

I went to stay with my mum for a while. She was happy I was home safe and cooed gentle words of love, letting me rest as much as I needed. I slept for what seemed like a week in her spare bedroom. I couldn't get out of bed, and I couldn't slip out of the not-with-it feeling that consumed me. So I stayed in that room, afraid I'd have another seizure if I left the house, hoping every time I woke up that I'd feel normal again. Text messages and calls poured in from the Towers boys, asking me and Lori to join them at their gigs, their studio, their home. I wanted to—so badly—but I just didn't have the strength.

About a month later, still shaky and frightened, I finally decided to leave the house and go out into the world. Lori came along to look after me in case I had another seizure. We went to an EMI Records promo event in Leicester Square. And that's when The Rev called, telling us to go to their place in Buckinghamshire. Even though it was midnight, and I was yearning for pajamas and cuddly pillows, my heart got happy.

We jumped into one of the illegal private mini-cabs offered up by the greasy wolfmen lurking on the corner after midnight. I checked to make sure I'd shaved every trace of pubic hair and brought my condoms. By now I'd decided never to drink or do drugs again; the thought of another seizure terrified me.

The Rev texted me an address to meet them at, but it soon became evident that it was going to be one of those remote hide-aways that was near-impossible to find. The farther we burrowed into the womb of the country, the more the cab driver's rage flared, until he was spitting obscenities, banging his hands on the wheel, and stressing out about how the fuck he was supposed to get back to London. I didn't give a fuck; I was going to see Dirk. It would all come up roses in the end.

Dirk was waiting for me in the driveway with a straw farmer's hat on. He ran up to me as soon as the cab driver angrily kicked us out. I straddled him right there and then, in the middle of night, amid the thicket and the flowers. Inside the dorm-like building that the band lived in, I was quickly introduced to real pain when Dirk slipped his cock into me. His dick wasn't normal; it was animal. It felt like being fisted by a very plump wrestler.

In the distance, I could hear Lori getting fucked good by The Rev in the toilets. I was relieved I managed to stay awake without a seizure. When we were done, Lori and I said our good-byes and got a cab back to London.

CHAPTER
31

A couple weeks later, Lori and I decided to get on the tour bus. The problem with home shows—as we'd learned the hard way—is that girlfriends are inevitably resident pests, sticking to the band like leeches and scanning every female. We couldn't even go near the boys in case the glimmer of memory in our eyes and the smell of familiarity on our body was detected by their girlfriends.

Away from home was where the real debauchery could safely take place. We took a train from London to somewhere called Morecambe in the dire north of England, which by a bad stroke of luck turned out to be The Rev's hometown, where a Bambi-eyed childhood sweetheart waited for him breathless. We were advised by the other band members not to linger around him.

The tour bus, sleek and gleaming, sprawled on the curve of the pavement like a Christmas box full of vile secrets. The band lounged in a pub down the street, their skinny denim legs spread across red plush Northern sofas.

We were dressed in identical outfits, except that Lori's hair was like Bettie Page's and mine was layered like trifle. That was the first time I properly met Mad Pete. I had seen this geezer hovering around the band at every Towers gig I'd attended, jubilant as a kid in a sweet shop, fanatical and adoring of the Towers boys. In turn, they made him feel a part of the family. He was probably in his late thirties, with years of tattoos stretched over his body, including one of Axl and one of Sid Vicious. Now here he was in the pub in Morecambe, sitting with the band, ecstatic, childlike joy sparkling in his eyes. I sat across from Dirk, posing while Mad Pete snapped pictures.

"You've got such charisma," Dirk said, flirting with me in his soft, camp voice as I did my narcissistic poses. "You're such a rock star, Roxana."

I was really beginning to like Dirk—and that was when I finally learned never to judge a rocker by his magazine photos. The Rev may have looked the hottest in *NME*, but he didn't have Dirk's rock-star charisma and sexuality. I pretended to be busy and not notice Dirk's fawning. This Mad Pete guy was quite a cheeky, chirpy, Cockney type anyway—so cute I wanted to squeeze his cheeks and eat them up. He had an athletic body, close-cropped hair, and a funny little face with flush, dimpled apple cheeks.

"Why are you called Mad Pete, then?" I asked.

"Dunno. 'Cos I'm not. I'm not mad."

"I know. But how did you get that nickname?"

"The band gave it to me."

The reason, it turned out, was that he was mad enough to follow the band everywhere. Mad Pete lived in London, but he drove to every single gig—and then usually drove home the same night, sleeping in his car along the way if necessary. Some nights, if they were feeling generous, the band let him stay on the tour bus. The band and its entourage seemed to be the essence of his existence; he followed them around the world.

The band's entourage consisted of Mad Pete; Stoksie, the tour manager, the most patient and caring roadie I'd ever encountered; Phil, the pink-haired guitar tech, who always had a smile on his face despite working his haggard bollocks off every night; the Kid, a childhood friend of Dirk and Donny's who always wore a fedora and a ravaged leather coat; Bertio, a big, curly-haired Italian dude who stepped into the middle of even the most vicious fights to bail the Towers boys out; Pug, a Lemmy lookalike who was supposedly the band's dealer and as camp as a drag queen; Punkrokka and Dyler Plummer, two eccentric, middle-aged men who were friends with Mad Pete and traveled to almost all the shows; and, now, Lori and I. It was a whole new family, and I loved them all.

And then there were the girls: porn star girls; indie girls; fat girls; schoolgirls; actress girls; goth girls; married girls; hippie girls; Chav girls; old, skanky girls; even skinny, geeky librarian girls. Everywhere we went, it seemed, every type and shape and age of female was willing to do anything to fuck the Towers of London—and every guy wanted to hang out with them. What baffled me most, though, were the middle-aged men who got so excited and jittery about hanging out with five young punk rockers.

The Rev, Dirk, and Donny took full advantage of the available women. But I never saw Snell with a girl, and Tommy just talked about his goat, which he called "the goat." It was quite disturbing. I had taken a liking to Dirk, who was probably the biggest whore in the band. I was fucked.

At the Morecambe show, I watched the opening act with Dirk and we talked about Axl. (He was one of many guys who must have gotten sick of me going on about Axl.) Finally, I managed to stop my mouth and follow Dirk into the dressing room, where girls fawned over Donny. The Rev sat quietly with his girlfriend while secretly wishing he could stick his hand in the cookie jar.

After the gig, the girls swarmed around Dirk and I started to get jealous. So I parked myself right next to him, just like those girlfriends that I detested so much. I shooed the little girls away with a motion of my hand, like I was flicking at flies. Dirk, on the other hand, encouraged them, loading them with crotch-pulsating compliments in his breezy way. Lori, Mad Pete, and I were staying on the bus that night as the band traveled on to Hull. Mad Pete had his own bunk, which made him endlessly happy.

Before the bus took off, the band brought some people on for drinks while The Rev and Dirk played guitar. Donny picked one girl out of the pack outside and took her to his bunk. Lori and I sat downstairs with Dirk, The Rev, and Tommy as an assortment of drunk, scantily dressed girls filtered through the bus doors and climbed all over Dirk for further helpings of compliments. He just smiled, letting them think what they wanted, while I sat across from him, watching like a bitter rhinoceros.

"You're gorgeous," I was told by a curvy young blonde who'd been flirting with Dirk all night while trying to position herself on Dirk's lap.

I told her to fuck off and leave the bus.

Around seven A.M., the bus started to move. The grateful boys and Donny-fed girls stumbled out of the bus. I hadn't slept, so I climbed into Mad Pete's bunk and cuddled up with him, the bus vibrating so violently I felt it in the marrow of my bones. Mad Pete was a gentleman throughout. He asked me about my childhood in Iran, and I told him about my father and how that whole experience, combined with my recent seizure, had made me hate drugs. Lori was in The Rev's bunk; Dirk had passed out; and Donny's dick was probably falling off from the five or so girls he'd ravaged that night.

We arrived in Hull—or Hell. The city was an absolute shit hole. We headed for the hotel room so the boys could take a shit, shower, and spray their hair to the high heavens.

"I came so hard this morning thinking about you," Dirk said, taking me aside to make me feel special. "Where did you sleep last night?"

"I was in Mad Pete's bunk," I said. "You were already asleep."

"Are you gonna come to my bunk tonight, then?" he swaggered in his fantastically overblown sexual way.

Sex on a tour bus bunk is fucking hard enough with two people, let alone a threesome. After the Hull gig, The Rev, who'd taken an E, was all lovey-dovey. Donny was in his bunk with a rotund Chav girl, whose fat spilled out the sides of the tiny sleepwear chemise she wore as outerwear. "Kellllyyyy, Keeeellyyyy!" We all heard him screaming her name as his balls slapped mechanically against her pussy.

Kelly's friend waited patiently on the upper deck hoping one of the other band members would take pity and have sex with her, but she was even more oxen-built. Soon Kelly came out of Donny's bunk with a proud smile on her face, on cloud fucking nine.

Our legs swinging from The Rev's bunk, Lori and I nudged each other and stifled sniggers. The Rev pulled us into the bunk, and the three of us packed like tuna into the coffin-size space, trying to have a threesome. Lori was on the wall side of the bunk, with The Rev in the middle and me on the outside, my legs spilling out of the curtains.

"Suck his cock," I instructed Lori; then I started kissing The Rev. I didn't actually fancy him, even though he had the rock-star look in every sense—arms packed with tattoos; hair long, black, and spiked, falling over his eyelinered eyes. His guitar fingers alone should have done it for me. But the chemistry just wasn't there. I did enjoy those fingers, though; they played my vagina like nimble toy soldiers, like Maradona dribbling his way through a whole team. Drummers have the big arms to hold me down, but I decided that night that guitar players—or anyone who uses their fingers so intricately and creatively on an instrument—could play my clit just as well. Just before the bus started to move, the two Chavs were kicked off.

"I really wanna fuck you both," The Rev purred to me in his northern accent. But we didn't have the space to move our limbs. For a moment we lay there like three hot dogs, frustrated. Then I strained my neck to put The Rev's cock in my mouth and sucked it as yummily as I could, giving it all my love and attention.

"How's your girlfriend?" I asked, looking up at him.

"C'mon! Being with you is like being with a porn star compared to her. No one is like you, Rox."

"Thanks, mate," I said, and slid out of the bunk to go sleep with Dirk.

Dirk and I fucked like animals. Once again his unhuman cock hurt me to the point of tears, but I didn't care. Even in the drawer-like narrowness of the bunk, he managed to slide himself on top of me and look into my eyes. I moaned, my breasts slithering with his sweat, nipples red-raw and standing up for attention. He wanted to keep me quiet, and put a finger over his lips as soon as my moans became howls. So I put my hand across my mouth, stifling my cries of pleasure.

When we were both done, we lay back, orgasmed out and simmering like tender cabbage.

"Can you go and find me some food, Rox? I'm starvin', babe."

So I ventured out. Everyone was asleep and the bus was silent. Among the crushed Red Bull cans and empty vodka bottles, which the band had guzzled like tap water, I found a can of soup and some sandwiches. I microwaved the soup and took Dirk the sandwich. I looked into Tommy's bunk and asked him if he wanted some cheese, knowing how much he loved it.

"Yeah, can you get us some of that packet noodle as well, Roxie? Cheers," he said in his little boy voice. He was so cute and adorable. I wondered if he was still thinking about his goat.

I went to the kitchen area and fixed him some food. I loved being the band's incestuous mummy.

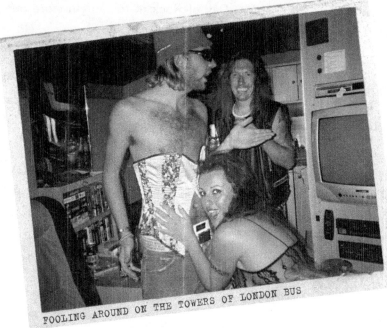

FOOLING AROUND ON THE TOWERS OF LONDON BUS

AS DONNY'S GIRLFRIEND WAITED NEXT DOOR, HE FUCKED LORI IN OUR BATHROOM.

Bloody hell, it was hot that day. Fuckin' 'ell, I was up for it! I'd just gotten back from Greece, and I was all tanned and lovely, with long, wavy, highlighted extensions galore and a new black-lace-and-scarlet corset and denim mini-skirt. I had just moved into a shared house in Highgate. And I had two all-access wristbands for the *Kerrang!* Day of Rock at the Virgin store on Oxford Street. That day was caviar with chips.

Towers was playing with Bullet For My Valentine and some emo bands. Unfortunately, *Kerrang!* sucked the cock of anything remotely emo, so I'd have to rely on Towers for my rock 'n' roll.

Lori and I arrived around three P.M. The first thing we saw was Mad Pete loitering at the store, looking jolly as usual, lost in his Towers euphoria.

"I been queuing up since seven this morning," he told us. "I got two more wristbands for Punkrokka and Dyler Plummer as well. Wot you doin' 'ere, fish legs?" I was used to his endearing jibes about my body.

"Where're the boys?" Lori asked, wide-eyed and peachy.

"They're signin' stuff. There's a barbecue an' all up on the roof."

"Free food! Let's go." I was starving, ready to wolf down anything I could get my hands on.

"All right, saggy tits. We've got to get the lift, mind."

As we stepped onto the roof, Mad Pete announced: "Ladies and gentlemen, Roxana is here. Can everyone pay attention?" There was a mini buffet of up-and-coming rockers, gorgeous food and drink, and Stuart Cable was there as MC of the event. I was too nervous to eat. After saying hi to Punkrokka and Dyler Plummer, I grabbed a piece of pineapple and watermelon, just for show, and made a beeline for Stuart to make out with him. He looked fucking horny. Before I could reach him though, I saw Dirk following me.

"Roxxxxaaannne!!" he exclaimed, singing the Police song in his effeminate way.

"King Dirk! Baby! Fuck me right here. Now!" Plate of watermelon still in my hand, I put my tongue in his mouth. We kissed each other's necks. Out of the corner of my eye, I saw Matt from Bullet For My Valentine watching us. I knew everyone on the rock scene hated Towers with unparalleled passion because the band was always starting fights, trashing every venue it played, and fucking every girl it could. Just to make things worse, I led Dirk to Stuart and introduced them, then proceeded to get between them and flaunt myself shamelessly.

After kissing them both in front of everyone, I promptly made my way back to Lori and told her we had to go have group sex with Towers at their hotel. They were playing a gig at the Camden Barfly that night, then going to Japan the next day. Tonight they'd be at a hotel near Heathrow airport.

A bunch of us—Lori, Mad Pete, Punkrokka, Dyler Plummer, and others—hopped in a van to the Barfly.

It was a hot night. Every Towers hanger-on was outside the venue drinking and hanging out. Pug, the gay Lemmy guy, was there with an older hippie woman who reeked of coriander. There were the teenage Japanese twin girls, the band's families, a scary-looking fetish model from Hong Kong, some circus-performer types, and, as usual, girls of every type, shape, color, and motivation, including the older groupies, wobbly in their best knickers and their hope for a bit of young punk meat.

The Hong Kong fetish model's face was set in a frozen look. She stood motionless in front of the mosh pit with Lori and me, cartoon-size mammaries on display. She kept staring at Dirk. I retaliated by elbowing her in the chest with all my might—accidentally on purpose—as I danced up and down and screamed "On a Noose," "Good Times," and "I'm a Rat" as loud as I could, right in her ear.

Because we were known to be with the band, random girls kept coming up to Lori and me and telling us how beautiful we were. "I can't get you backstage, sorry, sweetie," we'd say laconically. We were so happy then, hugging and dancing, unified in our love for this band—these boys who ran our lives.

That night was the first time I saw Janie. She was clambering onto the stage, a tall redhead with plump, crimson cheeks and all-white clothing, looking like a lost little puppy. She grabbed a pair of spare drumsticks by Snell and danced like a fairy by his side. Then she went and sat sidestage, swinging her long legs like a boy. She irritated me instantly. She didn't belong in this kind of scene.

Later I joined Dirk in the dressing room and we talked about life. Dirk always spoke as if he were on horse tranquilizers, which I never understood, since he was constantly hoovering all of Peru. He had a habit of looking so deep into your eyes when he talked that it felt like he was looking for more drugs in there. Poor Donny had his girlfriend with him that night, so he looked on wretchedly, a destitute kid, as Dirk drifted into the club to smooch and flirt with any woman he could find. This really upset me. Even though I knew I wasn't with him in any formal sense, his constant roaming around to perform his brazen seduction technique hurt—especially when it was done right in my face. But that was Dirk. He had to have sex with every female he saw: fat, ginger, blond, old, brunette, young, thin, unconscious—even my best friends.

I walked into the club that night to see him hungrily eating the face of the old hippie woman Pug had brought. She was in heaven: this middle-aged, saggy, henna-stained, herbal-tea-drinking, day-time-TV-watching, fat-arsed, farty old woman. My heart sank. Why would he do that? I just didn't get it.

⊰⊱

Their white van waited outside the Barfly. Stoksie was stressed as usual. And Lori wanted us to go to Japan with them the next day.

"Awww, let's get in the bus!" Lori squeaked, a pretty but annoying doll. She really needed the band: With no family of her own, she was the ultimate orphan. And I was her Fagin.

"We have to ask them first," I said in my mommy voice.

Lori scampered off to find a band member to ask, and I floated around the bar, trying to be as cool as the Fonz while desperate hope wriggled like maggots in my gut. I preferred to be asked by a band member.

I was eating Mad Pete's soggy chips when Lori popped up. "They're leaving!" she panted. The night creatures were still hanging around, desperate for a scrap of Towers—a chat, a comment, a smile; any Towers residue was licked up with relish.

"Come on!" Lori yanked my arm. Stoksie was huffing and puffing over the band's itinerary. Snell, happy-go-lucky as ever, already on the bus, sat in the seat next to the driver. Snell was the oldest in the band and the most down-to-earth. He was also the most level-headed and quaint coke snorter I had ever met. I always secretly wondered if his cocaine wasn't lemon sherbet.

The Rev climbed in, followed by Tommy, tall, posh, shy, and model-boned. Donny's girlfriend sat next to him with love in her eyes, and Lori jumped in the bus so confidently, as if it were her right. I knew she did this because she had to: It was a matter of survival. Without the band, she would simply die inside.

Tommy pulled Dirk into the bus, stumbling and giggling, drunk and still rancid—freshly unstuck from the lips of the old hippie woman.

I scanned him with nausea, unable to understand why he had no standards whatsoever, why he didn't differentiate between cool and white trash. Just as we were about to take off, Sasha, a skinny goth girl, slithered her way onto the bus like an eel. No one said anything to her. Maybe they were just being polite. Rolling into a corner, she hid herself in the inky shadows and dissolved out of sight.

That was the first time I noticed the band's manager, Nathan—a slick, older, Prada-decked smoothie who used to manage the Happy Mondays. Even in the dark of the bus, I noticed a cinnamon glow to his skin. So did the band.

"You been on a sun bed, Nathan?" they taunted him. "You weren't in Cyprus, really, were you? It was the sun bed!"

Nathan absorbed the ribbing elegantly, with a sort of fatherly pride. I wondered if it violated groupie etiquette to fuck the band's manager. Maybe it would be okay if the band watched. I'd never done a manager before. As I sat across the aisle from Nathan, I opened my legs and wet my lips, looking him directly in the eye.

Suddenly I felt something shuffling on the ground. I jolted back. "Did someone bring a pet?" I asked. "There's something moving on the floor."

"It's that girl from the show," Lori whispered, elbowing me violently in the ribs. "She snuck in."

Sitting ghostly next to the goth girl, I saw a pig-tailed Asian girl hiding in the shadows, trying to camouflage herself. She opened her mouth and let out a giggle, but said nothing. She knew her place.

At a gas station stop, Donny's girlfriend skipped out to get cigarettes and Red Bull. She was the ultimate fresh-faced girl next door. I felt so bad when I talked to her, knowing that I—and so many other girls—were fucking her boyfriend. I wondered if she knew. As soon as his girlfriend was out of sight, Donny's hands spread all over Lori, jabbering dirty filthy talk fast and furious in her ear in the limited window available to him.

At the hotel an hour later, Lori and I were hurriedly ushered upstairs by The Rev and Dirk, who were sharing a room. I knew The Rev was dying to fuck me, as he was the only one who hadn't yet (apart from Tommy, but Tommy didn't count). I was still really into Dirk, though, so I snuggled up to him while Lori and The Rev left us to it and went downstairs to join the others for a drink.

While I rubbed Dirk's back to melt the kinks, I promised him that I wouldn't try any funny stuff—just the massage, because he was exhausted. But I had a plan. Massaging him with one hand, I briskly whipped off my corset and skirt with the other, swapping hands rapidly so he wouldn't catch on. Soon, all I had on were stockings. When he rolled over and saw me, he had no option but to get turned on. Exhaustedly, he flipped me around and climbed on top of me. He held me down, because he knew I liked it. And I pulled his blond, punky hair.

DIRK FROM THE TOWERS OF LONDON

"Don't touch the hair, Rox. Don't. Touch. The. Hair." He was panicked his punk spikes would go limp. I should have realized how much hairspray it took for those blond tufts to stand starch-stiff.

He spread my legs open. I forced them shut. He forced them open again. Then he slapped me, and I whacked him back. I told him to punch me ("not too hard"), and he laughed that boy giggle; this was all a little weird for him. But he did hold me down, and fucked me so hard with that canoe-size museum piece of his that I got pissed off that my vagina was so tight. My knees were weak, and my heart—my heart liked him. I wanted to cuddle and kiss him. I wanted tenderness, but I had to behave myself and not show emotion. Especially to Dirk Tourette.

We heard a knock on the door and I grudgingly peeked it open. Donny stood there sheepishly. His girlfriend was in the room next door.

"Can I come in?" he asked, shuffling nervously.

He was miffed that he wasn't getting any playtime. Seeing as I'd only been sandwiched between two brothers once before, long ago, I gave it some thought at first. But tonight I only wanted to be with Dirk. I don't know what was wrong with me, except I was getting warm and fuzzy toward Dirk, which was as vile as getting addicted to smack. Donny got the vibe and left.

We were lying on the bed when The Rev and Lori barged in. "Everybody was asking where you two were," Lori cooed over us in the bed. "Everyone is always like, 'Oh, Rox and Dirk have disappeared again!'"

The Rev gazed hungrily at me and Dirk lying in the sheets, and climbed into bed with us. Lori followed him.

The four of us lay there in mutual, silent erotic repose. With The Rev on my left and Dirk on my right, soon I was being fingered by them both. I spread my legs as wide as physically possible, cursing myself for not taking those gymnastics classes my mother had insisted on when I was younger.

The Rev was ravenous for a piece of me; on his left, Lori was whimpering for him. "Go on, Rox," Dirk goaded me. Secretly I wished he wasn't so willing for me to get it on with The Rev. I wanted to be alone with him. But with Dirk watching me, I climbed on top of The Rev and slid myself on his cock. He swept his hair, languid and lovely, out of the way. And I kissed him as I let him thrust hard and fast into me. After three minutes, he let out a tell-tale groan.

"What the f—," I said to myself. I pulled off his cock and swallowed every last bit of his cum. Then I rolled over and went back to cuddling Dirk. Sweaty, sleepy, lovely Dirk.

"Open the door! I wanna come in!" A girl pounded on the door.

We were all in bed, trying to sleep. Sasha the Goth had arisen with the moon like a possessed doll.

"We're going to have to open the door." The Rev got up angrily. "She's gonna get us thrown out."

So in she came, scraggy arms everywhere, drunk and disorderly, ranting that she couldn't find a place to sleep and couldn't go into the streets, because we were in the middle of nowhere and it was four A.M.

"Here's a pillow." Rev threw it at her. "You can lay your head down in the corner."

"Ooh, you're so beautiful, look at you," Sasha said, gawking at me as she stumbled around our bed. "You...you are like the Queen of Sheba."

"You still can't sleep in this bed, luv," I said, smiling back. It made me laugh, the way these newbies tried to butter me up.

The door opened again, and a slab of light wedged its way in. Donny entered the room. Walking over to the bed, he grabbed Lori and took her to the bathroom. As Dirk, The Rev, and I lay there in silence, we could hear echoed moans coming from the bathroom and Donny barking out dirty, nasty words.

"You like that cock? Yeah? Do ya? Do ya?"

Silence.

After a few minutes, I heard Donny say in a more somber, childlike voice, "After you've been with someone for a few years, sex isn't the same."

I wondered if his girlfriend next door could hear him. A few minutes later, he came out, wiped his dick, and went back next door to her.

Lori stumbled out of the bathroom. Now it was The Rev's turn to start fucking her. I walked over to them and gently pushed Lori out of the way, so he could stick his dick in me instead. I hoped this time he'd last longer than three minutes. He alternated sliding his cock in and out of me and Lori until he couldn't take it anymore. We knelt down in front of him until he gave it to us. We swallowed it all—plenty. The whole time Dirk just kept on snoring and sweating, and Sasha kept coming in and out of the room.

<hr/>

"Anyone wanna cuppa tea?" The Rev was up bright and early, pouring cups of tea for everyone.

Lori began harassing Dirk, wanting to see his museum piece. "I've heard so much about it," she whined.

We all sipped tea while Sasha sat in the corner quietly. The Rev didn't offer her any tea as punishment for shredding the ambience during the night. We all went down for breakfast and found Tommy, Snell, and Stoksie. I kissed them one by one as they climbed on the bus for the airport.

"Don't do any Japanese groupies," I whispered to Dirk.

"Not into Japanese girls anyway, babe," he lied and gave me a kiss.

was standing with Lori on the side of the stage under a marquee tent in the cloudy, humid Belgian summer. I wore my new corset from Sluts R Us, also known as a Camden market stall. It was scarlet, with black lace on top worn with the vapor of hope and the sweet sweat of Cacharel's Amor Amor. My denim skirt, also new, made itself useful by being short and starched. Inside, I was happy but Lori was ecstatic. We loved our boys, their songs, their playing, their stage presence. And we loved and supported them everywhere they went, sending out our energy and vibes to them, inspiring them, making the crowd go even wilder for them.

That day, everything felt different. For a start, it was the first time we'd gone abroad to see the band and the first time we'd been with them at a rock festival. The band had started saving us a bunk whenever we wanted to travel with them. They'd asked us to come to Belgium, and then travel back with them.

Lori was newly platinum blond after I persuaded her to dissolve her raven-black locks so we could come as a blond-brunette pair. Right then, at that very moment, our long hair was congealed with sweat and orgasmic thrill. In her borrowed blue outfit, with her peaches-and-cream skin, Lori looked more like a kitten than ever. I hugged her against my breasts, and we giggled like crazy children. Mad Pete, who by now was the only person following the band to more shows than we were, lurked around snapping photos. The Kid, in his cowboy hat and weathered burgundy leather jacket, walked out of the boys' dressing room. It's an unspoken rule: whatever you might be up to in the dressing room, when it's showtime, you just get up and leave. No words required.

Pink-haired Phil had set up everything onstage, including beer, water, ciggies, and us—and, for the first time, Janie, the new girl. She was comforting and childlike—a strawberry milkshake with red hair and girly white vintage dresses. And, more important, she knew her place. This weekend on the tour bus, if she proved she knew the rules of being with the band, we'd let her hang around.

Janie liked Tommy, who was equally comforting. Lucky for her, his girlfriend wasn't there. Lori and I always did our best to make sure there wouldn't be any girlfriends suddenly turning up—that's why home gigs were a no-no. We'd made that mistake once at the Garage in Islington.

We grabbed a hot dog, then found our way to a field of tour buses parked side by side on Belgian stones and dust and fuel-stained balding grass hosting rock stars for two nights under the stars. The family rushed up to us. They were so happy to see us. Having these five hot rockers love us injected Technicolor into our lives. I gave Dirk the present I had bought for him, a View-Master with a Pink Panther cartoon. He dug it, and I loved seeing him happy.

After a day of walking in the grass and mud, eardrums perforated with gasoline rock 'n' roll, hair smelling of barbecued meat, brains fuzzy with wine, I stood on the table in the front end of the tour bus. I wore a black, lacy, crotchless catsuit, and even though I was wearing super-high heels I danced and danced and danced. Watching me on the surrounding red sofas were Phil, Stoksie, the Kid, Mad Pete, two photographers, Janie, and Lori.

Outside, the grass was wet and the sky lulling and soothing. An hour passed, and the band hadn't appeared. Someone said they'd gotten into another fight in the backstage area. Lori and I had been there earlier, and it was all industry types sitting around pretending to look important. No debauchery of any description whatsoever. The band were probably sniffing for a fight anyway, as they usually do. I felt so shallow, I wanted an orgy.

The band finally showed up, drugged up to their eyelashes. Especially Dirk. I hadn't been with him since the airport hotel three weeks earlier, and I'd missed him. It was poison—you cannot miss, or have feelings for, a rocker. I wanted to be with him so badly, but he was so full of chemicals that his eyes were whirring like cuckoo-clock birds and his walk and talk were comedic. When he flirted with other girls, I didn't care—not this time. He was twenty-five, after all, and in a rock band, with girls throwing themselves at him. But when he made out with my friends, it hurt badly. I knew that it shouldn't, that he wasn't my boyfriend, but when it was right in my face, it shredded me like the abrasive side of a scouring pad against my wrists.

Until December 2005, I hung out with Towers in every city in Europe and even Canada. Fucking on tour buses, trashed hotel rooms, backstage love-ins, and fistfights—it was all rolled into one kaleidoscopic photoplay before my eyes like the hum of the projector all those years ago.

But, along the way, I realized I still wasn't rock 'n' roll. I couldn't bear to see Dirk with other girls. It hurt too much. I was a wuss. So I turned to a teenage glam band: Kid Ego. They were just starting out—and therefore ripe for corruption. Their songs fucking rocked. I wanted to take advantage of them all.

CHAPTER

34

TONIGHT, I WILL DO THE WHOLE BAND. FIRST, THE SIXTEEN-YEAR-OLD DRUMMER MUST BE HAD.

had never slept with a sixteen-year-old boy. But tonight I was gonna do it. Nickky was Kid Ego's drummer. His face looked like it had been carbon-copied from a photo of a teenage Jim Morrison, and he played drums like Tommy Lee. He was a miniature miracle, and everyone stared gape-jawed when he played.

Rookie, the eighteen-year-old bassist, like so many male rock-star wannabes on the planet, used the Nikki Sixx formula to create his image. Zakk, the lead singer, also eighteen, was a bit tubby—he looked more like he had shouted at the donut than the devil—but his voice was magnificent when he belted out their sleazy rock numbers. And there were two others: Phil, with dreadlocks, and Birdy, a dirty, nasty, sleazy, hot motherfucker.

Their songs were volcanic, and swung me to roller-coaster heights. They were playing Cardiff, and even though Cardiff was bleak in my memory—all grayness, dirt, fucking, and seizure—I went there alone. I was nervous as a rabbit, and felt as if my knees had been sucked hollow. My bones were like tea biscuits, ready to snap. I hoped this time Cardiff would be kinder to me.

The Barfly, proud owner of the sallow and constipated, repulsed me, as it had before. I entered the minute back room with Kid Ego and their support band. It was full of the evil drink, and although I'd promised myself I'd stay away, I smuggled swigs of whiskey into my mouth. A photographer snapped away with deft precision—capturing me with ten boys full of raging hormones and unruly erections, all wanting to put their teenage, throbbing, quivering willies in me and suck my boobies, which they proceeded to do.

The young girl fans, all milky and full of stripy tights and *Kerrang!* posters, didn't even try to enter the room; instead, they just peeked in and saw me getting my breasts sucked and my body mauled by all ten boys. It must have looked like a cat with a litter of kittens. Then, in one swift motion, the band's manager slammed the door shut and all the boys gathered around, with me standing in the middle. With the sixteen-year-old drummer Nickky helping me, I unzipped and stripped off the remainder of my clothes. I took off my panties and stood there in my high heels. I wasn't sure if I had the energy to take on ten teenage boys.

Kid Ego, their support band, and I were taken by van to their hotel. I was surprised to find it was the same hotel I'd been in nine months earlier with Towers. Was it compulsory for me to do whole bands in this hotel? I saw the receptionist and wondered whether she recognized me with my clothes on. I was sure she hadn't forgotten the smell of congealed vomit and sperm and red perfume I'd left behind last time, and was still furious at the degree of my obscenity. But she looked at me with a motherly tenderness and addressed me with a knowing smile.

And I loved it. I loved it. I loved it.

We went to a room where one of the guys from the opening act was staying. I felt seventeen, shy but omnipotent. I was one girl in a room with ten boys—sweaty and unpredictable, hormone-buckled and leather-clad young boys. I was kind of scared, though I shouldn't have been. Both the bands were crammed into the room, impossibly wanting, waiting for something to happen.

I felt like I should start something, maybe fireworks and a show. I was the only girl. I felt as though I was in a desert at midnight with a group of Arabian smugglers. I suddenly became protective of my body, my womb, my femininity, as if it were in danger of being tainted. I folded my arms over my breasts and crossed my legs as my skimpy clothes clung to my body.

After a few minutes, though, I got bored. And I realized: these weren't Hell's Angels. They were just teenage English boys with tankfuls of sperm. And I could have any one of them. A gleam singed my eyes. I could choose whoever the fuck I wanted.

I thought. I decided. Tonight, I would do the whole band.

But before I did that, I did something nasty. I left the room to walk around for a minute—and got laid by one of the guys from the support band. He was cute, and horny as hell. But in my gut, a spew began to rise, produced by a rule embedded in my brain: Never fuck anyone from the support band.

We'd gone to his room, and when we were done I left him to go find Kid Ego and he walked off into the Cardiff streets to find a low-rent prostitute to administer things I wasn't capable of.

"The support band, Roxie!?" the Kid Ego boys sniggered when I entered the room. I hung my head in shame.

The lights were low, and as the boys taunted me, I started to play with Birdy. His loyalty to his girlfriend made him even hotter. I made him sit on the bed, and I sat in front of him and opened my legs as the others watched.

"Fuck, I can't," he said. "I really want to . . ." He looked pained, torn between loyalty to his girlfriend and my open naked body spread in front of him. "You're a fucking fag, Birdy," the others jeered from all directions. Birdy looked at me, aching desire dripping off his face, and tried not to cry.

I was cruel. How could I do this to someone who'd heroically managed to remain Super Glued to his love despite the hordes of girls chasing him every night?

"I'm so sorry," he said, crushed. I left him lying there, and went with Zakk, Rookie, and Nickky to their room of fun. Once inside, the boys ripped off my clothes in seconds.

"Do you think she's ready for us?" Zakk asked, way too confident for his age.

I felt all giddy. Should I be acting more responsibly? If I were a man with three teenage girls, I'd be in heaven. Fuck it, I thought. I'm a legend. My reputation in rock precedes me.

First, Nickky must be had. He was a wasted, staggering child. I took him to the bed and climbed under the sheets with him. I must be gentle, I thought. I don't want to scare him.

But he was dirty as hell. His fingers and tongue were everywhere, like a young, wild jackal. As Zakk and Rookie watched from the other bed, I slipped Nickky's cock in me. He thrusted a few times and came.

I threw the condom aside and opened myself like cake for Zakk and Rookie.

Zakk took me doggy style, penetrating me anally while Rookie fucked me so good that I took Nickky's cock in my mouth. Three childhood friends. They will never forget me. We fell into a sweet sleep: them dreaming of Mum's cooking up north and me having had my fill of three young boys.

JAILBAIT DRUMMER BOY FROM KID EGO

I HAD TO REMIND MYSELF THAT I WAS HERE IN A GROUPIE CAPACITY, NOT TO HAVE A FUCKING ROMANTIC TIME.

 had just recovered from my night with the Kid Ego boys and started to walk properly again when I got itchy—and it wasn't from an STD. Like an inmate from *One Flew Over the Cuckoo's Nest,* I paced and jumped around, brittle and bitchy, to get a new hit of action.

In December 2005, I started my MA in English Studies in Bath. I felt safe and happy being swirled into academia again. It was a fairy-tale world that nourished my soul; I gobbled up one book after another, those beautiful literary works dancing through my head. Returning to school allowed me to see my mummy more often than I used to, but my relationship with my stepfather was still sour and dreadful. Every time he surfaced in the living room, I felt a spiky concrete pole shoot up my spine, and I stiffened with discomfort.

One Wednesday evening, Lori and Janie were waiting in Euston Station when I came up the escalators with my tour-weary, concrete-heavy bag. They looked worn, like rag dolls hanging limply from a peg: Janie from touring with Towers of London and Lori from working like a battery hen in some college-administration office. She was still in her work clothes: a navy trouser suit with an icing-white, polyester blouse. We kissed and went to get fried chicken from a Somalian fast-food restaurant around the corner. The two men working behind the counter asked me where I was from, and were happy and proud to hear that I was from Iran.

Lori, Janie, and I hadn't been together for a while, so as we sat facing each other around the table, our genetically modified chicken was served with verbal diarrhea. Words toppled out of our mouths, competing for space: the Towers boys, Towers boys' cock sizes, Towers boys' girlfriends, tour bus stories, and anal sex incidents all crashed into each other like a train wreck, polluting the Halal air. The two Muslim men in traditional attire behind the counter looked on with disappointment as the Iranian girl talked quite scientifically about the techniques of how not to choke while deep-throating.

We seeped into the Wednesday night stuffed with manufactured chicken, and each called tour managers and roadies to find out if they were working with any bands that night and where. Nothing. Every band we wanted to see was either out of town or just about to go onstage in some hick town miles away. Eventually, out of boredom and frustration, we opted for a last resort: Brides of Destruction, the band Nikki Sixx had formed in 2002. Although Nikki had left the previous year to rejoin Mötley Crüe, the band had remained together.

I thought of Camden Underworld as home number two. As I stood outside the venue planning my living arrangements there, complete with cutlery and a kitchen sink, the doorman told me the gig was at capacity and we couldn't go in until afterward, when the crowd had thinned out.

With her usual military strategy, Lori suggested going next door to the World's End pub to wait, then trying to get backstage.

With my rock handbag an extension of my hand, Super Glued to my skin like love, I headed straight to the toilets to whore myself up. In the Victorian lavatory, I started the process: bee-stung flesh-pink lips, eyes dressed in soft kohl and shadow. I changed into a skirt, thin as an anorexic belt, and a jubilantly slashed top. I didn't care about the freezing weather breaking my body anymore. Lori and Janie didn't give a shit about how they looked; I wished I had their bravery.

When I rejoined them, they were hoovering alcohol as fast as they could. I missed drinking. That floaty, warm feeling, like nestling in my mother's warm bosom, had detached itself from me. It felt like a cold, hard slap. I couldn't even turn to cocaine anymore to comfort me.

Around eleven P.M., it was time to penetrate the Camden Underworld. The venue was packed to throttling. Even though the gig had ended, music boomed from the beatbox, blending with the crowd's voices into a milkshaked frenzy. Brides of Destruction may not have had Nikki Sixx any longer, but people wanted to see them anyway—mostly because of Tracii Guns, a cofounder of Guns N' Roses and the original guitarist of the '80s hair-metal band L.A. Guns. As we pushed our way through the crowd to find the backstage area, I prayed he wouldn't turn out to be like Steven Adler. I wasn't in the mood to play along with the demands of another junkie.

Brides' lead singer was London LeGrand. I hadn't heard of him, but all of a sudden a raw throbbing formation of fine rockers on stage began to take shape in front of my contact-lensed eyes. At the front of the stage, I grabbed some kid and asked which one London was; he pointed out a guy who was as tall as stilts, wearing giant, square, black-rimmed comedy glasses. He had a top hat, a zebra-patterned coat, massive platforms, and lips thick as squid. He stood on the small stage, surrounded by people and popping cameras, all wanting a piece of him.

From some corner, Sasha appeared, still skinny as an eel. Her hair was dyed sherbet-pink, falling down her back like a champagne waterfall. She wore tiger-print hot pants and jumped up and down excitedly, with a devilish Joker smile. "Hey, Rox!" She ran toward me and gave me a love hug.

"London wants me to go back with him, but my boyfriend's here," she said. "What should I do?"

"Is your boyfriend in a band?" Lori asked the necessary question.

"Yeah, but they're unsigned."

Lori and I looked at her sympathetically.

Janie and Lori followed me toward the stage, beating off little eyeliner boys and wannabe groupie girls. The three of us together were like a Nazi force no one would fuck with. Up by the stage, the guys from the band were having photos taken and signing limbs, asses, shirts, and photos. Lori and Janie started talking to various band members and I aimed straight for London. Then I saw a goth named Mimi. She was so fucking maternal. I loved that girl.

BRIDES OF DESTRUCTION SINGER LONDON LEGRAND

"Hey, Rox, you *have* to come meet my friends. You would love them. They're really wild."

"Are they in a band?"

"Yeah, they're the support band."

I balked, but she dragged me to the corner of the stage anyway, where four guys in leather trousers complete with thick chain belts and aviator shades started to hug and kiss me. They were warm and friendly scallywags, clownlike and down to earth. But they were the openers. I said my greeting and went to meet the Brides of Destruction.

I turned around and noticed a slim, lanky guy with swaggering snake hips, kohl liner, and a cluttered mane of raven hair. Something he was saying to Lori was making her throw back her head and laugh.

"This is Scot," Lori said, introducing us. "He's the drummer in Brides."

He was incredibly beautiful, with a joyous smile lighting up jade green eyes enhanced by kohl liner, and photo-perfect white teeth behind full lips. He made me quiet. I walked away to find London.

"Hey, I'm Roxana," I said, looking up at him and rubbing my hands along his naked, heavily inked six-pack.

"Hey," he purred in a wide American rock-star grin, made nerdy by his giant square glasses, all the while squeezing Janie by his side like a schoolgirl.

"She's so fuckin' cute, man. I'm really digging her," he whispered in my ear. "Are you girls gonna come back with us?"

"Sure," I said. "But you need to sign my tits first." I knew full well that he'd have to take me somewhere private to do so.

"Yeah, but you know, I can't do it here. Let's go back in the dressing room."

"I'll be back in a minute, hon," I whispered to Janie.

"Go for it, babe." She gave me a triumphant smile and a peck on the cheek.

"You cannot come in here. You have to go back out *now*," said a black security guy by the backstage entrance, as patient as a psychopathic bear. He wouldn't let me through.

"She's with me, Kekone. It's cool, man," London said, stepping in. As I walked through, Kekone gave me an evil look that inhabited me. Backstage was a mess—bottles and coats and people scattered everywhere. I loved it. Holding my hand, London worked fast and methodically, pulling me past people sitting around playing guitar, smoking, play-fighting, and screaming, to a tiny room with a sink in the back. London clicked the door shut, clean as a surgeon. He pulled out a black marker just as I pulled my top down.

"You have fuckin' beautiful tits," he said, breathing in close to the side of my neck, gently and softly kissing me there and on my chest.

"I know," I whispered, pushing my breasts tight together for him to sign and feeling the cold rush of the pen soaking through my skin.

London didn't hesitate. He took off his coat and started to massage my breasts. We kissed, fooled around, unzipped things. He slid his hand between my thighs and his fingers found the slit in my crotchless panties. Then someone knocked on the door.

A little boy fan, standing there enviously, told us that everyone was going to the Crobar. So a fistful of us took a cab there, to the west of the city. The Crobar made me ill; every time I'd gone there, I'd vomited from its virus. It is the size of my hand, yet armies of people manage to squeeze their bodies in there night after night to soak in putrid smoke and damage their eardrums. The urine yellow lights are hospital bright and it's impossible to move unless you possess the ability to fly or are comfortable being violent.

As soon as I walked in, Scot Coogan, the Brides' drummer, had to be helped; his knees had just abandoned him.

All I wanted was to be with London in the men's toilets, but I had to keep propping Scot up and helping to keep him from passing out. London was downstairs with Janie anyway. He seemed to relish the knowledge that they looked like a circus act together: seven-foot, bug-eyed, top-hatted London as the hot ringmaster, with a flowery, fragile Janie as his baby doll.

Right then, in that moment, London was the only one I'd set my sights on. He was my project for the night, I'd decided. I stumbled down to the toilets as Janie was leaving his embrace. But then, as I locked myself in his body, I discovered that, close up, he was as dull as paper. He was mechanical and robotic, devoid of any natural wildness. It was just his image and lead-singer status that I had wanted. I was disappointed and I didn't know what to do. I decided to get Lori, who was nursing Scot, and head to the hotel with the band.

Many hotels in London—and one particular one in Cardiff— know my body intimately. I have spent a significant amount of my life in those corridors, running half naked from one room to another, trying to find friends, lovers, or a lost shoe— sometimes bumping into a musician or roadie and getting his rocks off or having disgruntled hotel staff threaten to call the police if the noise and obscenity are not put to bed. I have walked past one cliché after another: fists through windows; trashed rooms; girls patiently lined up outside a lead singer's door; random people being hit and cut; tour managers losing it because of lack of sleep; roadies going out in the middle of the night to find snacks or KY Jelly; false promises; moans and groans and lost property, including girls' dignity. But I've always managed to come out of it with inner thighs aching and soul flying.

Lori, Janie, and I rode to the hotel on the bus with all of the band except Tracii, who was already back at the hotel with some German girl and Kekone, the scary-bear security guy. A couple little goth girls had sprung out of nowhere and sand-wiched themselves between members of the band. A tubby one had taken a particular interest in wet-pasting her body onto Scot's and was talking very loudly in a Texan drawl that only she found hilarious. We all couldn't wait to get rid of her.

I know that most of the girls who hang around bands hate me, because I'm the girl who gets it all. Girls show their deep-cut fury in various ways: sometimes with just a look, some-times by darting venom from their coarse tongues to rattle my bones, sometimes by physical assault. Usually their plan is to butter me up with words swathed in syrup, telling me how beautiful I am and what beautiful corsets I wear. It's not just the little girl groupies and female friends of the band who say this. Sometimes the girlfriends—threatened that I might suddenly decide to abduct their rock-star boy—feel the need to soothe the flames of their nervous innards and keep me happy.

When we reached the hotel, Kelly—one of the goths—got out of the van with her sweaty, jiggly little agenda. Lori and I went with Scot to get liquor and snacks, and Kelly stumbled behind in hot pursuit. We wanted whipped cream to play with, and she was in our way. So the three of us ran out of the store after we'd paid, leaving her all alone. I didn't have the patience any-more to stop and be nice and sacrificial to anyone who wasn't an ingredient in the baking of this happiness cake.

In the beginning I was everybody's friend, ready to help—whether it was the band's extended family or the little boy fans standing outside the backstage area waiting for auto-graphs. Now I didn't care about anyone's happiness except my own. I was on a ravenous hunt to experience sweetness in my bitter rush of life, and the love of rock bands had become my sugar. Week after week, I went face-first through a nettle for-est of raging rejection and unpredictable moods, yearning to reach and touch the yolk of love I hoped to find inside.

I hadn't been to the Camden Lock Hotel since the first time I met Towers. The hotel wasn't my friend. It was hostile to me, like an indie crowd. I couldn't wait to get inside and amend that by giving its heart and walls the best entertainment it had ever seen.

Inside the lobby, Kekone pushed money at the receptionist to keep him saccharine sweet, deaf, and blind to the extra people about to occupy the band's rooms. I caught sight of London taking Janie upstairs. Lori, Scot, and I staggered upstairs like three hobos, with Scot carrying my pink bag. As I walked up those familiar burnt-toast and cigarette-stained stairs, I spotted Kelly walking into the reception area and looking up at us. I felt really bad.

In his room, Scot was gentlemanly, making sure we had whatever food or drink we wanted. It was odd. I was used to rougher, more sullen behavior, and impersonal rock stars as conceited as wild orchids. But he was adoring and considerate. I looked at this achingly beautiful boy and wondered why he was behaving this way, if he had a different agenda.

Lori and I showered in the eggshell-white bathroom, slipping on the tiles and wondering which towels were appropriate for use. Our black makeup slid off like mud slipping down marble, reminding us of the many times we'd spent scrubbing ourselves in hotel showers to make sure we were clean as a whistle down there for girl-girl sex.

We heard Scot talking to Kekone, who had entered the room. Then there was a polite knock on the bathroom door, and Kekone left us some towels by the sink.

"Do you girls need anything? Just yell if you do."

We stepped out from the bathroom apprehensively, nestled in plump white towels like cream puffs. Would they expect us to do what we'd heard Marilyn Manson did to groupies, like making them hold cereal and milk in their vaginas?

"Hey, I'm sorry if I was a bit mean back there at the club," Kekone said. His face had transformed from angry bear to loving uncle.

"You were mean. And scary." I started pulling on my negligee.

"Sorry, that's just my job," he said softly and expertly, without even a smidgen of desire for my lingerie-ensembled body. "You girls are cool, man, and I'm gonna get outta here and leave you to it."

"Where're you gonna go? Do you have another room?" I asked.

"Nah, I'm just gonna go find a room and hang. You guys have fun." He blew us a kiss and left, his neck chains clanging down the hall.

Lori took out a camcorder sitting on top of Scot's bag.

"Hey, can we film with this?"

Scot, who had been lying on the bed sobering up, sprang to his feet. He took the camcorder from her and began shooting. Automatically, Lori and I positioned ourselves at a good angle for the lens and started to kiss and lick each other. Silent as a boy, he filmed Lori and I sixty-nining each other like two cats grazing on tender beef. We went through the motions, the ritual, blah, blah, but I didn't like it. I found myself craving intimacy again, just with one guy, without a whole gang-bang porno scenario. I wondered what that would be like: to be alone with someone you were attracted to. Without a word, I stood up mid-lick, pushed Lori away, and walked up to Scot. I kissed him silent and deep, without permission.

Up close, his skin felt slithery soft and lionesque. His hair smelled of Elvive shampoo and boy sweat. I watched his smile, innocent and boyish, light up his whole brilliant face. I felt strange kissing him, because he was so nice and tender for a rocker. Lori sat watching as I cuddled him and he gently put the camcorder down to kiss me back. This performance that was imbedded in us was becoming a tired act. Even though I loved having sex with her, I wanted to change the routine, I wanted to be the selfish friend and the etiquette-snubbing groupie.

I felt a shock and a huge rush of relief when Scot was so responsive to me. I was so used to the Towers boys giving Lori and me orders like porn directors that I'd forgotten the sensuality of being with someone passionate and giving. I was glad I was with a friend who loved me—who was more selfless and patient than I could be.

Lori lay on the bed like a child watching two other kids eating the best lollipops. I knew how much she wanted that, too, with Scot. My insecurities were poison, and they contaminated my friends' souls. My roaring beast of desire for intimacy had reared itself like a hook-nosed pedophile.

Eventually, Lori grew bored and took over as director, filming close-up shots of Scot and me, from kisses to penetration to cum shots. But being with this one was making me shy, so I decided to get my act together and stop dreaming, to remember my place and my role. So I worked it for the camera, turning away from Scot and positioning myself in reverse cowgirl to get the best penetration shot. Then I ordered him to fuck her. I stood in the corner of the room and cheered them on, watching as Lori, too tight for Scot, winced in pain when Scot tried to have gentle sex with her. I hated how nice he was to her, apologizing and asking if she was okay. I hated that he touched her face and slowly kissed her neck. The whole scene made me want to throw up, as if I'd just guzzled a gallon of petrol. In the end, the only thing left for me to do was to turn quietly sadistic, triumphant in the knowledge that his penetration was hurting her, that she was no good. So when Lori decided she wanted to go up to London's room afterward, I didn't persuade her to stay. All I said was, "Okay, bye," as I locked the door behind her.

I turned around to see Scot lying on his back, looking at me. Without a word, he held out his hand. It felt very natural. As soon as we opened our mouths to talk, we couldn't stop. We talked about poetry and Jim Morrison and the Beatles. Then he hugged me, and we held each other for what seemed like an hour. He stroked my hair and kissed me, my arms, my back. He looked at my face and held my hand.

"You're so nurturing. I love that about you," Scot said as he held my face in his hands. I had to remind myself that I was here in a groupie capacity, not to have a fucking romantic time. It was three A.M.

Minutes later, there was a knock on the door and half a dozen people arrived. I was glad to let normality return. Snapping back into my role as wild rock chick, I entertained the crowd. There was London, Janie, Lori, Kekone, and Jeremy the bassist. The camcorder was once again our playmate, and everyone was begging me to ejaculate on camera. I lay back on the pillows naked, with everyone around me, as Scot quietly left me to do my show. I let Jeremy film me with my vibrator; he was just a kid and hungry for mischief. Soon the others got involved: zippers were unzipped and belts were unbuckled. London made out with Lori and Janie. I was loving the attention—until I noticed Scot watching me from the corner of the room, and suddenly I felt uncomfortable. For the first time, I'd met a guy I didn't want to see me in this way.

Forty minutes later, after my show, after I'd been kissed by nearly everyone and blushed for it, after everyone had finished gossiping about the weird German girl Tracii was fucking in his room, they all left Scot and me alone together. I couldn't believe Kekone, exhausted after weeks of touring, was so kind to let Scot and I have the room, even though he was supposed to sleep there that night.

"*Before you slip into unconsciousness,*" I sang the Doors song as Scot shut the door on everybody.

"I'd like to have another kiss, another flashing chance at bliss." He joined me in the song, and we sat there quoting Doors lyrics. We didn't sleep and were on such a high that we went downstairs at eight A.M. to have breakfast.

I finally left him a couple hours later, sleepless, but as awake as a hyper child on a sugar buzz. My heart flew through the morning rush of Camden market. I was in a kind of shock; I'd never met someone like Scot in the band world—or in the real world, for that matter. C'mon, you idiot, snap out of it, I admonished myself. It was so hard to detach from that kind of bonding experience, to make myself believe it wasn't real. But, still, I couldn't wait to see him again.

CHAPTER

36

The black carpet, stretched taut over the frame of the stairs leading up to the Bierkeller in Bristol, feels like its skin. Years of beer-barrel stench stain the bowels of the building, which is on the same road as my old gym, next to the club that held Arabic nights, where I did my belly dancing.

The walls of the club are big hunks of granite rock, '70s style. It is successful in being exactly what is says: a beer cellar. PLEASE DON'T DO DRUGS IN OUR CLUB, a piece of cardboard at the bar says in neat, thumb-thick letters of black. The bar is a wannabe star. It tries so hard.

It was here that I fucked up.

I recognized the signs that I was falling. That familiar honey gush raised my heart right up to my throat like candy sickness when I arrived and saw him backstage for the first time in a few days.

He was surrounded by people, laughing and larking, hips swaying, raven-black tresses gleaming and soft liner blazing his feline, jeweled green eyes, which should have been illegal to display and parade around. His lips were identical to mine—big, with an obscenely perfect cupid's bow.

When he saw me, he stopped still. "Hey, baby," he beamed, walking away from the crowd toward me. Right there, in that tight overcrowded backstage room, he hugged and kissed me hot and soft. I knew then that he was going to be *that* person—and my fear was second to none. Wednesday night had been so beautiful; this was dread. My feelings were going to wreck me like a car crash. I should have left the scene right then.

The venue wasn't full that Sunday night. Instead of brimming and overspilling, it was receding and balding. I watched from the wings as he played, and I couldn't look at him—the drummer boy. I danced to the music of the night, focusing my gaze on London, Tracii, and Jeremy. I had a kind of rock burlesque look going on, with a baby pink corset, pink bow, trousseau mini-skirt, and thigh-high leather boots. London came over to me in the middle of a song, hugged me, and smothered my face in salty kisses. My carefully scrubbed, mango-buttered skin grew sticky from his dripping man-sweat, and for a deranged moment I panicked that Scot might hate the taste of London on my body.

After the gig, I put Aerosmith on the backstage CD player. The room was packed with bodies, snacks, beer cans, dirty towels, and luggage. Wrecked jackets and leather accessories decorated a uniform-blue sofa stained with white marks. A white fridge in the corner, graffitied with years of band names and lost people, had filled its square belly to bursting with useless lager.

There was a blond girl showing her tits to Tracii and Jeremy. "Fuck off, I'm with the band," her T-shirt blared. She came to the show with her boyfriend, a wretched-looking bloke who stood outside the room looking on as she straddled Tracii. She got up and walked over to him calmly. "I think I'm gonna stay with the band at their hotel tonight," she told him matter-of-factly.

"What do you mean?" her boyfriend demanded. "What about me? Are you not going to come home with me tonight?"

"I wanna stay with Tracii tonight. You can go home."

I had to feel sorry for the poor guy. He looked devastated. "What about us?" he said. "Is this it? After five years, is this it for you?"

"I really wanna stay with the band tonight," she replied. As he walked off, she turned to me and said, "Didn't really like him anyway."

I had never seen the support band, the Red Star Rebels, play. And although they were down-to-earth and heartstoppingly funny guys, I was just dying to be with Scot, who was surrounded by randoms. So I danced to Aerosmith, as I always did when feeling jittery, and let Jeremy take pornographic photos of me. I knew Scot hated that, and I felt bad for acting this way. I just thought all rockers would be devoted to any behavior that was wild and decadent. And I was determined to bury this rapidly intensifying feeling poisoning me. I had to have a cigarette to suppress the feeling—because I loved him. He was brilliant—the worst thing that could happen to me. Backstage was chaos, and he held my hand and my body, and it just was *not* going to happen to me.

I had come to the gig with Ostara, the girl with the angel face and curls of sun-blond hair tumbling down her back whom I'd met at Adler's Appetite. She had the demeanor of Princess Diana; I'd discovered she was also very bisexual and preferred wild and exotic girls to vanilla. I left her and followed Kekone to the van. The Brides were going back to the hotel, and I needed to ride with them. Thankfully, they weren't sleeping in a tour bus that night but a hotel room. The tiny bunks may have been concentration camp chic, but they were too tight to play in, and the vibrations when the bus moved shredded my insides like stew.

I bounced on Scot's lap in my heavy thigh-high boots and corset. I'm sure his legs died that night. Outside, clotted fog seeped thick over the city. Bristol had never looked so good.

"I'm sorry the bed was so small last time," Scot said. "This time, I made sure it's a double bed, so we can be together all night." I couldn't believe he'd planned ahead so we could be alone.

Outside our room was chaos. I opened the door to peek. The Red Star Rebels were running naked down the corridors, pushing each other in wheelbarrows and discussing racquetball. Every two minutes, Blacky, the lead singer, naked and drunk out of his mind, knocked on our door.

"Can Scottie come out and play?"

"No, he's busy. Shut up and go to bed." I slammed the door.

Then I opened it again to whisper: "Please, please, please, can you leave us alone to be together?"

But Blacky was not to be denied. Eventually, I broke down and let him in, because he was dying to play with Scot. Together they became a comedy duo, with Blacky having a conversation with the coat hangers in the closet and Scot fueling him on. I still wanted to be alone with Scot, but it was the last night of the tour and they were having fun playing together like naughty little boys. So I let them be and went to find Ostara.

I hadn't bothered putting on my top, so I walked along the corridors, my watermelon tits swaying in the breeze. Stepping over the drunk and the undressed, the loud and the lewd, I marched past the staff, who threatened to call the police, and stumbled into Tracii and Jeremy's room.

"Does anyone have a bloody cigarette?" I asked four bodies in mid-copulation. I saw Abigail—the one who'd deserted her boyfriend—grinding on top of Jeremy. Thank God the boy was getting some this time. Next to them was Tracii and some goth girl who was giving him a halfhearted attempt at head.

"Hey, Roxie, have you been walkin' around topless like that?" Tracii said as he tolerated his blowjob. "Fucking love this chick, man! I thought you'd be with Scot."

"That's not how you deep-throat, honey." It pained me to see someone giving such bad head. "You have to loosen your throat and breathe through your nose." Even in the murky shadows of the room, I could see her justifiably give me a fuck-off look.

I walked back into the corridor, where mayhem was spreading; the police had been called. Body after body scampered off into one room after another. What a fabulous sight! I walked past a room and spotted Ostara sitting on a bed, surrounded by four members of the Rebels. She looked so serene that she reminded me of Titania, the queen of fairies in *A Midsummer Night's Dream*. The hotel staff, hunting for any further signs of mischief, passed by in the corridor and saw me topless, so I decided it was time to go back to Scot.

Inside Scot's room, I found Blacky squatting in the bathroom, and Scot telling him to be quiet. I told Blacky playtime was over.

"But I can't leave. The hotel people will kick me out 'cause I already got a warning."

I felt bad about getting rid of Scot's little play-buddy. I turned to look at Scot and saw the sweet way he was looking back at me—and it scared me. I had to keep it together. He was leaving in the morning.

He held me so tight that night, like lovers in a video for a sugary ballad. We kissed and had sex, and I cried at the insane intensity.

"I've been feeling like shit," he said. "When I saw you tonight, I almost didn't want to spend it with you."

"What's wrong?"

He looked at the wall.

"It's because I'm feeling things," he said in an almost whisper. "I like you."

"You mean you like me as more than just a friend?" I asked, even though I knew the answer.

"Yeah," he nodded and looked away.

I hugged him and kissed his cheek. I just wanted that moment. I didn't care about tomorrow or consequence. I wanted the smell of his hair, his sweat, his chest.

That night, he joked about the phrase "I love you," but I had to believe in this fairy tale. The way he looked at me and held me and kissed me that night, I knew I had fallen for him, and I knew it was going to be a glass ride to misery.

In the pale sunshine of the morning, I walked hand in hand with Scot in his woolly hat and baggy coat to get coffee. We were silent as thieves. People gawked at me in my thigh-high boots and tiny skirt, but even the old lady who stopped in her tracks and shook her head at me didn't matter. I was angry and bitter, knowing I wouldn't be with him again—my darling, my love, the one who had taken my heart.

Disneyland was officially closed.

I cried so much when he left. I had an audition that day for a short film, and on the train there I couldn't stop crying. I failed the audition: it was for a happy part.

SCOT COOGAN—EPITOME OF BEAUTY

SYNYSTER GATES FROM AVENGED SEVENFOLD UNLEASHED HIS HOT PEE ALL OVER MY BREASTS IN THE MOONLIGHT

fter Scot, I was like a blind bull in a china shop. Rock 'n' roll was supposed to be a wild and free playground, but all those warm romantic feelings kept getting in the way. I needed to have some fun. I needed to forget Scot. I could not miss him. So I went to hang out with Avenged Sevenfold. I'd heard from girls on the scene that they were the kind of boys who'd show you a good time, the kind who'd make your troubles disappear.

They were from Huntington Beach, California, and they looked like an instant cake batter mix of inbred serial killer: part white supremacist with a pinch of rabid animal. Even looking at a photo of them for too long scared me—especially the lead singer, M. Shadows, and their drummer, who just happened to have the same name as the Towers guitarist: The Rev. I wasn't a huge fan of their sound. Even though they had ditched their hardcore screaming, they were still too nu-metal for me.

Though their look seemed aggressive at first glance, their reputation for excessive behavior unfortunately reeked of public-relations press release. Like many young metal bands, beneath all the biker grease, charcoal-thick eye makeup, and metallic teeth, I had a feeling they were just soft, Cheerios-fed, Californian beach boys.

I got ready for the gig with Lori in her windowless room in a basement flat she was renting in East London. I wore a buckled and belted metallic dress.

The Forum loomed dark and large in Kentish Town, a rough part of London. Litter and dog shit decorated the ground in proud detail. We walked to the side of the venue: me marching ahead of Lori, swaying my hips and sticking out my chest on an adrenaline-pumped mission to find the backstage doors.

I found the backstage entrance on a drab and industrialized little street on the side of the venue. The all-too-familiar site of tour buses, roadies, and technical gear gave me a head rush of endorphins, and I felt lured into a warm cocoon. I banged my fist hard against a huge set of dirty blue doors with a security camera fixed overhead. A concrete-bodied but cuddly-looking guy opened the door with amusement, like a giant looking down on a mouse. I hated dealing with security. It was futile and unnatural.

He looked us up and down. I wished Lori had also undone her coat buttons, so he could see her in all her beauty. She was very slow sometimes.

"Hi." I smiled, tender but self-important. "How are you?"

His smile was a half moon of gapped teeth. I could tell he was sweet and lovely, and hoped he'd be easy to deal with.

"Can we come in?"

"And who are you?" Another guy appeared behind him with an equally warm and kind face.

"We're the band's entertainment."

"And what would you do for the band?"

"Entertain them."

"Are you groupies?"

"Ha! Ha! Ha!" People were so '80s.

Since it was murderously cold—and we had tickets in our hands—they let us in. Just inside, there was a little area with security cameras and orange lights, with a set of huge doors on the left and a set of steps to the right.

"Can we go upstairs and say hi to the band? The main band, I mean. Avenged Sevenfold." We had to be direct and to the point, and my lack of clothing supported me in that.

"I'll have to go and talk to them. You wait here."

People with laminates and glasses scuttled and bustled between the stairs and the doors, which led to the side of the stage.

A few minutes later, the security guard returned. "You have to wait a few more minutes. But only *you* can come up," he said, pointing at me. Lori was on the verge of throwing a tantrum.

I heard a voice crackle on his radio, and he motioned for me to go up with him. I bet he just wants me to suck his cock, I thought. Nothing comes this easy without favors. We climbed past the first floor, past the opening act's dressing area, past tiny rooms with mirrors and graffiti and belts on the ground, until we reached the third floor.

"Wait here," he said, then walked up the stairs and knocked on a lone door tucked in at the end of the corridor.

Waiting mid-stairs, underneath oily orange lights, I noticed that the corridors looked and felt Victorian, like an old opera house. Avenged Sevenfold came down, silent and heavy. They looked prettier in the flesh, especially M. Shadows, whose face was actually less that of a ravaged serial killer than that of a lovely little boy. That damn marketing department didn't do them justice.

"Hey." I looked up at them. Smiled. Chatted with M. Shadows a little. They were about to go onstage, so I asked, "Do you guys wanna party with me and my friend after the show?"

"Sure. But first we just have to go to an industry meeting thing right afterward."

As they made their way to the door leading to the stage, I kissed them one by one on the cheek. Cute as puppies.

As Lori and I watched from near the stage door, they roared, raged, and rampaged through their set, entertaining and enflaming the young crowd into sweaty hysteria and ecstatic fury. I watched Synyster Gates and his fingers make that guitar wail and moan, seducing and hypnotizing the audience. He had smelled of blue-collar machismo when I had kissed him earlier. His guitar fingers danced a frenzy on those strings. I wanted him to play me.

Five blond girls with piercings on their face, white hair bleached within an inch of its life, and black, gritty jeans began to make their way to the side door where we stood. The security guy didn't seem happy about this fivesome of Barbie dolls. He gestured a "no" to them. I didn't understand why: they were hot, in a synthetic kind of way.

"You'll have to stand back," he told them sternly, beckoning me to come forward. "Don't worry. You're the only one that's gonna go upstairs." Again, I hoped he wasn't expecting any sexual favors.

After the lights came up, people emptied the venue in droves as security guards hollered at them to vacate. Lori and the per-oxides were tipsily fooling around and dancing with each other. I stood still and sober, waiting impatiently by the door. Finally, the security guy's scratchy radio talked to him, and he signaled for me to go up.

"The main band has gone to an—" he started to say.

"I know. I know. An industry thing. Can I go up anyway and see the other band?"

The name Bullets and Octane was printed on the white paper on the wall. I hadn't heard of them, but I didn't care; I just wanted to get out of the audience area and into a dressing room.

"Have fun, naughty girl." The security guy winked at me as I walked upstairs.

"Thank you for being so nice." I waved.

As I walked up, I saw a guy with a laminate around his neck. He told me he was Brent, the bassist in Bullets and Octane, and sweetly offered to take me up to their dressing room.

When we got there, three other guys looked at me timidly amid the clutter. The room had a Victorian texture, with deep velvet sofas and ruby curtains.

"You want a drink?" a voice offered. I shook my head no to an alcoholic beverage and nodded yes to a soft drink.

I was sitting on the sofa, trying to remember who was who and wondering what I was going to do with four very gorgeous rockers, when the drummer decided to take a chance. He was the drunkest and therefore the bravest. Sitting me on his lap, he stroked my thighs. And I, in turn, started to rub the torso of James, one of the guitarists. Brent the bassist was such a gentleman. And Gene, the lead singer, could have been London LeGrand's double. He was tall and lanky like London, and his face and mannerisms were similar.

"So you're here!" Lori blustered in, breathless.

"You better not have done anything with the security guy," I snapped.

"No, they just let me in!" she protested. "Honestly."

For the first time, I really noticed how beautiful she was, with her natural flawless skin, apple cheeks, and long blond hair thick as chips flowing around her face like a mermaid's.

"Come join us," a voice from the back softly commanded. A fucking roadie had succeeded in camouflaging himself into the furniture.

"Hey, this is our tour manager, Bobby," Brent said. "He's the fucking best, man. Fucker has had to put up with us." It wasn't the first time I was struck by the pure affection between bands and their crew. It was an intimacy only achieved by having to witness every experience, every emotion, and every bodily fluid on a tour twenty-four hours a day.

I felt uncomfortable with the crew being present in a situation where physical intimacy was about to occur with a band. Lori was already whispering sweet nothings into my hair and hugging me. I wanted to suck her perky tender breasts like they were chicken.

I liked the company of this lovely band. They were fresh meat. They had an air of all-American wholesomeness and fresh-cut grass, which made them pheromone-crazed for a girl in rain-soaked, sleazy London. We partied a little, but a couple photographers and more crew filtered into the dressing room. It felt invasive. Secretly, I wanted the intruders to leave. They slowly trickled out but the odd amateur journalist-type remained, mulling in the corner.

This scene—inside a band's dressing room—was the one place I felt truly comfortable and content. Watching rockers playing their instruments onstage was foreplay. Making out with the ravishing rockers afterward was the only way I got off.

I placed tiny kisses on James' naked back, and he turned around to face me. From behind, Ty, the drummer, slid his hands between my thighs while Gene fooled around with Lori. The remaining intruders left to the drone of moans and kisses. We were all at play, tremoring to pre-orgasm, when a 250-pound, tattooed, white, skinhead security guy crashed into the room.

"Get out!" he trumpeted. He looked like an escaped convict.

"This is our dressing room," Gene said.

"You have to leave this place," he insisted vacuously, as if quoting a manual.

"Why? What's wrong?" Ty asked from behind me, although his dick had gone soft by now.

"Just leave," the security guy echoed.

"Hey man, this is our dressing room. Can *you* please leave?"

It was a standoff: a tableau of soft-spoken Midwestern gallantry amid topless girls versus a mentally challenged Cockney skinhead. What a damned pleasure.

The skinhead shuffled closer. "You better get your stuff and leave the building." His pink cheeks were fluffed up like dough.

"What have we done?" Gene and Ty asked, trying to sound chivalrous.

I knew what they had done. They had dared to make out with girls in their dressing room. I could tell from the way the skinhead feigned a pantomime baddie look for Lori and me, that seeing other people engaged in sexual activity twisted and gnarled his insides.

"It's okay, guys," I said, grabbing my clothes. "We'll go. You stay. It's your dressing room."

"You're not goin' anywhere." The guys stood up, pissed off that their pussy was being taken away.

The guard waddled after us and held us back as the band left the building and climbed aboard their tour bus.

"They're not comin' in." He pushed Lori and me into a fenced-off coop, where hundreds of fans stood huddled in the freezing blackness with markers and cameras. In a flash, Lori made a run for it, slipping through an opening in the fence. I felt my arm yanked as the guard's sausage fingers dug into my flesh. I screamed, surprised and confused by his intense force. I tried to wriggle my arm from his grip, but he was still as stone. I then tried to appeal to his sense of logic.

"Please. Why are you doing this? I'm just standing here."

I looked around at the scattering of fans, and everything became a coal-smudged blur. His fingernails, deep in my skin, had me choking back ribbons of tears. Suddenly, he started whispering obscenities in my ear, calling me every foul name he could. His words came thick and fast, unexpected, as if I were his sworn enemy. I looked over the fence to the tour bus, and saw Ty and James running over. They started pulling my other arm.

"If you take her on your bus, I'll make sure you never play on a stage in this country again," the guard announced. Fortunately, the band didn't care. They just wanted to get me out of his claws. My bruises stung raw as I climbed on the bus. Leaning my head outside the window, I saw the fans still waiting and screaming, and I soothed my arm against the cold of the glass.

The bus stood still, waiting for the Avenged Sevenfold boys to get on the neighboring bus so both bands could make their way to Heathrow together. Ty got me a cranberry juice, and Lori and Brent were fascinated by the vast amounts of pubic hair abundant in the old German magazines they were looking at. Gene was in his bunk with a girl.

Under the table, James slid his fingers in between my thighs, but he was too all-American lukewarm apple pie to take it further. He needed more time. And I needed him to lay me. So I tried as hard as I could, kissing him and moaning so he would put out. But he wasn't man enough.

So when the Avenged Sevenfold boys came on the bus a little later, I readily agreed to go with them back to their bus.

"The Rev"—Avenged Sevenfold's drummer—"wants us," Lori whispered excitedly.

But I wasn't interested in him. His face was squished and angry; he looked like a rodent on crack. I dug Synyster Gates. So I walked over to Synyster, who was standing by the bus door.

"Hey."

Beneath all that rock-star image, he was just a young boy. I wasn't sure what he thought of me, but I wanted him.

I was polite.

"Would you like to do some water sports?" I asked charitably.

Water sports was something I'd been curious to try. It was a power thing as well as a submissive thing, which I enjoyed. It was also dirty and sleazy, which gave me a throbbing clit and made me want to conquer the world.

"You ever done it?"

"No. I haven't," he whispered with a cute twinkly smile. God, he was hot.

"Let's go, then."

I was low-key, trying not to be too loud. Synyster followed me outside, and it occurred to me he might feel obliged to do this to preserve his bad-boy metal persona, just like Donny had. I felt bad.

I kneeled in the grit and took my clothes off, anxious to avoid soiling my hand-embroidered corset. It was freezing cold, and my nipples stiffened into bullets. Synyster put down his beer and unzipped his heavy-metal pants, full of chains, studs, and assorted accessories. I smiled up at him and he smiled back. He reminded me of Slash: quiet and reserved, but with a heavy presence.

"Do it to me, baby," I purred with my boobs pushed together for effect.

"Are you sure?"

"Yeah, I want it."

He unleashed his hot pee like a fountain all over my breasts, white and firm in the moonlight. I held my head back to expose my neck. The rush was like a roller coaster. I felt so turned on doing water sports with Synyster Gates. When he was done, we both stood up silently, and he took me on the bus to clean up.

Afterward, I could tell he was shy about what had happened. He was mumbling, and I just wanted to hold his hand and tell him it would be okay. The bus was sleek and bright and clean, laboratory-like. It was crisp and flowery like Korn's tour bus, which I had been on uneventfully when I was in Belgium. What had I expected to find? Dead animals and blood smeared on the walls? Just then I heard Lori drawl, "Oh my god, this is such a cool bus." The alcohol had put her in airhead mode. The ratlike Rev, holding her hand, pulled her upstairs. I didn't like him but a niggling sense of adventure made me follow them. It was the wrong move.

I can only describe what ensued in the next half hour as nerdy frustration. The Rev tried to fuck me while the singer, M. Shadows, watched. When Synyster showed up, though, The Rev's dick died. He kept trying to fuck, but his dick was spaghetti limp. He tried to shove it in again and again.

Because of all the chemical substances he'd consumed, he began foaming at the mouth. All of a sudden, his face went pale and twisted in deranged psychosis, and he slammed me onto the ground. I hit my head, then stood back up in a daze. I was angry, but mostly because I hadn't gotten proper sex. I turned to leave. This made The Rev livid.

"Just go, then!" he shrieked.

As I grabbed Lori and my clothes, one of the crew guys thought it would be hilarious to draw swastikas all over my body and came after me with a black marker. I tried to push him off me, but he was really strong. My head was still sore from hitting the ground and my arm was hurting again. I ran out in the freezing cold, my body stained with swastikas and still horny. Apart from the water sports, it had been a very un-rock-and-roll night. I felt like I'd spent the evening with children.

or four months after that I kept my head down, continuing my MA studies in Bath and participating in animal rights campaigns. I immersed myself in academia and felt instantly alive again. At the time, I was thinking about teaching gender theory at university and wanted to do my PhD. I was happy reading Virginia Woolf and Michel Foucault. Writing theory essays and joining discussion groups brought out the dorky real me. The university environment gave me stability and a self-love I'd rarely felt before. It was a welcome break from dumbing down my conversation every time I was with rock bands; I could never discuss poetry or postmodernism in their company.

But I still got off on rock 'n' roll, and I listened rapt to my friends' stories every time they came back from a tour. Though I loved university, I was still addicted to my other life. It was a drug that made me euphoric and free, that made me feel like I belonged, although it was only a temporary high that wasn't healthy for me at all. I got to have amazing sex on the road, but it wasn't fulfilling, only momentarily amazing and wild. It was like planting the seeds of love, but then severing them at the source just as they were about to bloom.

I still thought about Scot, but choked out the feeling and stopped my heart whenever it fluttered. From now on, I decided, rock 'n' roll would be just a splash of fun with a dash of sweat. No one was gonna take my heart again.

Then I met Dizzy Reed.

PART 4

DE

CHAPTER

39

HAVE A WONDERFUL TIME ABORTING YOUR CHILDREN, YOU PIECE OF SHIT.

 hope you go through more abortions to be honest. . . . Have a great life. Have a wonderful time aborting your children, you piece of shit."

It was a February night in 2007. I was holed up in Hollywood and Guns N' Roses keyboardist Dizzy Reed was sending me text after text. Each one was intended to annihilate my spirit, which was trying so goddamn hard to be strong.

I was down on the floor. My body, ox-broad, concrete, coarse-spined, nonexistent. All I was aware of was the existence of my knee joints.

The square carpet under me was faultlessly cut. The orange lamp bled light above me, and I saw the walls with perfect clarity. It was two or three A.M. I was alone, wearing a starched shirt-dress covered in an epidemic of tiny white dots, red velvet platforms, spaghetti hair drizzled in spray, eyes caked in kohl, and lips gummy with coral gloss. I had to be strong. I wasn't going to cry.

"I fucking loved you," I texted him back. "I wanted to have our baby." My heart was bursting. And if I jolted, it would overspill into my chest, a sea-bucket of emotion.

"You never loved me," he replied. "You're incapable of loving anyone you cold piece of shit."

I couldn't stop Dizzy Reed. It had been five months since the abortion and I still endured his abusive behavior. I just didn't want him to hurt me anymore. I wanted him to stop. I wished he could be kind, the way he'd been back in England. It couldn't all have been an elaborate masquerade. He must have some humanity somewhere. Inside, I had strength: I hoped God would help me not to fall apart. But my stupid eyes had a life of their own. My tears felt warm and free as they flushed down my face, swimming past my neck, itching my collarbone. I couldn't stop them.

With my hands shaking like crazy, I sent him a long text back about what he had done to me, how he hadn't been there for me after the abortion.

"I went through a lot because of this abortion. I just needed your emotional support. That's all I wanted. Stop this."

"Stay out of my life, you urine semen pussy-stained whore," Dizzy texted back. "You have no place on this earth. None."

I had this terror in my throat that was killing me. I couldn't stop the fear. It was a gargantuan wall in my chest. And I felt weak. I couldn't stop crying. I hated myself for being such a fucking wuss, for weeping so much.

I couldn't move. I didn't want to. I was fucking scared. That night the floor was my friend, my comforter. I didn't want to leave it. I tried to reason with Dizzy, to use logic. After all, he was a forty-three-year-old man. He already had four children by three different women.

My one saving light was that I'd recently found out that he'd done the exact same thing to a twenty-four-year-old girl. I felt strangely comforted knowing there was someone out there who had gone through the same experience. I wanted to find her, my other half, my twin, the only one who would understand my pain. She was younger than me. I kept thinking her abortion must have hurt her more.

"I know about the other girl you got pregnant. . . . know what you did to her life," I texted, inflaming him even more.

"So you and this girl, you're friends now? I hope you go through it again to be honest. I'll gladly write you a check for saving the world from your offspring. Enough. Good-bye."

My throat hurt. I wailed like a child when I cried. I didn't care if anyone in the room next door could hear. I felt so alone. It was just this room and me. Where could I go? I didn't want to face the morning.

The curtain displayed its curves in waves over the window with glee. Maybe Dizzy was right, I thought. Maybe I had no place on this earth. I wanted that baby so much. I loved it. What was left for me to do now but put myself out of my misery?

I put my phone on silent, peeled myself off the floor, and emptied a packet of pills in my palm. It would end the pain.

DIZZY AND ME ON THE GUNS N' ROSES TOUR

CHAPTER

40

The first time we met was in the summer of 2006 in Paris, a cloudy city, vast and rabid, stained with perfume and watercolors.

"Hi," I said.

"Hi."

I was in the VIP room at Paris' Bercy Stadium. The guy in front of me was staring wide-eyed and mute, his eyes so explicitly sky blue I thought he was wearing contact lenses.

"This is Dizzy." Chris Pitman from Guns N' Roses stepped in and introduced us.

I had vaguely heard of Dizzy Reed before—he was one of the many musicians hired by Axl Rose as part of the ongoing Guns N' Roses machine. Dizzy had highlighted dreadlocks, which was weird. He was in Guns N' Roses, so I couldn't understand why he was endorsing a rasta look rather than dressing like a rock star. Somehow he had managed to stay in the band for sixteen years, which interested me straightaway. But it wasn't just that: he had an overpowering and intoxicating sexual aura that even Izzy Stradlin, who was hanging around, didn't have—and even Tommy Lee hadn't had.

He wore a light blue denim waistcoat draped over his slight frame. He had a well-worn aura of staleness about him. His eyes gawked at me, fixed and vacuous, but they dripped sex in a dirty old man way. He didn't seem quite there, like he was on some secret cloud-nine medication.

"Hi and bye!" I said. "I have to go."

I was tired after standing around on my six-inch PVC heels for hours—first waiting for Avenged Sevenfold to finish their set, then waiting for Guns N' Roses, who came on more than ninety minutes late. Their show then stretched for two hours, with lengthy guitar and bluesy piano solos randomly spliced into sets by a medley of musicians I didn't recognize. I nearly passed out with hysteria when Axl came out to the opening bars of "Welcome to the Jungle," but by the end I was just praying for the show to end.

It had been a long journey to get there. Just a few nights before, I had been in Frankfurt for the World Cup. While I was singing the theme song from *Titanic* in a Thai karaoke bar, a roadie friend working on the tour had called to say he'd gotten me a pass. So the next day I took the train to Paris for the show.

In the VIP room afterward, a pair of gangly emaciated teenage twin girls in matching yellow lycra vests and microscopic black shorts, souped up with valley girl accents, were straddling Izzy Stradlin like he was this year's hot stuff in *Teen People*. They nuzzled him like two child giraffes, flirting in their limited teenage way. Silent, introverted, pointy-chinned and meek, Izzy tried to respond, coquettishly flirting back and smirking like a shy schoolboy.

By then I'd talked to various members of this new Guns N' Roses, especially Chris Pitman, one of the keyboardists, who for some reason was dying to introduce me to Dizzy.

It was mid-June and the steaming heat of summer in Paris had broiled my flesh. I was tired, but this Dizzy guy's intensely sleazy, sexual vibe and stare convinced me he'd be easy to get, that he was someone who could not resist pussy. I said bye to him, cursing myself for being too damn tired to even flirt, and headed back to my cousin's flat in Montparnasse to crash out.

"Did you meet anyone in the band?" my cousin mumbled from the dark when I crept into the room.

"Oh, just the keyboardist, Dizzy Reed," I mumbled disappointedly as I drifted into sleep. "Better than nothing, I suppose."

The next day, I went to visit Jim Morrison at Père–Lachaise Cemetery, which I always did when I was there. And, as always, I got lost trying to find his grave. Walking past my idols, Oscar Wilde and Edith Piaf, I decided to follow the debris of burger, fries, and cheap aftershave that trailed from a group of American tourists wearing Eminem T-shirts and the like, who were loudly making their way through the cemetery with their cameras and iPods, whooping and cheering.

The cemetery was serene and courtly, snug and dusky. James Douglas Morrison's grave seemed like one of the biggest tourist spots in the world. Thin silver railings at knee height had been erected around the grave itself to protect it from human copulation, bloodletting rituals, and general Morrison worship. I stuck myself hard and fast to the silver railing and vomited in my mouth a little as loud, fat Americans high-fived one another and took pictures. Jim's grave had become Disneyland and I had to cry just a little bit for that. The smell and noise and *click-click* of cameras drove me crazy. This was a carnival of the grotesque, the debris of an MTV version of Jim Morrison.

But then I was a tourist, too, gawking at a slab of cold stone. To comfort myself, I took a mental step back and chose to view the scene as purely postmodern.

A couple guards, looking like toy soldiers, stood by as more loud Americans sieved through with maps of Paris and ice cream. We all stood around staring at the grave, as if Jim might come alive any second. It was like some Brechtian play. And that's when I decided to get a closer look at the notes and poems left on the grave. I put one leg over the railing and one of the toy-soldier guards clicked awake. *"Non!"* he yelped, and proceeded to unravel a reel of French.

"He says you can't climb the railings, dude," a sleepy guy with an afro drawled.

"I'm just going to look at the writing," I answered affably.

"If you go over fence, I will get police," the guard said, switching to English.

"I'll just be a minute," I snarled and put the other leg in.

I walked over to the grave and read some of the writings. There were letters wailing desire and dirty laundry to Jim, notes of sexual innuendo and sorrow, candles with rainbows, child photos, lipstick tissues, some dead flowers, and a plastic bird.

Minutes later I heard what sounded like an army of footsteps behind me grinding on the gravel. I turned around to see seven French policemen standing against the railing, beside themselves with anger. I climbed back over the fence, nearly shitting myself.

"I was just looking at the poems," I stammered.

"You must come with us," one of them announced.

"Just because I climbed over the fence? I wasn't causing trouble."

"You must leave now," one of the security men repeated. "You have to come with us."

Suddenly, the number of uniformed men seemed to double, surrounding me in a flash. The spectacle had succeeded in making the American tourists shut the fuck up, and turned me into the circus freak. As the policemen took me away, I decided to add a P.S. to their postcard home, shouting, "Jim would have been so proud of me!"

Because I didn't struggle, most of the policemen dispersed and left me with just one guy. At least I wouldn't get lost this time.

"I'm sorry I don't speak French," I said. It was tacky that I didn't speak the language.

He seemed to like that—so he asked me out to dinner.

"I wasn't doing anything wrong," I insisted.

"Yes, but many people want to have the sex on his grave," he stated in his hard, sugary French way. "That is why we put fence."

As he led me through the cemetery, I realized that he might actually be taking me to a police station and not just escorting me out. I'd had enough bollocks for that afternoon, so I decided to make a break for it. I ran out of the gates, down the street, and into the fusty tubes of the metro.

hile I was in Paris with Guns N' Roses, my mum had a stroke. My brother called and reluctantly relayed the news: She was alive, but had lost some of her memory. I bawled as I waited for the Eurostar train back to London that morning. I loved my mummy so much, and I didn't want her to die. So much had happened in the past twenty-four hours. Paris was a bittersweet, twisted lover.

When she recognized me in the Bristol hospital, my jagged insides were anesthetized with relief. Her eyes, though, were vacant and her words slurred. My mother was my heroine. She had worked so hard while studying at university to provide for her parents, brought up three kids by herself when she moved to England, and sold her wedding jewelry to buy us food. Laying back, her hair floating about her as if underwater, her body was warm in the white sheets.

"Did you see anything exciting in Paris?" she whispered.

"I saw a band," I said. "They're called Guns N' Roses."

"Be careful." She looked right at me as she said it. I should have listened.

Guns N' Roses had a UK tour coming up. Their music had been my life and soul ever since I was a teenager. So I e-mailed Dizzy. I couldn't get his frozen-eyed stare out of my head. It seemed like an invitation.

"It was nice to briefly meet you at the Paris show in the 'little room,' " I wrote. "I was the one with the corset and heels in case u don't remember. Hope to see ya in England for 'proper' fun! Xx."

"God, I hope so, too!" he e-mailed back. "Let me know where you are going to see us and we can plan ahead so you're not disappointed!!! Message me and remind me when it gets closer to the gig. The girl I was totally in love with just blew me off for a baseball player but that's life. See you then. I'm an idiot."

I felt bad for him, but I figured after that experience, he might be in the mood to party. A couple weeks later he e-mailed me again: "We get to Sheffield tomorrow. Let me know if you want to come to the gig or if you want to meet up tomorrow night as well. The gig will be no problem except I don't think we are hanging around too long after so it might be cooler to hook up tomorrow. Let me know, Diz."

I couldn't make it, but I told him I would go to the Manchester show. Again, he responded right away with a sweet e-mail, signing it "Dizweiser."

I hadn't expected him to be so nice—or so interested in me. I was flattered that someone like him would be so willing to pursue little old me. It was out of this world—especially, a short time later, when he wrote to me again: "I think we are staying at some place called the Malmaison. When I confirm that, I will send you the address as well and my contact info. I need some fun too! We all do. Talk to you soon. Dizzy Fuckin' Reed."

I Googled him. Wikipedia described him as someone who was very loyal to his wife and enjoyed collecting stamps. That sounded nice.

I was delirious every time I got an e-mail from him; I would squeal with delight and clap my hands together like a child. Eventually he sent me—a complete stranger—his BlackBerry number, a second e-mail address, and the address where he was staying. "I will stay nice and sweaty for you," he wrote at the end of the e-mail. He remembered I'd told him I liked him sweaty.

In the back of my mind, of course, there was a nagging signal: Isn't this the behavior of a complete male whore? What kind of guy gives out all his details to girls on the Internet? But because he was in Guns N' Roses, it translated as sexual confidence. I was blinded by his breathtaking charisma, which was bound in the Guns N' Roses name. And I was intrigued that he wanted me so much when there were hordes of females of the model variety to keep him company in England. Of course, I realized that if this had been some random guy from the Internet asking me to come to his hotel, I would have freaked.

In hindsight, that might not have been a bad idea.

In the days before I was to meet him, I took out my collection of Guns N' Roses videos and watched them all again. Dizzy hadn't looked too good back in the '90s. He resembled a roadie, with his long, shaggy brown hair trailing over a tubby denim-clad body. Embarrassment burned over me.

"Why don't you hook up with Izzy instead?" Abigail chided when I told her about Dizzy. She laughed at me, thinking I was desperate.

"I don't find Izzy attractive at all," I replied. "Dizzy seems very sexually exciting and charismatic." I wasn't just defending my decision; it was the truth.

On Friday night, I groomed myself to perfection: skin apricot-scrubbed; hair glossed; brows and other hairs waxed, epilated, and shaved; body marinated in mango butter. Bitter butterflies zigzagged in my belly all day. That night I made my way to my mother's house for a family barbecue, and sat silently in the garden under my parents' little canopy as my stepdad grilled lamb and tomatoes in the twilight. I was so nervous that I couldn't even touch the feta salad my little sister had made. Sheer nerves froze me to my plastic garden chair.

Was I out of my depth? This was Guns N' Roses, after all, not some little band playing the Camden Underworld. Would I be glamorous enough? Would I have to mix with beautiful models? Did I have what it took? How should I behave? Was I pretty enough?

"Why don't you eat?" my mother asked. Though still frail, she was on her feet again and back to her signature scoldings. "You never eat anything. You have become so skinny. Look at your eyes!"

"How is your PhD going?" my brother asked. "Which university are you going to be attending?"

I ignored him and stared blankly at my family.

"You look so nervous," my sensible little sister said, gazing at me with concern.

"I can't eat," I told them. "I've been invited to hang out with Guns N' Roses tomorrow and I'm nervous."

And then I scampered off into the night.

CHAPTER
42

HE HAD A **KINDNESS MERGED** WITH AN **EXPLOSIVE** CHARISMA UNMATCHED BY ANY **OTHER MAN** I'D EVER **MET.**

'm in 304. Text me when you get to the station. I'm a wreck. It's neat." When Dizzy texted me, I got nervous. I felt like I was heading to a big interview, a high-stakes audition.

I was on the train from Bristol to Manchester, wearing a red polka-dot shirt-dress and carrying my pink goodie bag laden with lingerie, shoes, a dress, and a skirt. I felt weird. I'd never made a trip like this—in broad daylight no less—to meet a random guy in a hotel. I was so used to staying overnight with bands—on a tour bus, at a hotel—that I didn't even think about it; my loaded bag had become like an extension of my arm. But now I wondered why on earth I would bring all that along: it seemed so amateur and presumptuous. In the toilets, I struggled to put my makeup on as the train hiccuped and jolted. I came out of that cubicle looking very 1960s, with my hair high, my eyes feline and heavy-lidded.

I'd bought a movie magazine to immerse myself in—as if the old photos of Betty Grable, Ava Gardner, and the rest would soak their essence into my aura.

By the time the train arrived in Manchester, my heart was fluttering, my anxieties overwhelming me. I wasn't beautiful enough, cool or interesting enough, good enough. My one comfort was that I knew I could give good service in bed. That was my weapon to make me feel sturdy inside. So I walked more strongly, knowing I could use that whenever I felt scared.

I texted Dizzy and told him I'd be with him in thirty minutes. Here I was in Manchester again, the city that had given me my first glimpse of England as a ten-year-old political refugee. I looked at the gray skies and let the thick cream of hops brewing in the beer belly of the Manchester sky soak familiar memories into my snout: Thoughts of gloomy skies, dreary public housing, missing my friends in Iran, hospitals, hunger, and my grandmother—and my orgasms to Axl Rose.

Inside, the Malmaison was berry red and intimate, with velvet gouged in its core. When I pressed the button in the elevator, my hand slithered in sweat like baby oil. I found room 304, held my breath, and knocked. The door opened, and Dizzy fixed me with his familiar wide-eyed, sky blue stare.

I went into that room and my life was changed forever.

"Hi, how are you?" I smiled.

"You know, there's no air-conditioning anywhere in this country," he said. "I'm opening all the windows." He was so insanely stunning. Such a rock star. I felt like I was in the presence of something amazing. I was in awe of him.

"The air con and rail system in this country is so antiquated," I said, trying to be casual and breezy. With my big bag pulling at my arm, I felt stupid and rude, like I'd come to stay. This wasn't the normal band encounter after a gig in a club. It was daylight in a hotel room. It felt staged, like a hooker meeting her client.

But Dizzy had a calming influence on me. He gave me a drink.

"I don't usually drink," I said. "But I think I will now." I guzzled the red wine like it was hope. It tasted disgusting.

"So who's staying at the hotel?" I asked as we sat on the edge of the bed, Axl's name floating along the tip of my brain but my face not hinting at anything.

"The band."

He looked at me with those Slavic blue eyes, penetrating me like he knew what I was thinking and this was what he expected from girls who were with him. Wearily, he said, "Axl stays in London."

"Oh, okay," I said, my mind flying: *Where in London?*

"He has a helicopter that flies him over," Dizzy said, obviously chagrined that he had to automatically dispense this information to every girl he met. "We wanna go to a club tonight," he said. "Do you know any good places?"

I called a boy who used to be a regular Towers of London hanger-on and he gave me a name: Jilly's Rockworld.

"Can he get any blow?" Dizzy asked, looking at me like a lost child. That bothered me for some reason; he looked too sweet, too calm, to be needing that kind of shit.

In his bathroom, I put on the appropriate club attire: designer, Baroque corset and a taut, stiff skirt that would make me a success.

"That looks great," Dizzy said with a mix of approval and relief when he saw me. His arm candy wouldn't let him down.

We went downstairs to the bar to meet a few others who were heading to the club. Around a tiny table with red murky lamps sat a collection of very ordinary people quietly sipping drinks. The whole scene felt very uncomfortable: I was used to witnessing a cesspit of activity, with filth on the band's itinerary and teenage girls giving roadies blowjobs in toilets. Now I would have to act like a lady. I was wild and stormy inside, but I tried to shift into my university-educated persona.

I sat cross-legged and straight-backed, sipping my cranberry juice, and wondered how the others nearby were seeing me—as Dizzy's road slut or as his date.

I was introduced to Tommy Stinson, formerly of the Replacements, now in Guns N' Roses, looking kind of grunge; an older woman with white-blond mermaid hair and a slight overbite; and Del, a round, balding, fragile-looking guy with glasses who was as warm and smiley as a teddy bear. Del had an elevated, authoritative energy about him, and I got the feeling that he was someone important, someone in charge. I was introduced to a few others, and as we all sat there drinking from our posh glasses, I went into lady-mode, drawing on my demure, educated side. The older blonde was Italian, and she maternally stroked my arm to approve me and make me feel welcome in their circle.

Soon we slipped into the warm pool of the Mancunian night to an open-air bar full of office types. A gaggle of mousy female students hugged Del ecstatically. They were the tour catering girls, their severe attire a blend of bland and blander: hoodies accessorized with greasy, limp ponytails and pallid, blotchy complexions. You could've made an effort, luv, I thought. This is Guns N' bloody Roses.

Down Princess Street, in the epicenter of gay Manchester, everyone was out on the raz, on a mission to get as obliterated as possible. Past the Chavs and emos, past loitering football fans and trampled döner kebabs smeared like roadkill on the pavement, past teenagers getting pissed on passion fruit alcopops and looking for a Saturday night shag, I walked with Dizzy. I was elated. Here I was, walking through a city I had only known as a scared, hairy-lipped refugee, with a guy who was being so nice to me and making me feel safe.

At Jilly's Rockworld, Del had a word with the bouncer. "This is Dizzy Reed. We're on tour and we're just—"

"Fuck me, yeah!" the bouncer jolted, looking at Dizzy in disbelief. It was so funny. I didn't know Dizzy was that well-known. I hated being a blagger; it was tacky, the kind of thing Z-list reality TV stars did. I felt bad for the broke students waiting outside after their beans-on-toast dinner.

The club had three separate areas: '80s hair metal, death metal, and emo crap. I dragged everyone into a large space where they were playing Mötley Crüe, and I dirty-danced with Del, who I had completely taken to by now. Dizzy stood by the bar watching me dance the seventh veil to Mötley's "Girls, Girls, Girls." He seemed so timid, calm, medicated.

"Did you get them to play this song?" he asked me deadpan.

"I love the Crüe," I said, swinging with my glass in my hand.

"I fucking hate them," he said, staring in the distance angrily. The band had treated him like shit when they'd toured together in the '80s.

Dizzy wanted to leave and so did I. I hated clubs, and wanted to cuddle. I felt strangely comfortable with Dizzy. When we walked out, he sweetly took my hand and we walked through the Saturday night—stepping over inebriated beer fans, lipsticked girls, soiled burgers, spoiled cabbage from the Turkish takeaway—all warm and fuzzy along Princess Street.

Back in Dizzy's room I was nervous again. I didn't want sexual intimacy, just cuddles. For the first time I could remember, I was with a rocker and I wasn't horny. I wanted the coherent structure of getting to know one another—without sex involved. Perhaps somewhere in the back of my mind, I might also have stopped believing I'd be good enough in bed for him, since he had fucked so many chicks. But I was here to fulfill a task. Showing up with my bag and wearing provocative clothes signified an intention—even a duty—to perform sexual acts. He had given me shelter for the night, so there it was.

I reached in my bag for music, but the only CDs I'd brought were *Appetite for Destruction*, Velvet Revolver, and Mötley Crüe—none of which went down well with Dizzy.

"You *cannot* play Velvet Revolver or Mötley," he said. "Velvet Revolver are frauds. Scott Weiland is a fraud. They've stolen their songs from other bands. Can you please put on a CD that *I* am on?"

I tried to calm him down.

"Have you fucked Slash?" Dizzy suddenly asked.

"No," I said. "Why?"

"Have you fucked Duff?"

"No, I haven't," I said. "Why are you asking me this?"

"Please don't tell me you've fucked Vince Neil. That would be gross."

"Oh God, no!" I laughed. "It's Nikki Sixx that looks good."

"*That* guy? Fuck, please don't tell me that. I see that guy all the time in the mall. He dyes his beard," he said, as if that would seal my repellence to Nikki Sixx.

A naughty shimmer slicked my eyes. "Axl's always been it for me—Nikki and Axl," I purred wantonly.

"Oh God," he sighed. "I can't believe you're saying that to me. Axl? The guy who's fucked me over money for years? Fuck, that really hurts to hear you say that!"

"I'm sorry," I said and hugged him.

We were sitting next to each other on the bed. He had the most powerful, charismatic hold over me. The air around us felt precious—sweet and simple. Dizzy had a sexual, romantic magnetism that no person I'd ever met had. He lay me down, and I looked up at him with wide eyes. I dared not blink. My heart pounded like I was a rabbit stuck on a highway. He just looked at me with that deadpan muted stare as he placed his lips gently on mine.

There was no need for sex, but being as scared as I was, I used my weapon of choice anyway. Even though I hadn't had sex in over a month, I wasn't turned on at all. But it was the only way I could think of to get him to approve of me, to think I was a cool chick.

Dizzy was childish and dorky in his seduction. It felt awkward and innocent. We didn't speak at all. It was all done very quickly and methodically. I turned around, rubbed my ass over his crotch, and he slipped his cock into me. I wasn't on any contraception, and we went with the flow.

Once his breathing and moans became heavier, I knew he had come inside me. "You're not gonna get pregnant, are you?" he asked.

It was the first time a guy had ever ejaculated inside me without any protection. It felt scary but safe—because of something a doctor had once told me.

After my seizure, for the entire year that followed, my periods became a one-day event. When I asked my doctor about it, he said I had Polycystic Ovary Syndrome, which meant I wouldn't be able to conceive naturally. It didn't mean I was infertile, but it was something I had to live with. So when Dizzy came inside me, I didn't think about pregnancy. I answered his question by explaining my condition, and he was cool with it. That first night, and for the rest of the week, there was a flood of him swimming in me.

That night, he held me and kissed me all over my face. I was taken aback by how lovely and protective he was as he rubbed my back and stroked my hair.

"Have you ever thought about settling down with someone?" he asked.

"I don't believe in monogamy," I said. "I think that even if you're in love with someone, a person has a human need and a right to be able to experience sexual variety."

"That's exactly how I feel." His voice shook with relief. "I believe in an open marriage, but my wife and I are separated now."

I loved how honest and open he was with me, despite the fact that we'd just met. I think he needed to pour his heart out to someone. He seemed lonely, sad, and fragile.

By now I was getting sleepy. I lay down on the bed and Dizzy cuddled me, holding me in his arms and stroking my hair. I snuggled into him, feeling his coarse dreadlocks on my skin and his soft chest against my naked breasts.

"Did your dad molest you when you were a kid?" he suddenly asked.

I was shocked. "I don't know you well enough to answer that."

But he made me talk. About my childhood. About everything in my heart, my soul. About my parents, my life. It felt so good. He knew exactly how to get into me, how to make me feel wanted. I told him about my mother's stroke.

"Why didn't you tell me before?" he exclaimed, strangely shocked.

He seemed genuinely interested in knowing everything about me. I was on such a fucking high lying there next to him. It felt like the little girl part of me had finally been given everything she'd never had in life. It was better than cocaine, better than every happiness I'd known put together. He had a kindness merged with an explosive charisma unmatched by any other man I'd ever met. Nothing bothered me: not the noise of the buses on the street; not sleeping in someone's arms when I normally wanted my own space. Dizzy was so gentle, kissing my back, my neck.

"Would you still like me if I wasn't in a band?" he asked.

"If you were how you are now—the same guy—then, yes, I would," I said truthfully.

"So it's not just because of who I am and the band I'm in?"

I didn't know how to respond to that. I actually didn't even know the answer. I wanted to be honest but not cruel. I wasn't even sure myself if I only liked him because of Guns N' Roses. Either way, I was floating over the bed with adrenaline.

———————

I checked my phone's clock when I awoke. It was really early. I'd only slept for about four hours. I looked over at Dizzy. He seemed to be asleep. I couldn't let him see me without proper makeup on, so I grabbed my bag and shot through the room to the toilet. I crayoned on my thick foundation paste to cover up my acne scars, retouched my now Alice Cooper-esque eyeliner, and applied a light daytime blush. If I didn't look good when he woke up, he might think, "Lord, what have I done?"

I slunk back into the sheets and lay still as concrete. I touched Dizzy's dreadlocks. They were fuzzy and rough and itched my skin, which was still raw and tender from the elation of being with him. Dizzy had taken sleeping pills, so I didn't want to disturb him. I was so happy that morning, but nervousness was creeping in again like a hail of darts. Today was the day of the concert. What was expected of me? I was used to small, beer-stained hotel rooms, hordes of young, half-dressed, drunken groupies, and angry tour managers. This hotel room was so pretty. And clean. I cuddled Dizzy's back tightly and placed kisses all over him until he woke up.

"Do you want breakfast?" he asked as he kissed me. "I can order room service."

"Oh, don't order room service," I said. "It's expensive. I'll go get us some Starbucks. Would you like that?"

He kissed and hugged me again, and I ran out in a denim skirt and red shirt into the sunny, smiling Manchester streets.

Strolling through the city center was like walking in the past. I was ten years old again, smelling the leather of new shoes, eyeing toy shops full of glamorous dolls, and gazing at brand new toasters and kettles in the Argos store, the kind we could never afford growing up. I remembered how my cousin and I used to go and look at the porn magazines in comic book stores and steal them because we were too young to buy them. I'd jack up my hair with stupendous amounts of hairspray, and wear purple eye shadow, long lacy white gloves, and thrift-store jewelry as I walked through these streets.

I remembered my mother calling me a whore when she saw my tiny ripped skirts, fishnet tights, and ripped tops. Stung by her words and unable to contain my tears, I began to believe her.

As I grew older, I transformed myself, within and without. I changed from proper clothes to my shredded outfits in public toilets in the park, where I smoked cigarettes and drank cans of Guinness. I embraced a life in the shadows.

The thick smell of coffee at Starbucks snapped me back into reality. "Chai latte, please, and a decaf caramel macchiato."

On the way back to the hotel, I saw Tommy Stinson shopping with the big-toothed, blond mermaid woman. Then I bumped into Del.

"I bet you've been up all night," he said in his sweet, uncle-type way. "You kept him up, didn't ya, you bad girl?"

"Yes, we're both tired." I blushed.

"See ya tonight, sweetheart."

Del was so adorable. I still didn't know who he was.

"I need to go shopping for my kids," Dizzy said when I got back. "Will you come and help me? I have to get Manchester United stuff for them."

"Are you sure you want me to come shop for your kids? I don't want to intrude."

"I really like you. It would mean a lot to me if you came." Dizzy looked at me dead-on. His honesty was so refreshing, so endearing.

Going shopping in the Arndale Centre mall with someone from Guns N' Roses was surreal. The place epitomized the unpleasantness of my childhood life in England. It looked exactly the same to me: the same smell, the same hollow lights, the same gurgly echo of kids' voices and Mancunian accents. We went into a sports shop and started picking out Manchester United shirts for Dizzy's children.

"Do you think this would fit a nine-year-old? Would she like it, do you think?" Dizzy was intense. We'd only been together for one night; I didn't feel I had any authority to shop for his kids with him. But, at the same time, the fact that he would ask me made me feel good about myself.

As we walked back to the hotel, Dizzy took my hand. It melted into his with trepidation and joy. Then, as we reached the hotel doors, he suddenly stopped and faced me.

"Why do you like me?" he asked. "I want you to be honest. Why me?"

"Why *me*?" I said. "You can have models if you want."

I didn't understand this at all.

iding on the Guns N' Roses tour bus felt grand. Dizzy and I sat at the front on the way to the Manchester Evening News Arena. And Del gave me a gold laminate granting me VIP access for the European tour.

Back at the hotel, we had bumped into Izzy Stradlin outside. He was with the most beautiful and fragrant Frenchwoman and a young girl of about twelve, who I assumed was their daughter. They were traveling in a separate car because Izzy was higher up in the band's ranking system.

I wondered how the rest of the band viewed me. I wondered if they were aware of the state of Dizzy's supposedly open marriage. Each band member seemed to be in a world of his own, like office workers shuffling in quietly to do their day's work. It all felt very corporate—so different from traveling with other bands, where it felt like one big family.

When we reached the venue, the bus went through giant metal gates. We parked next to Bullet For My Valentine's bus, which was a vomit-inducing emo surprise. If they hadn't shared the same management company as Guns N' Roses— Sanctuary—they probably would never have gotten the support slot.

Towers of London was also supporting Guns N' Roses. It would be weird to see them in these circumstances. Usually I'd be so excited at the thought of seeing my boys—I was as proud as a mother hen to know they were playing such a huge venue—but this time was different: I was with Guns N' Roses. As we got off the bus, I kept wondering where Axl was and whether I'd meet him tonight.

After walking down a labyrinthine maze of fluorescent-lit stone corridors that felt like a maximum security penitentiary, we entered a dining area where the catering girls from the previous night ladled out soup and distributed shepherd's pie, crunchy veggies, and puddings with custardy things. The whole band—minus Axl—sat down for supper.

Afterward, I followed Dizzy to the dressing room. I felt like I was walking on eggshells, as if at any moment someone would jump out and say, "Hey! This isn't right. You're not hot enough. You shouldn't be here!"

WITH ROBIN FINCK

So I entered the room meekly. A long table with a vast array of fruit, a juice extractor, finger sandwiches, hummus, and other dips awaited the band and its entourage. There was a shower room and a large bathroom. In the corner, Robin Finck, the lead guitarist, was doing leg lunges and yoga stretches in his white long johns, looking like a yeti. Dizzy introduced me to everyone he could.

Then he brought out his keyboards and put his headphones on for a warmup before the show. I knew it was time for me to leave, but I didn't know where to go, so I decided to venture out into the corridors.

Just as I came out of the dressing room, there he was—Axl Rose, striding briskly toward me like a cougar, surrounded by a wall of security. He was wearing shades and smirking. His face was alabaster white. He was still as beautiful as Dionysus. I felt my body lengthen and bloom like a glowing flower. I smiled seductively, presenting myself to Axl with kittenish fuck-me eyes. He looked me up and down and smiled back. My heart beat super-fast and I was so happy that I was looking hot as fuck.

I glided on through the corridors, every bend and intersection occupied with security guards poured into elephant-gray uniforms. They were so courteous and gentle with me because I was with Guns N' Roses. Through those burrows of fluorescent-lit gray stone, I stumbled across the Towers' dressing room just as the boys were filing out to go onstage. I glanced inside their room, which was pocket-sized and tucked into the back of the venue like a redundant sandwich. *My boys.* Kissing them one by one on the lips as they scuttled off to play, I felt pride swell in my chest like a mommy watching her children at their first school play.

"Oi saggy tits, wot u doin' 'ere?" It was Mad Pete, the glue to the Towers family. The guy looked so bloody grateful and deliriously happy, as he always did when he was with Towers. I had missed him so much.

"Woz in Glasgow last night. Fackin' drove back to London and then back 'ere." He wasn't called Mad for nothing. "Had to go 'ome for somefin'. Anyway, wot u doin' 'ere, saggy tits? You're shagging Axl, aren't you?"

"I fucking wish. Actually, I'm here with Dizzy Reed. He's the keyboardist. He's really nice, Pete. Not like the rest of them you've seen me with. I'll introduce you later."

"C'mon then. Towers are on!" He pulled me along, his giant tattoos of Axl and Sid Vicious entertaining his arms.

I had to go get Dizzy. I wanted him to see Towers, the boys I had known for so long. Dizzy and I stood sidestage, Dizzy silent and me screaming hoarse to my boys' songs and jumping up and down like a teenager with Beatlemania.

Such a huge venue didn't suit Towers. They were too quirky and Donny's voice was too weak to fill such a large arena. They thrived in intimate venues.

At the end of their set, Towers covered "Free Bird" by Lynyrd Skynyrd. "They totally ruined that one," Dizzy whispered to me disgustedly as we walked back to the Guns N' Roses dressing room. I felt embarrassed that the band I loved so much had let him down.

I started massaging his tense shoulders and placing kisses on his head while the rest of the band warmed up, strumming guitars, doing yoga, and eating organic food. Dizzy kept looking up at me like a little lost boy with wide blue eyes. I started to realize that he was getting off on being seen with me. I got the feeling that it actually made him feel more important; even after sixteen years in Guns N' Roses, many people still looked at Dizzy as just another hired hand, especially since there were two keyboardists in the band. But he didn't need to feel that way. He was so lovely, so sexy, and such a dispenser of cool.

Waiting on the sidelines for Guns N' Roses to come on that night was one of the happiest moments of my life. The band had been my life since I was a teen. Axl had been my God, and their songs had resonated in my being. Now I was watching them from the wings in a huge arena. And even though it wasn't the real Guns N' Roses—with Slash, Duff, and Steven—it was still the music I lived for.

As I strutted on the edge of the stage in my starched skirt and embroidered corset next to Towers, Mad Pete, Del, and the sound technician, I was thrashed by a sea of thunderous frenzy roaring from thousands of sweaty humans chanting "Guns N' Roses!" from the dark innards of the arena, steeped in smoke and heat. It was a volcanic yearning so deeply emotional that it resembled mass religious zeal. I felt like this was the top of my mountain. I felt at home. Even Velvet Revolver was dribbing penny change compared to this.

When Robin Finck trickled the opening bars of "Welcome to the Jungle," the crowd poured out a soothing sigh of relief. It quenched the festering frustrations kept stacked and stagnant in their lives. Pyro kept going off every ten minutes, and I saw Dizzy pat on some bongos at the top corner of the stage for the opening of the song.

It was surreal watching the show with Towers. Here I was with a band that I had been everywhere with, sharing girls with, screaming hysterically to their songs; now we were the audience together, excited together, singing together.

Every Guns N' Roses song was a little plate of heaven—even though they never played my favorite, "Civil War." After the final notes of the closing song, "Paradise City," my body felt arthritic. I went to touch up my makeup in the Towers' dressing room, which was packed with people like steamed fish in foil.

"I'm so nervous. What should I do?" I asked The Rev while his girlfriend, a tanned surfer-type, soaked me in embittered looks.

"You're gonna be all right, babe. Give Dizzy a few minutes. He's just come offstage."

Just before Towers left, I asked if any of them had any Lynyrd Skynyrd or Stones CDs, because Dizzy didn't like my Mötley and Velvet Revolver records.

⸺

I treaded like a feather whisper into the Guns N' Roses dressing room, my cheeks blushed and burning.

"Hey, where'd ya go?" Dizzy looked up as I came in.

"I didn't want to intrude."

"Come sit down, honey. Do you want any food?"

I felt so shy and humble. It was weird being backstage with a band without sex, drugs, and naked girls. This was so proper, like being at my auntie's house for tea and biscuits.

I helped myself to some pineapple and sat next to Dizzy.

"Did you like my piano solo?" He looked at me expectantly.

"I loved it. And I loved watching the show. It was so exciting."

"When I was playing it, Axl kept saying in my earpiece, 'The guy who wrote that killed himself,'" Dizzy said, his eyes widening like an excited fan, as if Axl were his spiritual leader.

Then Axl walked into the band's dressing room from his own dominion. "That was fucking great," he said, hyped up and excited, just like a normal human.

While he raved on to Tommy and Dizzy about the show, I sat there looking at them all like a nerd. I had to be normal even though I wanted to look at Axl's face with awe, kiss him, and tell him how many teenage orgasms he had given me.

"Last night I was in the lobby of the hotel and I saw these two girls," Axl said, smiling with relish. "We started talking and I took them to my room." He said this like a normal man, even though he wasn't normal; he was a god. I was surprised he seemed so proud of such an accomplishment.

I was nervous and just wanted to cuddle Dizzy and so we decided to head back to the hotel. First, though, we stopped by Del's room, where we started making out as Del played Lou Reed on the stereo and watched us.

"Are your friends hot?" Del asked me as Dizzy kissed my neck.

"Yeah, they're coming to the Birmingham show on Tuesday," I said. "They're all really into Axl and Sebastian." Sebastian Bach of Skid Row was slated to join the band on the road in Birmingham.

"Does Axl have a girlfriend?" I asked, hoping I wasn't being too obvious.

"Axl has a lot of girlfriends," Del smirked. I felt crushed; I wanted Axl to be a one-woman man.

As Dizzy kissed me and fondled my bare thighs with Del looking on, I suddenly felt strange as if I were sirloin steak dripping in sauce, a spectacle for these two men's amusement. Dizzy looked so smug in front of Del, as if he were showing off to him. His usual wide-eyed, frozen look had morphed into a blazingly dirty sexual one.

Back in his room, the lights were low and I bounced on the bed like a kid. Then I spread my legs and made Dizzy watch me. He looked at me more hungrily than he had the previous night, his eyes fiery like a silent predator's. I could tell he was less stilted than the night before. He had a raw, yearning, almost animal energy about him that was crazy. He held me down and climbed onto my body like a sheet of love falling all over me.

"I wanna come inside you again," he kept saying as he fucked me, his eyes carnivorous.

I leaned back, legs up, back arched. And we locked eyes like two rabid animals. He came in me hard, and the sperm ran down my leg when I stood up.

"Have you even been with any of the guys from Towers of London?" he asked in a snap.

"Yeah," I said. "Four of them."

"That's hot," Dizzy said. "They *are* good-looking guys."

"Why do you keep asking who I've slept with?" I asked. "You fuck a lot of women yourself."

"I can't imagine you ever feeling jealousy," he said. "You don't seem like you'd ever be jealous of who I fuck."

"I'm the most romantic person ever. I've just had bad experiences. I know the game now. It's just fun and sex and it's all good," I said happily as I cleaned up my thighs.

"Why don't you just settle down with someone?"

"Because musicians are no good," I laughed. "No offense."

"So you're not gonna be with someone just because he's in a band?"

"Just for fun and that's it," I said.

"That's great," he sighed.

"What?"

"Please don't freak out, but I have to tell you something," he said quietly. "I really like you."

Inside, I was laughing. I never took anything a musician told me seriously. I saw it all as fun and fluff because they lived in a make-believe world; only the music was real, not the offstage theatricality of its performers. And if I let my exposed heart's fibers get intertwined with theirs, the pain would surely impale me. I knew enough not to take that kind of talk seriously. My heart couldn't afford it. I didn't want to get hurt again. This had to be sex and nothing more; that was the only way to preserve my heart.

So I asked him to do water sports with me to steer him away—away from entering the emotional pool. It was the only way I could turn this thing around.

I took him to the bathroom and put down some white towels. I knelt on the floor and told him to do it. Dizzy looked at me skeptically, with trepidation. He said he'd never done water sports. So he looked at me and I at him. I prayed that he would do it so I could make him forget about that stupid emotional "liking me" bullshit.

I couldn't understand why he would be so caring. I still didn't know why he wasn't like other musicians. In bed, he held me and talked to me and I told him more about my childhood and my father. When I woke from a bad dream in the middle of the night, he rubbed my back and held me tight.

"It's okay, baby, I'm here," he said, cuddling and kissing me. I wanted so hard to believe that this caring, needy persona was just an act, but it was the most comforting seduction in the world. It made me feel safe.

In the morning, Dizzy ordered eggs Benedict and told me some girl was planning to come see him in Birmingham the next day.

"I'm gonna tell her not to come," he said.

"Why not?" I asked as I gobbled up buttered toast.

"Because I just want to see you." He looked embarrassed.

"Really?" I was surprised. I assumed he'd be looking forward to getting a different variety of pussy.

"I'm gonna call her now and tell her not to come. She's driving from London." He got his phone. I thought it was a bit drastic.

"If the poor girl has already made plans to see you, don't be mean. Let her come, and I'll just make plans to see you another day." I actually felt bad for the girl.

"I don't want her to come. I told you I really like you," he said as he texted her ferociously.

I didn't say anything. I just sat there and ate my breakfast, still wondering why he was so nice. There had to be something wrong with him.

Then Dizzy looked up at me. "Just say it," he said angrily. "Just say you're not into me!"

He picked up his plate and threw it on the bed. The runny eggs rolled and splattered on the white cover.

I was a bit scared, but I loved his intensity, which matched my own temperament. To me, it was passion and creativity, a rush of ferocious, romantic feeling for me.

"I'm not saying that," I said. "I do like you. I just feel bad for the girl."

"Fuck!" he shouted, livid. I wasn't sure if that was because he really liked me and felt conflicted, or because he hadn't taken his medication.

"What's wrong?"

"Just fuckin' tell me you don't like me. It's fine." He paced across the room.

I immediately rushed to comfort him, to calm him down and reassure him that I did like him.

"You have to eat," I told him. "You need it."

"I don't feel like eatin' now." Dizzy looked so hurt. I felt like a witch.

And I felt helpless. I had no idea what to do or say. It was too intense. I wolfed down my eggs Benedict, and then I left, confused, bewildered, yet still on a high.

Later, on the train home, I received a text from Dizzy: "Sorry I flipped out earlier. I can't help it. I really dig u."

My body felt like a furnace. My head was concrete. He was so intense.

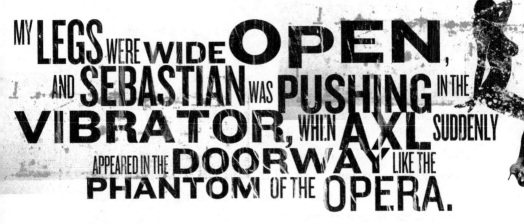

MY LEGS WERE WIDE OPEN, AND SEBASTIAN WAS PUSHING IN THE VIBRATOR, WHEN AXL SUDDENLY APPEARED IN THE DOORWAY LIKE THE PHANTOM OF THE OPERA.

n Birmingham, I brought my friend Ostara as a present for Dizzy. Dizzy had e-mailed me to say: "I told that other person not to come. I can't wait to see you, bring your schoolgirly friend." (Months later I learned the girl actually did come to see him—and darted off just before I arrived.)

But I had my own plan for that day—to get Axl.

I was meeting Abigail at the venue with her new boyfriend, Warren, who was Sebastian Bach's promoter. Sebastian was opening for Guns N' Roses, and I was looking forward to meeting him. Even though he had pretty hair, I never understood why chicks found him so hot. He was too much like a big kid for me.

Even though it would be nice to see Dizzy again, he was getting too intense and too needy for me. My plan was to distract him with my friends while I tried to get Axl. I put on my Victoria's Secret corset and did my hair and makeup like the girls from Russ Meyer movies.

Outside the venue, as I asked Padge from Bullet For My Valentine for directions, a bleached-blond Chav, whose skin looked like it had been dyed with carrots, started shoving me around for talking to her boyfriend. I was used to being pushed and hit by girls whenever I talked to any member of Bullet For My Valentine.

In the warehouse-like area behind the stage, where dozens of roadies milled around fixing and dispatching stage equipment, Ostara and I strutted around in our minis. We looked like such groupies in our slutty rock gear, heavily made up and accessorized with our Guns N' Roses laminates. Among the stressed-out roadies in their Megadeth T-shirts and the catering girls in their little caps and aprons, a photographer snapped away greedily as we posed in naughty positions beside the broad rubble of metal equipment.

I couldn't wait to take Ostara to Dizzy. I knew he'd love her schoolgirly looks and bright young disposition. I wanted to make him happy.

"I'm taking you to Sebastian after the show," Warren, the tour manager, kept telling me. He followed Abigail around like a little lamb despite the fact that she and Ostara were crazy in love with Sebastian and were wetting their knickers to say hello to him and fuck him.

The dull thud that pounded from Bullet For My Valentine's set was about as pleasant as being a factory worker in Hull. Ostara and I left our spot to hang out in the catering area. As we wolfed down yummy shepherd's pie and cake, Dizzy and the band arrived. Dizzy looked withdrawn and hung his head, his straggly mane of dreadlocks drooping low. I didn't want to bug him, so I just waved from across the room. Two minutes later, he texted me: "I don't even get a proper hello? Fuck!"

I went over immediately and gave him a hug and kiss in front of the band. "You made me look like an idiot," he said quietly. "Everyone knows I'm with you."

"I'm sorry, so sorry," I said. "Are you okay? Have you been sleeping okay?"

As he prepared for the show, I hung out with Ostara and Abigail. But as I watched Dizzy playing the piano later that night, I realized for the first time how heartbreakingly talented he was. He was an artist, with a raw creativity so unkempt and free, and the aura of a wild tiger.

"Look at your face." Warren elbowed me in the ribs. "You have a look of lurve . . ."

"Shut up, Warren," I said. "This is not love. It's lust. Now take me to Seb's room."

After the show, Dizzy came to the VIP area where fans and contest-winners waited to get autographs and photos. Clusters of drunk young girls in clothes so slutty they were offensive even to my eyes were sprinkled around the room, giggling and talking to members of Guns N' Roses. I waited quietly in the corner for Dizzy as he chatted with fans and signed autographs. Next to me a pair of slutty young girls giggled.

"I am so gonna fuck him tonight," one of them said, pointing at Dizzy.

"How are we gonna get him?" her friend asked excitedly. "You go talk to him. Ask him for a photo and then flirt like fuck. Go on."

"Oh God, I can't. Do I look okay? I really want him. He's hot."

One of the blondes seemed close to exploding with excitement. All I felt was jealousy and fury, but I decided to stay silent because I wanted to see what Dizzy would do.

The girls flirted with Dizzy, giggling and touching him. An overwhelming rush of relief washed over me when I saw that he wasn't flirting back or making arrangements for the girls to come back to the hotel with him. Then I kicked myself for the pang of jealousy that had managed to slither in.

Although I was excited at the prospect of meeting Sebastian, a feeling of attachment kept confronting me. Dizzy's behavior started to affect me, and for the first time, I felt safe believing it. I loved his company, and I couldn't wait to get back to the hotel and be with him.

After forty-five minutes, Dizzy still hadn't come out and I'd grown tired of lurking around the corridors like some teenage fan waiting for an autograph. Dizzy texted me saying they were all going to a party, but I would have to wait awhile until he was ready to leave.

Just then, Warren invited me to go to Sebastian's room. I deliberated for a couple seconds and then my excited curiosity got the better of me.

———————————

Sebastian Bach's dressing room was a godawful mess. Pizza crusts, cigarette butts, dressing gowns, filth-ridden T-shirts, and empty beer cans congested the room. Battered sofas and ramshackle chairs with blackened petrol-looking stains were encrusted with a gaggle of strippers who said they worked in the local Spearmint Rhino. They draped themselves over Sebastian with their spray-tanned arms, giggling toothy smiles as he got stoned and sipped expensive red wine. Now I could see why other women found him attractive. He had beautiful boy looks, with a sun-kissed golden mane cascading down his back like a shimmering waterfall in a shampoo ad. His face was cute and modely and squishy. I had heard he was a complete asshole, but in real life he was fucking endearing. I wanted to gobble him up and kiss his squishy little face.

I was not in any way attracted to him sexually, however. Even his rock-star status didn't excite me. But Abigail and Ostara were salivating from the corner of the room. As one chipmunk-cute stripper got the most attention, the two of them seethed in the background.

"I'm gonna have some fun tonight!" Sebastian said in a singsong voice. The stripper giggled, young and devoid of rock history and Sebastian Bach.

The rest of Sebastian's band mooched around like unwanted gristle to Sebastian's lean, raw steak. They were outgrown, hairy beasts, and I wanted them to leave. Warren watched Abigail like an obsessed teenager, and I knew tonight was the last night they'd be together. She didn't give a shit. She was gonna fuck Sebastian one way or another. She lay back and put her legs in the air, and right away Ostara got on her knees and started to lap up her pussy. My girls—I was so proud of them. They were both after Sebastian like frenzied terriers in heat, caged and unfed for days. Abigail threw her head back with a curdling yowl, which made Ostara lap her up even more. Suddenly, Sebastian's attention snapped to them. He began goading them on, whooping and cheering. The strippers were instantly forgotten. Not knowing what to do, they quietly dispersed. It floored me that all it took to grip the attention of any man was a bit of cliché hardcore girl-on-girl action—even if he had strippers on his lap. I started laughing at the predictable simplicity of it all.

I uncrossed my unpantied legs, exposing my bare crotch. "What are you gonna do, Miss Sharon Stone?" Sebastian chortled.

I was bored of waiting for Dizzy, and paranoia began to gnaw at my insides, whispering that Dizzy was fucking someone in the dressing room. So I locked eyes with the shampoo-ad boy, my chin in my palm, and replied, "What do you want me to do, Sebastian?"

I knew how to get my girls off. I grabbed Ostara's hips from behind and went down on her as she licked away at Abi. My vibrator was in my bag, and Sebastian grabbed it and started sticking it into me.

The dressing room doors were open, and within a few minutes I started panicking that either Del or one of the Guns N' Roses guys would walk in and see. Here I was, fooling around with my girl-friends in Sebastian's room—with the backstage pass Dizzy gave me.

My instincts were right. My legs were wide open, and Sebastian was pushing in the vibrator, when Axl suddenly appeared in the doorway like the Phantom of the Opera. He was wearing shades, and his strawberry-red hair, which I'd loved for so long, was neatly bunched in cornrows and pulled back in a shoulder-length pony-tail. He was wearing a leather jacket and ripped jeans, his body packed tight like meat into clean, crisp designer wear.

I shut my legs as fast as a whip and covered my breasts. "No, I don't want to," I said firmly, standing up and fumbling to put my corset and skirt back on. I didn't want Axl to see me this way, amid this disarray of stacked flesh. I walked over to him, smiled, and said, "Hi."

Then I shook his hand and told him something else: "Thank you for inspiring so many volcanic orgasms in me since the age of thirteen."

He smiled. "I'm flattered," he said.

I lifted up my skirt and asked him to sign his name, because I wanted to get it tattooed. Someone handed him a black marker and he signed my flower.

Later that night at the hotel, the signature was rubbed off when Dizzy made love to me.

BACKSTAGE WITH OSTARA IN SEBASTIAN'S ROOM

I WOULD NEVER HURT YOU. I WOULD NEVER FUCK WITH YOUR HEAD AND HEART LIKE THOSE OTHER GUYS HAVE.

hortly after Axl branded me, Dizzy texted that he was back at the hotel. He wanted to know whether I would come over. "Either way, I dig you," he wrote.

Ostara and Abigail wanted Sebastian so badly, they were tugging at my skirt to go with them to his hotel. So I decided to join them—because they told me there was going to be a big party and because I thought I might catch a glimpse of Axl there.

The "ugly syndrome" is what we call the bewildering phenomenon that occurs when rock stars pick the ugliest girl out of a group of super-hot women. It's ridiculous, but also perhaps understandable because the ugliest girls are the most grateful. They don't expect much, and therefore they'll put up with anything. In other words, they're the easiest lay.

So that night, the ugly syndrome struck again, and Sebastian chose to focus on the lumpy, greasy, ponytailed catering girl over all of the sexy strippers—and over Ostara and Abigail. My gob was smacked. But I understood.

We followed Seb and his ugly, annoying band to the van Warren had ordered. He was sedate and defeated after having seen Abigail be herself: a tiger. As we neared the Hilton Hotel in Birmingham where Sebastian was staying, I realized there wasn't going to be any party, and Seb's band had brought us there only because they thought we would sleep with them. How dare they think I would fuck any of them? They were gross, slimy, creepy, and repulsive. Even if they were beautiful, it wouldn't have mattered. I wanted to be with Dizzy.

I found myself back at the Malmaison again. In the lobby, I saw Dizzy sitting with the stripper girls Sebastian had dismissed. Jealousy like I'd never known blinded me; I went weak at the shock of it. How dare those whores think they could even try and get Dizzy! I walked slowly up to him.

"Hey, you came!" He looked tired, but so damn happy to see me. I had actually missed him. I sat in his lap and draped myself all over him, giving him a kiss while a brunette stripper shot vitriolic looks in my direction.

"It's so good to see you," I said, and I meant it. I wanted to be blanketed in his comfort.

"I brought my schoolgirly friend like you asked me to," I whispered, pointing at Ostara. "Do you like her?" All I wanted was to make him happy and keep him interested in me. He glanced at Ostara and looked pleased. I was relieved.

"Shall we go back to your room, *hon-eee*?" I soaked every word in raunchy syrup, just to annoy the strippers.

"Yeah, let's go," he said. His bandmates looked at him in envy: having been in Guns N' Roses for sixteen years, he automatically got more pussy than them. The brunette stripper was left with Chris Pitman.

Dizzy's room still displayed his devout loyalty to Jägermeister, which occupied every corner like it was nectar for soothing a cold. It was the first time I'd had hard alcohol in a while, and it was syrupy and delicious. He was tired but he got on the phone straightaway to order room service for Ostara and me. We couldn't decide what we wanted, so Dizzy ordered nearly everything on the menu, allowing us to pick and choose.

Ostara drew a bath and a musky smell filled the air. I flopped down on the bed, exhausted.

"Are you gonna get in the bath, too?" Dizzy whispered hopefully to me as Ostara cooed from the blur of raw velvety steam.

"No, I'm really tired," I mumbled sleepily. "I'm just gonna rest a bit. You should get in with Ostara. I don't mind."

Of course, I *did* mind. I wanted him to be with me, not her, even though she was my friend and I loved her. But I had to demonstrate that I was a maestro in the rules of groupiedom, that I hadn't let myself become emotionally attached in any way, that I was okay with sharing. But, in my heart, I wanted to see if he would fuck her in there without me.

As Dizzy got in the bath with Ostara, I lay in bed, still as meat. Every second ripped my insides to shreds, but I had to stay strong in this boot camp because this was the game, and I was not to get emotionally attached to a guy in a band. This was rock 'n' roll.

But I was so upset, I wanted to die.

After only three or four minutes, Dizzy came to me. I was lying facedown on the bed, my neck growing stiff from keeping still. But I didn't turn because I didn't want to show him I cared. He climbed on the bed beside me and just held me in silence, laying kisses all over my face. I turned around.

"Why didn't you stay in the bath with Ostara?" I whispered. I wanted to be casual, but I was shaking.

"Because I wanted to be with you. Just with you," he whispered back. And it was then that I knew. I knew I fucking loved him. There was a naked, young blonde in the bath, and Dizzy could have had her, but he came to me. He just wanted to be with me. I was falling for him so fucking hard and I hated it. This wasn't part of the game, but that feeling of love just swept over me, and right there, at that moment, I felt safe and whole, and sure he would never hurt me.

"I'm gonna sleep on the sofa so you guys can have some space together," Ostara said. She got out of the bath and curled up like a newborn kitten in the corner of the sofa. Ostara, the sweetest angel and the most loyal friend anyone could ever wish for.

That night, I felt a degree of intimacy I'd never experienced before—the kind that can only be achieved one-on-one. But in the back of my mind I knew I was letting my barriers down too fast, and I cursed myself for it. I needed to keep my guard up because I had to live in reality.

"You know, you can have Ostara if you want," I said to him. "Would you like me to get her?"

"So you don't want to be with me alone, is that it?" He looked hurt.

"Come on, I do like you. But I *can't* like you."

Dizzy sat up and took a big swig from a bottle of bourbon by the bedside. He looked really pissed off. "Fuck! Why?" he spat out the words.

"You're in a band. You live in LA. This is just fun and sex." I couldn't let my heart get hurt.

"So you can't like me *because I'm in a band*? Fuck!" He looked so upset. I didn't understand why he didn't see the reality of the situation, why he couldn't just leave things as they were so that no one would get hurt.

"We can't get involved with guys in a band," Ostara said from the corner, echoing my case. "It's just rock 'n' roll. It's just fun and that's it."

"I would never hurt you," he said. "I would never fuck with your head and heart like those other guys have. Can't you just believe that I like you? Fuck."

I really wanted to believe him. It felt so good just to let go and be the innocent me again—to reject the cynicism and the bitter liquid rush of rumor, suspicion, and resentment that prevailed in the rock scene. It was like he wanted to prove himself to me. Yet I didn't understand why he liked me so much. He touched me, kissed my face, and looked at me when we had sex. My body burned like a furnace. I had never been so turned on. It was the first time I'd felt security and trust. I was opening up and letting go, and it was so freeing to feel safe with a man who I liked and who liked me.

I opened myself wider to him, as if to absorb his being into me. He ground himself in me so hard that a volcano exploded lava and fireballs in my tummy, and I screamed, my vagina convulsing as I came so hard I cried. It was the best sex I'd ever had.

"I want to come inside you again," he said.

"I want you to. I want you to come in me." And I felt him explode in me. He looked at me. He looked beautiful. And we both just smiled. I put my legs up and let his cum rush through my body. He held my hand and we fell asleep in each other's arms. I had crossed the line I had once drawn for myself.

<hr />

I awoke to the phone ringing.

"Your friend is gonna get raped," Del said when I picked up. "She's walking around the hotel naked."

I always had to babysit her. I knew this would happen. She always got like this after the evil drink.

"Stay in bed," Del said. "I'll bring her to your room."

Abigail was naked, except for her cowboy boots. Her tits, ballooned and tanned, had handprints on them. Her platinum-blond hair was matted and congealed around her face. Del smirked as he looked at the scene sprawled before him: Dizzy with three naked chicks. It paid to have endured sixteen years of Axl: you got more pussy coming at you.

I placed Abi next to the sofa and put a burger in her hand to help her absorb the alcoholic spew. I could smell roadie sperm on her. Or maybe it was Sebastian's band. I was so disappointed in her. She fell asleep sitting up, still clasping the burger. I pried it away from her, then I climbed back into bed with Dizzy and went back to sleep.

The next day, as soon as I returned home, a text from Dizzy appeared on my phone: "I can still smell your body. It's in my hair.

Come see me. I miss your body, eyes, hair, boobs . . . all of u. And just so you know, I do dig u, and I would never fuck with your head and I would never fuck you over."

I slept sweetly that night. But at around four A.M., Dizzy called. He sounded upset. He was in Nottingham, and he wanted me to come join him. I imagined girls lurking there, stumbling in and out of his room, and camouflaging themselves in his wardrobe as we spoke. But he didn't seem to have anyone else there. His voice was pleading, reeking of neediness. We talked on the phone for an hour; he snapped at me angrily, pleading with me not to break his heart, not to let him down.

"Fucking blow me off then," he said. "I treat you good, unlike those piece-of-shit men who have fucked you over in the past."

"I really like you, too, but you live in LA. What do you expect to happen between us?"

"So you're breaking my heart?" he shouted. "Just tell me to fuck off then! I can't believe this!"

"I am just being realistic," I said. "This is fun. What else could it possibly be?"

I tried to remain logical, but I knew it was too late. My heart could not take even a feather stroke of pain. I just wanted him to understand the reality of the situation—in a few days he'd leave for home.

CHAPTER

46

couple days later, just before the Guns N' Roses shows at Wembley Arena in London, one of Dizzy's children came to visit him. She was in her teens, and he hadn't seen her for a few years; he was ecstatic at the prospect of seeing her. I was bringing Lori to the Saturday show and another friend on Sunday. I wanted to be with Dizzy so much, I couldn't wait for Saturday.

Late Friday night, he called me, crushed. The meeting with his daughter hadn't gone so well.

"I'm so fucking down," he said. "I wish you were here. I'm feeling pretty alone." He said he would give the hotel receptionist my name, so I could hang out in his room if he wasn't there.

The next day, I bought a fuchsia corset and a Playboy bunny polka-dot skirt from my usual Sluts R Us stall in Camden Lock. I couldn't wait to see Dizzy. He'd been telling me how much he wanted to see me, as he needed some serious cheering up. So I was determined to give him the best cuddles and massages I could. I would melt away all his hurt.

Later that night, he told me, the band was going to play a secret acoustic show in a small club called Cuckoo's in Mayfair after the regular gig, and that Lori and I should meet him at the Soho House Hotel, where he was staying, and we'd all go together.

I couldn't wait for Lori to meet him. I gushed to her about how I had finally met a rocker who was genuinely lovely and good-hearted, and who treated me nice. Lori was dying to see what this rare amulet looked like.

The Soho House was a Kinder Egg surprise. Hidden in an alley off Dean Street, it reeked of film-industry types and its foyer was engorged with scorching crimson trinkets. Lori and I sat in the waiting room, a cleft off the reception area, and waited for Dizzy. The room was so exquisitely white, fluffy, and Peter Pan–like—a deviant in dirt-and-smoke-saturated Soho. But by the time Dizzy texted me that night, it was nearly three A.M. and I wanted to go to bed.

"We are not going to hotel now," his text read. "We are going to Kabaret and then Cuckoo's for the gig. I am so down. My kid blew me off tonight. I want to die. Sorry."

Kabaret was a little celeb-type club that was always in the gossip mags, usually because reality TV stars were constantly falling out of it. To get there, Lori and I took a rickshaw: I loved going through the intestinal tubes of Soho that way, smelling the night—the Chinese-Italian-Turk brothels, Albanian pimps, gay boys, cocktails with olives, Essex boys and girls, and excited Euro tourists—of a typical Saturday.

The tiny club was packed sardine-tight with the remnants of an Essex pub on football night. I saw Axl sitting in a roped-off area with two brown-haired girls laughing around him.

Here was Axl about five feet away from me, and all I wanted was to be with Dizzy.

After scouring the club, though, I couldn't find Dizzy anywhere. It was now about four A.M., and the paparazzi were waiting outside the club. Lori, in her hedonistic pink heels, was melting with exhaustion. My eyes were shutting down when I received a message from Dizzy: "Sorry, honey. Now we're going straight to Cuckoo's. It's completely out of my hands. No one knows what the fuck is happening. Do you want to ruin my night, simply because I was nice to you and didn't treat you like a piece of garbage like all the other men and women you have fucked in the past?"

I couldn't understand why he was texting that when we'd been waiting around for him all night.

Five A.M. A lovely Sunday morning. Church day. Birds were chirping for their Sunday brekkie in the light outside. Inside Cuckoo's, Guns N' Roses were finally about to play and it seemed like anyone who was awake in London wanted to see the show. Bunches of the band's crew members were scattered outside the club, harassed and hijacked from their sleep. Paparazzi lenses fed on whatever fodder they could serve the tabloids, so I stood in front of the lenses, pouting like I was sucking on lemons and peacocking my being so the bulbs would flash when Dizzy walked into the club. A petite, dark-haired Italian girl who did public relations for the band fingernailed a last-minute guest list, saw me, grabbed my hand, and pulled me through the crowd. That got me happy quickly: Finally, I felt like part of the Guns N' Roses family. I reached for Lori's hand and whipped her neatly into the club.

The club was a tiny space, intimate, with peach lighting and rustic, tangerine-peel walls. All the crew I recognized from the tour were there. A Chinese photographer who had taken a series of shots of Ostara and me in Birmingham was sizzling in the shadows, observing. Sebastian was swaying in the middle of the crowd, bouncy and jovial, like a big happy-go-lucky kid trailing the scent of Herbal Essence shampoo. He was adorable and fun; I wanted to kiss him all over, like a puppy, but his shampoo smell put me off. It was like smelling a girl. Hard as I tried, I still couldn't find him sexy.

Suddenly Axl rolled in with a couple girls swept up in his tails. He came over to us and, as the room went crazy, Lori took his hand and kissed it like he was Henry VIII or something.

"I want that Indiana boy, Sebastian," I panted, conflicted between my youthful desire and the new feeling of love-fueled attraction I was experiencing with Dizzy. "I want him. Get him for me."

"I'll try. Did you get his signature tattooed on your pussy?"

"No. It got rubbed off when Dizzy went down on me."

Sebastian howled with laughter. On a tiny, impromptu stage, Dizzy played the keyboards, pale and haggard. Robin and Tommy played along as Axl sang a salad of Guns N' Roses medleys, while Sebastian and I kept shouting for our favorite, "Civil War." I looked at Axl like I was a teenager, and his gaze lingered on me. I flushed the same vermillion as my corset and lips. His aura and talent drilled through and punctured that small lair. He was majestic, and I was in dripping awe.

As I stood there with Sebastian, the catering girl he'd been hanging around with at the Birmingham show appeared, docile and domesticated, and tried to grab his hand awkwardly. Sebastian ignored her and moved away. I assumed she was his date, and I felt bad for her. It was a further reminder of how rockers pay attention to women one minute, then treat them like shit the next.

But then I looked over at Dizzy. He looked so broken. I knew it for sure: I loved him.

The catering girl inched closer to Sebastian, with faith and optimism in her eyes. As she reached out again to him, Sebastian's glance suddenly webbed on to a crust-ridden toad of a blonde and he promptly started paying attention to her. My heart melted for the catering girl as she walked off in tears.

After the set, I waited for Dizzy so we could leave. But when he still hadn't come out after an hour, I was filled with fear and dread. I was sure he was upstairs in the dressing room area, fucking the girls Axl had brought to the club. I knew he would do it. Despite his kindness and promises that he would never fuck with my head and heart, it started to dawn on me that maybe I didn't really trust him at all. So I compensated for the sinking feeling by flirting with Sebastian.

I stepped outside. The Sunday morning sun was bright as a lightbulb. I tried to stay calm, but my heart hurt with fear as I wondered where Dizzy had gone with those girls. They were beautiful models, and I was just a nerdy Iranian girl with big facial features.

But when I checked my phone, I saw message after message from Dizzy landing in my mailbox; they'd been stacking up there while I was out of range in the club. He was back at the hotel already, wondering why I wasn't there with him. Relief warmed my heart, so sweet and soothing. I smiled so wide that my mouth stretched like a facelift.

When Dizzy opened the door to his room half an hour later, I nearly collapsed on Del. The two of them were in the middle of a heated discussion.

"I have to call my manager," Dizzy said, in a panic. "The fucking band owes me thousands of dollars." His face was white and drawn.

"Are you okay?" I hugged him close, trying to calm his anger. But he was furious, so I went to soak in the bath while the two of them talked in private. I was dying of fatigue, but happy to be with him at last.

Eventually Del left, and I ran into the bedroom to hold Dizzy tight. God, I had missed him so much. And it wasn't just love: I liked him properly, as a person.

The room was splendid. Creamy curtains and plush decor set the tone. Despite our fatigue, we made sex-love. I was finally under his spell and I was so fucking happy. I knew he had many women, but the way he was with me was real, beautiful, caring, and protective. It never once occurred to me that it could all be just a con.

———————

I had to leave before noon on Sunday because Dizzy's daughter was coming to the hotel to see him. He was planning to take her to Camden for a tattoo.

That night, I went to see him play the last show of the tour in Wembley. I met Janie there, and we skulked around the catering area; her raging, brilliantine white dress dazzled like a snow-storm in the heat of backstage. I watched the show with Warren. As I gazed at Dizzy playing a beautiful piano solo, Warren teased me again.

"Look at you. That is the look of love."

This time I blushed and scowled, squelching my face like a kid. Axl was ill that night, so Del had to fill in on vocals for some of the songs. When Axl passed out in the sidestage area later, Sebastian took over for the last song.

Afterward, the crew looked exhausted, and I couldn't wait to get out of there. Dizzy called and told me to hurry.

AT THE GUNS N' ROSES SHOW

CHAPTER

47

hat night, back at the hotel, Dizzy was super-hyper. He talked like a woodpecker on fast forward. He discussed his child-hood, and how his grandmother saw him play the piano when he was little and marveled at his natural talent. He talked about one of his first bands, the Wild, and his own cover band, Hookers N' Blow. He had a bunch of their songs on his laptop, and he kept nagging me to listen to them. "Do you wanna hear my band?" he asked over and over. "I want you to hear my band."

I hated cocaine so much at that moment; it gave people verbal diarrhea, which bored me to tears. "I think you got a bad batch there," I said, pointing at his stash. He thought that was the funni-est thing ever.

Dizzy rambled on about how dorky he was as a child and how badly he'd been bullied. It was as if he were trying to tell me his whole life story in one big roller-coaster breath. He particularly rel-ished telling me little anecdotes about things that had happened to him in Guns N' Roses. I absorbed so much information, I felt like alphabet letters were swimming in my eyes. And then, right in the middle of his autobiographical rant, he skidded to a stop.

"What if you're pregnant? I've come inside you so many times." He looked at me dead-on, and I got worried.

"Yeah, I got a bun in the oven!" I patted my stomach jokingly.

"I'd have kids all over the world then! This one would be half-Iranian. That's fucking cool." He smiled. I was so relieved.

By now I was tired and I just wanted him to stop talking. I rolled over onto the other side of the bed.

"Do I have to text you to come over here and cuddle me?" he said. I rolled back and we held each other as we had every night we'd been together.

Only this was different: It was his last night before going home to Los Angeles. I wanted to tell him so badly. I wanted him to know. "I love you," I said, looking straight into his eyes, without emotion, but with raw honesty.

He went quiet and stared at me for what seemed like five minutes with that wide-eyed stare of his. I didn't know what that meant.

We fell asleep around six A.M. and got up at noon so he could go to the airport.

"I miss my dog," he said as he started packing. "Oh, and I have to leave this girl's shoes at reception for her to pick up." He casually picked up a pair of candy-style, wooden-heeled pumps.

"Whose the fuck are those?" I screamed. "And what the fuck are they doing here?"

"Oh, that girl I told you about. The one who was driving over to Birmingham to see me. They're hers." He was so nonchalant about it.

"But you told her not to come. You texted her that in front of me!" I was shocked, and soon I was in tears. "You lied. You even e-mailed me telling me that she wasn't coming. Was she in your hotel room just before I arrived?"

I couldn't believe it. Why had he gone to such elaborate lengths to lie to me?

He just shrugged. I had a fast choice to make and I made it: I decided to let it go.

As we hugged good-bye, Dizzy made me promise I would text and call him all the time. I didn't feel a thing. I had mentally prepared myself for his departure. I was already shutting down. I was going to be a robot.

He picked out two teddy bears from a bag stuffed with cuddly toys that his kids had given him to keep him company. "These are for you to look after. But only for a short time, because I know I'll see you very soon. I'm so happy we met. Those days and nights were amazing. I will see you very soon. I promise."

I told him the pain was a motherfucker.

Later, he texted me from the airport: "I already miss you so much. I am going to make sure we will see each other soon."

I didn't cry. I just drank the rest of his Jägermeister and cuddled the teddy bears he'd given me. This was life. It was rock band reality. Subreality. I was ready as rain to walk the wobbly pavements of Soho and lose myself in the daze. People, shops, the Tube, colored lines on the route map, my body, sex, going dead inside—all these things must exist without emotion, with precision and tidiness. Because this is life. My heart must not miss or long.

time I'd get the real results: *Please, God, let it be a minus blue line. Let it be a minus blue line when I look.*

I looked. It was a plus blue sign. I screamed. "No, God, no. Please, no!"

I was terrified. I didn't know what to do. I was so angry at myself for being so irresponsible, and angry at my doctor for telling me I couldn't get pregnant. So I could, after all. And I was. I was having a baby.

Dizzy was going to fucking kill me.

I was shaking like a lamb on her way to slaughter when I called him. I left a trembling voice message. Fifteen minutes later, when I was out wandering the streets—looking for new pregnancy test brands, as if that would fix everything—he called back.

"I'm pregnant," I told him, terrified. "Are you mad at me?"

"Fuck! You told me you can't get pregnant."

"I know. My doctor told me I have very low fertility. Listen, I'll take care of it. I'm so scared, Diz."

"I'm freaked out," Dizzy said. "We can't have a baby. Fuck!" He went on and on, but I couldn't hear him because it felt like my head was underwater.

I was crying, standing in a back alley with people unloading meat and garbage all around me.

I knew what I wanted to tell him: *I'm sorry. I'm sorry I fucked up. It's my fault. I love you, Diz, and want to have this baby, but I know I can't because you don't want me to. You would never look after me and take care of our baby, because you already have four children by three different women. You have all this stress from touring. You don't need this shit.*

After we hung up, I called my doctor and tried to be a rational human being.

"I need to make an appointment with a clinic. I am pregnant and . . . I don't . . . want to be." The National Health Service offered the service for free, but because of their waiting list, I was told, I wouldn't be able to have the termination until late October. By then, I'd be three months pregnant. That was not an option. No way did I want this baby to grow, to continue forming an identity. I called every help line listed in the phone book. Finally I found one that told me they could do it in a few days. It would cost about £500.

That night I dreamed I had a baby boy. He was running in a forest and had blondish hair and intensely wild blue eyes. He was creative and intelligent, and he talked to me and laughed. He looked at me, and I knew I loved him. I loved my boy. His name was going to be Tiger.

When I woke, I e-mailed Dizzy. I didn't know what to do. I wanted this baby. I told him about my dream, and I couldn't stop crying as I wrote. I could barely see what I was writing because it was like a rainstorm on the screen. Everyone at the Internet café looked at me with such curiosity as the tears streaming down my face fucked up the keyboard.

"It was good to hear your voice, although I couldn't hear what you were saying very well," I wrote. "I'm kinda scared. I have to be honest with you and say that all I wish is that you were here with me when I go to the clinic. I have never done this and it upsets me that I have to kill my baby, especially because it's yours. It's kind of heartbreaking, but I know I have to do it. I wish you could hold me and comfort me. I cannot tell anyone apart from a couple of girlfriends. I need to see you very soon. I can come over in mid-September and we can have lots of fun. xxxxxxxxx."

Dizzy replied the same day: "I'm sorry you have to go through all of this. I'm pretty freaked out. I'm in the middle of a U.S. tour with my other band trying to make some $. Totally burnt. Let me know how you are doing and we will hook up when u get over this way and when I know my schedule. I wish I was there, too. We do need to talk. I hope u r okay. Fuck."

I walked all over town, through shops and past people under the clouds. People with McDonald's and sugared cereals and children. I was terrified. I didn't know what to do or where to go. I just needed Dizzy. I needed him to help me get through this. And he was so far away. I decided to see my mum.

"You have to get rid of it," she said. "It'll ruin your life."

"But I love this baby."

"You love it, but think about your future. Is this man going to help you? Will he support you? He has four children by three different women. He doesn't sound like a very responsible person. Please don't keep this baby."

"You don't understand. He's on tour. He can't do anything now. He's a very kind person. He's so nice to me." I was conflicted, defensive, anxious.

"Do you know how hard it is to be a single mother? This man is unreliable. He's not going to be there for you. You'll have to do everything by yourself, just like I did when I had you."

"I love my baby. Dizzy will help me!" I screamed and ran out like a teenager.

The day before my appointment at the clinic, I went to my university to walk along the river. I was going crazy. I loved my baby so much. I wanted to keep him. I was hysterical. How could I do this by myself? It wasn't the right time.

There was no one on campus. I walked around the forest and the hills and I talked to my baby: "I'm sorry I can't keep you. I love you so much."

That day, I had an appointment with my tutor to get feedback on my final paper for my master's degree. Throughout the meeting, I bit my tongue so hard so I wouldn't weep. I had to keep the lump in my throat from exploding, or my tutor would think I was mad for crying in the middle of discussing my essay.

Later that night, I texted and e-mailed Dizzy. I was desperate for anything—a single shred of hope—to change my mind.

"I am going in tomorrow," I wrote him. "If you want me to keep the baby, tell me now."

"We can't keep the baby," he replied. "Please don't wig out on me. I got your text. I feel awful but there's nothing I can do about this right now. We can meet when you come over here. I'm still waiting to get our tour dates but we don't officially start the tour until Oct. 21 so I don't know where I am going to be yet. I flew all night, haven't slept in two weeks. Call me when you get out of the clinic and please leave me a message if I am asleep and I will call you back."

I texted Diz again a few hours later: "I'm going in to the clinic tomorrow morning at nine A.M. if you still give a shit. If you want us to have this baby, you have to tell me right now."

God, please let him want me to keep our baby.

Dizzy replied: "I don't think either of us should have a baby. I do give a shit. I'm 10,000 miles away at this time. I just returned from a tour in a van this morning. My contact via e-mail, myspace, etc., was very limited. Let me know how you are doing 2moro, or I will call you. What time do you go in?"

I was fucking crushed. "What if he is a talented piano player like you?" I pleaded with him. "God, this is so hard."

All night, I cried and apologized to my baby for killing it. "I'm sorry," I told him. "I can't keep you. But it's for the best. I love you so much."

CHAPTER

49

he taxi picked me up at eight A.M. I wore a light pink shirt and wide black trousers. It was sunny. I took my checkbook. We drove to a lovely part of town with lots of trees and posh cream buildings. We walked to a tiny cobbled road and there it was: "The Clinic," all prim and proper and tucked within the shadows. The door was river blue.

The receptionist took my name and told me to sit in the waiting room. There was a teenage girl with her mother, an older woman, and a hot model type with long legs, long hair, and designer sunglasses there. I filled out the form.

"It's five hundred and five pounds, please," said a matronly woman in a sectioned-off area of the waiting room. "Will you be paying cash or card?"

"Can I pay in installments, please? I don't have the whole amount right now."

"You'll be pleased to know that we have a monthly plan, but you need to give me three backdated checks now."

I wrote the checks out as if I were in an office and it was the start of my working day.

"Thank you. Please have a seat in the waiting area again and the doctor will see you in a few minutes." Then she called in the next person.

A nurse took me into a room. I filled out more forms. "Please lie down on the bed and I'll take a scan," she said. I lay down and she put this cold jelly stuff on my belly, then rolled a long silver device on it, attached to a monitor.

"Yes, I can see it. It's there. See?" She pointed at a tiny, white bean shape about an inch long, lodged into the gray mesh of the scan of my womb.

I looked at the monitor, and there it was: my baby. Created by Dizzy and me. Inside me, feeding off me. Needing me. Tears rushed down my face. I was so embarrassed. I felt like such an idiot. The nurse must have thought I was an idiot for crying over something an inch long. I could tell she felt uncomfortable. She was just there to do her job, not to babysit an emotional wreck. She said nothing as she printed an image of the scan.

"Can I have one?" I asked, trying to jostle some sort of emotion from her instead of the money-in-exchange-for-terminating-your-baby transaction she had been programmed to implement. I wanted her to say something warm, comforting, even if it had to be clinical. I wanted her to present me with other options, to hint that I should at least think about this decision. But she didn't. I knew she wanted to get on with it, move on to the next person waiting, and finish for the day so she could go home and put her feet up and drink a cup of tea. I clutched the picture of my baby.

"His name is Tiger," I said defiantly. It was a last-ditch attempt to extract emotion from her, tenderness that surely all females must possess.

"Ahh," the nurse said. "Do you want to think about it a bit more, miss?" She stood in front of me, broad-shouldered, tidy, sanitized.

"I have to call the father," I said, and walked out.

Outside on the cobbled street, amid the Georgian buildings, law firms, and petite office girls with salon hair, I called Dizzy. My fingers pushed the call button like they were squeezing the life out of a fruit. "Pick up, pick up," my mouth tripped into the phone. *He's the only one who will understand. He's my lifeline.* I needed him so much.

His usual voicemail message clicked on: "I can't answer the phone, I'm losing my mind."

I wailed into my phone like an animal in pain. "Please pick up, Dizzy, please. I'm at the clinic and I just saw the baby. It's tiny, Diz. You don't know. It was so beautiful. I don't know if I can do it. It's so hard. Please call me. Please. My phone is on."

I huddled down by the clean white pavement. My body was a burden I couldn't escape from. It enslaved me to decisions I could not make. I needed Diz. I wished he was here to hold me.

I walked across the street to a café to think. By day it was a café for office types; by night it was a hip-hop joint. I called Dizzy six or seven times but he didn't pick up. He was with some girl; I just knew it. He knew that if he picked up the phone and I heard his voice, I'd get all lovey and emotional and change my mind and keep the baby. I wanted him to like me, but I knew if I kept this baby, he wouldn't. He'd be mad. He'd shout at me. How would I live then? How could I be a single mother and have no one but my mum? How could I ever laugh with him and be in his arms if I kept his baby?

I walked back to the clinic with the most disgusting fear I'd ever felt. I felt like I was going to the butcher. If he had bothered to pick up his phone, to talk to me, to be there for me, then I would have kept our baby. I wouldn't have had to kill it. This was his responsibility, too.

After I filled out more forms, a nurse took blood from my middle finger to check my blood type. My ears were deaf to the blare of white noise, white uniforms, and shrunken doctors around me. They took me to a tiny area next to the operating room and told me to change into a blue dressing gown. I complied. This was my fate, after all, and I must proceed in order to be successful, to get on with life and the order of things.

In the few minutes they left me alone to change, I clasped my hands together to pray. I sobbed hysterically into the cup of my palms, so that if they walked in they wouldn't see how pathetic I was. "My baby, my baby, I love you. I love you so much. Tiger, Tiger, forgive me. Forgive me, please." I rocked back and forth. My dressing gown, flimsy and blue, was soaked at the sleeves because I kept wiping my nose on it.

"Dear God, please make me strong. Give me iron strength, because this is what I have to do."

———————

They were waiting for me when I walked into the operating room. It was the length of a small bed and the width of another. There were three people: the doctor, a nurse, and an anesthesiologist. Next to the operating table was some kind of machine thing.

A huge man with a mustache gave me instructions: "Lie here and put your legs up on the stirrups."

My knees buckled. I'm so pathetic. I thought I was brave.

I lay on the table, obedient and still. When I put my legs up, I noticed I hadn't shaved. "Will I still be able to have babies?" I suddenly cried and stupid tears streamed down my face.

"Yes, you should be able to," the doctor said kindly.

The huge man was the anesthesiologist and he slid a needle into a vein in my left hand. "It'll just make you drowsy," he said. "It won't put you to sleep. You'll be half awake."

"So I'll be able to see everything?" I asked.

My left arm froze, and I felt like I was drunk and floating in the sky with balloons. There were flowers underneath me and my skirts were light. The doctor, a short bony man with canals of wrinkles gouged in his pointy face, smiled at me.

"Are you okay?" He had an Italian accent.

I nodded. He put something in me, and twisted and turned it. He kept twisting and turning, like he was a plumber or something. I squeezed my eyes tight. I thought of my grandmother smiling and holding my hand. I thought of our house in Iran, the sunny garden where I played all the time. I was losing Tiger. The doctor was pulling, twisting, pulling at my insides. Then he removed something. It was my fucking baby. I knew it. It was out of my body.

He placed it in a container. The container was metal.

"There. It's done. You can go."

Slowly, I stood up. I was so woozy that I stumbled like I was doing a comedy walk. A nurse held my arm and helped me to a room to sit back with other women who'd also just come out. There were scores of them scattered around the airy, sunny room, lying on lounge chairs and drinking tea. We were women in unison, lolling around, dazed and drunken, quietly mulling over the decision we'd all just made that had changed our fate. The nurse handed me hot water and biscuits, and said I could leave when I felt ready. I was in shock, my body hummed like a fridge, buzzing serenely. I did my best to leave.

At my mother's house, she made me soup. I lay on the plaid sofa and slept. Later that day we took a bus to my flat, where an e-mail from Dizzy awaited.

"I'm worried about you," he wrote. "Let me know how you're doing."

Later, I was sitting with my mother, who was telling me how proud she was of me for making the right decision, when Dizzy called. He sounded terrified, as if he'd been holding his breath all day to see whether I had chickened out and kept the baby.

"I did it," I told him. "I went through with it."

I heard him sigh with immense relief. "We couldn't have had this baby, honey. The world is such a fucked-up place to bring a baby into. It wasn't the right time for both of us."

"I wish you'd been there," I said. "I really needed you."

"I am sorry I wasn't there. I've been so busy with Guns N' Roses. We're going on the road again."

"Can I come and see you? You said I could stay with you."

"I don't know my schedule."

"Okay. Let me know when I can come then," I said. "The clinic, it was really expensive. About five hundred pounds."

"I have to go," he replied. "I'm in the middle of rehearsal."

I just wanted to be numb. To forget. The only thing that would help me was being with another rock band.

MY ABORTION WAS RUNNING DOWN MY LEG. I WAS DEAD. I KNEW THERE WAS ONLY ONE THING THAT WOULD MAKE ME FEEL BETTER. I HAD TO BE WITH JOSH TODD.

y abortion was running down my leg. I was dead. I knew there was only one thing that would make me feel better. I had to be with Josh Todd of Buckcherry. It would smooth the pain like cream marble on dry rot.

I had nothing. I had lost my soul. It had dissolved into the fumes of garbage trucks, and it resided above them now, singing a homeless song. I was walking like a mannequin. I was relieved that my legs worked, because my brain didn't talk to my body anymore. My heart pumped out its wrenched pain. I needed to find Buckcherry's tour bus. It was the brilliant warm light that would heal me.

My abortion was thick and clumpy, heavier than a period. So I let it be, to run free. I wanted to liberate it. It was the remnants of my baby with someone I loved. I marched to forget, to numb and to deaden.

I had bathed myself that day. I had washed and scrubbed, and wished that my child would come back. I missed Dizzy so much. But I knew that being with Josh Todd would make it better. He would be the smooth pink pill of happiness.

I was a groupie. This was what I deserved. Pain and tears and heartbreak should not—could not—enter the sphere of groupie-dom. We were all meat. I had been slack, and I had paid the price.

So I focused on my destination: the Buckcherry tour bus, parked somewhere on the Nottingham streets, full of fish and chips and yellow lights and skint students on that September night. In my Tesco bag, I had a vibrator, condoms, wipes, and a vitamin shake my mother had made for me, worried that I'd become too pale from the loss of blood.

When I saw the tour bus, I smiled. Ever since I'd first met Josh Todd nearly a week earlier, and he'd played with my tits on stage during "Crazy Bitch" while I massaged his crotch, I'd known for dead certain that we were going to copulate. The attention felt good. He was a rock god. He was Steven Tyler—the way he moved, his swagger, his presence. Every inch of his naked, serpentine upper body was tattooed with runaway ink. Onstage, he roared with heartbreaking pain on a song like "Sorry" and with howling orgasms on a song like "Porno Star." But I'd gone to the show with my little brother, and I was still hurting and raw over Dizzy, so I couldn't imagine being intimate with anyone.

But four days later in Oxford, Josh had remembered me. He'd picked me out of all the pretty girls standing outside the tour bus. It had been two days after the abortion. I wasn't bleeding then, but my left hand was bandaged in white clumpy dressing because of the anesthetic shot.

I had thought I'd forget as soon as I got with Josh Todd.

On the tour bus, he kissed me and I massaged his naked snaked back. I told him he needed to eat a few more cheeseburgers; he looked hurt that I thought he was too skinny. He was perfection, I told him. It was a well-known fact on the road that he had a thing for raven-haired and sultry girls.

When he noticed the bandages on my hand, though, a fear—of sexual disease or domestic violence—thundered across his face.

"What's happened to you?" he asked.

"I just had an abortion two days ago." I conveyed the information as daintily as I could, so he'd still want to be intimate with me.

"Oh, I'm sorry. Are you okay? You have to look after yourself—your spirit."

"I'll try." I smiled with hope.

Josh led me to a bottle-green carpeted area in the back of the bus. Quietly, he undressed me and started to finger my vagina from behind while I bent over and rubbed my ass over his bulging crotch. At the clinic, they gave me a pamphlet warning of the danger of infection if I engaged in any sexual activity for two weeks after the termination. But this was Josh Todd. He would make me forget the pain.

Condoms were Josh's obsession, and he whipped one out like a surgical instrument pivotal to saving a life. We kissed hard and grabbed each other like two savage animals. Sweat dripped off his tattoo-covered torso. He sucked and devoured my body as if I were yummy chicken. His face was that of a rock god, and I wanted to look at it. But he turned me around and penetrated me. I moaned as he roared into me, holding my round hips tightly. My pornographic moans bore through the bus' corridor, and I felt bad. My bandage was unspooling as my body shuddered, full of Josh.

"Please let me swallow you."

I sucked and swallowed him like it was the last soup on earth. He had been affectionate. I needed that.

Somewhere along the way, my bandage fell off, revealing the puncture of the anesthetic needle on my hand. He saw the pain in my face and we talked about Dizzy. Josh was a master of spiritual healing, though he couldn't administer it to himself.

———◆———

Now, a day later in Nottingham, I drank my vitamin shake. I hoped my breasts were big enough. They'd grown huge during my pregnancy—ballooned and aching. I knew I needed to be home in bed that night, but that would be madness.

Outside the tour bus, I saw the band's crew. They greeted me beaming, like they knew. *I just want comfort tonight: I want to be with Josh.* I presented myself outside the bus as a beautiful glamour girl, my hair chestnut-brown and glossed, makeup a work of art, body voluptuous and ready. But Josh was still in the dressing rooms, so the band's tour manager, Kyle, escorted me there to meet him.

Nottingham Rock City's dressing rooms were a catacomb of naughty sex-play, with a beehive of squat, pocket-size niches tucked in the back of the venue. I found Josh in the Buckcherry dressing room with the rest of the band, stage-sweaty and signing posters for fans and taking photos with contest winners. He hugged me, and I removed my coat to reveal my corset and polka-dot bunny skirt.

"You look beautiful," he said. "How have you been?"

"The train journey was so long," I said.

He asked about my family and my background in a very concerned way, wanting details I didn't find interesting. But he was generous with me, so I felt high and happy, and began to forget the clinic.

"Keith really likes you," a roadie whispered in my ear, referring to Keith Nelson, the guitarist. "He wants to see you."

"I can't right now," I said. "I'm with Josh."

"I think you should go with Keith," the roadie insisted. "He's crazy about you."

Keith was stereotypically sexy, muscular, and rockerish, but devoid of the sexual aura Josh Todd radioactivated. I didn't want to be with Keith. I looked at Josh as Keith stood behind me waiting. I didn't want to offend anyone. I wished Josh would say something. Maybe this was a test: I was supposed to perform my groupie part. Keith took my hand and led me away. I looked back at Josh, and he looked at me. My blood flowed heavier, and I felt disgusted with who I was. I missed Dizzy. I wished he was here.

Keith took me to an empty dressing room and locked the door. Fluorescent lights on the ceiling kept guard over empty beer bottles, an eyeliner-smeared mirror, a pile of soaked sandwiches. I looked over at Keith. He had unzipped his pants. I didn't want to do this, but I wanted to be polite. He was a nice guy who always had to play second best to Josh. I couldn't reject him. It would've been cruel.

I could feel myself bleeding in clumps as Keith pushed himself against the door to keep it shut. *How can I be doing this?* He had his dick in his hand, and it had a huge ring through it. It repulsed me. I got down and began to suck it, and it hurt my mouth. I opened up wider so the ring could fit into my mouth and throat. I gave him the best cock-sucking I could, so he could cum and I could leave. But he didn't cum. He wanted to fuck me.

"Turn around," he said.

I didn't want to.

He lifted my skirt. My abortion was sliding down my leg.

"It's just my period," I said, not wanting to offend him.

He put a condom on and looked away from the mess as he entered me. That cockring choked my vagina, scraping my insides. He pumped away furiously and I felt nothing. I was dead. I closed my eyes and thought of sunshine, of my grandmother's house where I played on the carpets.

Keith couldn't stand the mess. He looked away in disgust. "Honey, it's too much blood," he said.

"I'm sorry it's grossing you out. You can finish if you want to. Or you can come in my mouth."

He finished in my mouth. He was such a sweet guy. I felt bad he was grossed out.

When I stepped into the corridor to find a bathroom, Stevie the guitarist—who'd been with Ostara in Oxford—came over to me and touched my leg.

"I have to go find Josh," I said, as if he were the only remedy.

On the bus, Josh was eating a sandwich and salad, and watching a James Bond film with the character Jaws in it. I think it was *Moonraker*. He offered me food and water. I wiped my leg with a tissue and started to put mango body butter on my skin. My blood was flowing heavier now. I hoped it wasn't too visible.

Stevie, Keith, Xavier the drummer, and a couple crew members were on the bus. They all wanted to watch me play with myself, and I obliged, spreading my legs and rubbing my dildo along my pussy for them. One of the crew guys asked me if I wanted to have some fun; I declined. Then Stevie and Xavier asked if I wanted to go with them to the Welbeck Hotel, which was located next to the tour bus. Keith wanted to come, too. I took a deep breath. I could always say no. I looked at Josh, but he was quiet, wearing his glasses. He didn't seem to want me tonight, but I wanted to talk to him.

Three of the other guys in the band took my hand and led me to the hotel. We took the elevator to a room that was so pretty. Keith turned off the lights, because he couldn't face the blood. His cockring hurt me again, but I was as quiet as a mouse. Then Stevie climbed on me from behind and fucked me as I tried to please Xavier, while he tried to enjoy a butch girl with a mound of crusty pubic hair and B.O. that nearly made me throw up. I wanted the band to be happy. Once they were done fucking me, they left. I gathered my belongings in my plastic bag and caught the early morning train home.

lthough the Buckcherry guys were nice, they didn't numb the pain for long. I still wanted to be with Dizzy, to have him comfort me. I needed him so much. In September, a few days after my birthday, I texted him.

"You forgot my birthday."

"Happy birthday," he replied. "Can we fuck soon? That would be neat."

I scolded him for being so blunt, then told him I missed him.

"U r beautiful," he said. "That's all I know."

"You should see me without my makeup. I look like Godzilla!"

"No u don't. I've seen u in the morning, more beautiful than ever."

Seeing a post-abortion therapist had helped a bit, but all I could think about was Dizzy. I would have given up everything to be with him, despite everything I knew about his women and his ways. I loved him with all my heart.

But he had become cold. He rarely answered my texts or e-mails, and I wondered whether I had hurt or offended him in some way.

In October I had to go to Toronto, Canada, for a family wedding and also to see Mötley Crüe in concert. I knew it would be the perfect time to fly to Los Angeles like he had asked me to. But all Dizzy sent back were vague, confusing messages.

"I have been through a lot because of this abortion," I finally texted. "I feel I need to see you. Just be cool with me."

"Why don't you hitch a ride with Mötley?" he responded. "Much cheaper. I'm sure they're heading back to the States." He seemed so bitter. I couldn't understand why. And then he continued: "I do like u and it would be neat to c u but I sort of feel like I became attached to the wrong person. U r somewhat of a notorious groupie. And I don't mean that in a bad way. I can't have you in on my pass hanging out with the openers anymore. That sucked. The more I thought about it, the more it just fucking hurt."

That made me furious, especially after everything I had told him about how much I adored him and how much I loved him. This was clearly just a flimsy excuse so he could evade his responsibility in the aftermath of the abortion.

"Please don't call me a groupie again," I texted back.

"Well, look it up in the dictionary. Would you prefer hardcore fan? I mean that's cool. I'll go with that. You are a notorious hardcore fan. Where would you like to meet?"

Nothing he said made sense to me. He was like an actor who had stumbled into the wrong theater and was spouting dialogue from another play. It scared me a little, his sudden shift in character, his silence. I just missed him so much and needed him to tell me everything was going to be okay.

By the end of my two-week stay in Canada, I was falling apart. Dizzy wasn't replying to any of my phone messages or e-mails. I saw babies wherever I went, and every time I burst into tears like an idiot. They seemed more striking and conspicuous than usual, as if they were all staring at me with the secret knowledge of what I had done. To explain to everyone around me why my eyes were streaming, I told them I was wearing faulty contact lenses.

I returned to London dazed and dejected. Strangely, that very night, a couple hours after I'd landed, Dizzy actually called.

"I am not blowing you off honey," he said. "I have just been very busy. I've been rehearsing with three bands. Our drummer quit."

"You know how much I needed to see you." I felt defeated.

He told me he was seeing a few women, and I didn't care. That wasn't the issue at all. It was that I needed his emotional support. He had brainwashed me with his persistent promises of tenderness, his constant imploring for my care and companionship, and his sincere pleas not to break his heart. He had conned me with a sea of love and trust, until the thought of having sex with anyone else repulsed me. It was my constant stream of bereaving for my baby that kept me thinking of him. All I wanted was for him to make love to me. It was insane.

We didn't talk for six weeks after that phone call. I hated myself for the abortion. I couldn't get out of bed because of the grief and aching. I was like a fly in honey, and my legs weren't strong enough to escape the density. My mother tried to help with kindness and comforting Persian foods. My friends tried to keep me sane with their talk and love. It was an ugly time, and it was about to get uglier.

In November, we finally spoke again. I had been through horrible times in my life and had managed to get by, but this abortion had fucked up my head so much. I had this idea stuck in my head that I needed to see him to get closure. So we made plans to meet in Canada, where Guns N' Roses were playing. "Quebec, Montreal, Ottawa, Halifax," he said, reeling off the band's itinerary. "Sure, I would like to see you, too."

I worked all night, and any day possible, belly dancing. I spent all the money I had in the world on the flight and hotel in Ottawa. I was buying my sanity, so it wasn't much to pay. I'd get to see him, find out why he had been so angry with me, be healed, and move on. How naïve I was.

CHAPTER

52

I LIKE ALL HUMAN BEINGS. YOU'RE A HUMAN BEING, AREN'T YOU?

Ottawa was glacial. Governmental gray buildings sprouted throughout the city like giant icicles. It was like walking around a city-size office. The only thing I found interesting was a bagel shop, which served the sesame bagels with cream cheese I loved. My hotel was grand, majestic even. I bought fake tan lotion so my skin would glow amid the November bleakness and make me beautiful for Dizzy.

The night before, I'd flown from Montreal to Ottawa on the tiniest plane. It had only ten rows of seats. Its old-fashioned propeller clunked and whirred during the half-hour journey.

"You must be in love with this guy to come all the way to see him here," the old man next to me said when I explained why I was going to Ottawa. But I knew it wasn't just for love. It was for peace of heart.

I waited for two days in my hotel room. I went to the bagel shop as often as I could. I found a movie theater and watched the only film showing apart from Disney cartoons, *You, Me and Dupree.*

On Friday night, Dizzy called. "I'm on the tour bus," he spat down the phone. "I have a little time before the concert. Come here if you want to talk."

"What? I thought you were going to be at a hotel."

As soon as the words came out of my mouth, he started screaming. "I fucking told you. I fucking told you we're traveling on the bus. Didn't I tell you? Didn't I? I fucking told you." He was like a madman, screaming so much I had no chance to speak.

I took a deep breath. Then, as calmly and lovingly as I could, I said, "Okay. You did not mention one word about the fact that you were not going to be at a hotel. But tell me where to come and I'll get a cab, okay?"

It was ten P.M. and freezing cold. I put on my special new coat, new jeans, and a pink corset, and I got in a cab. I was nervous and excited. I wanted answers. I needed to know if he was still the guy who had been nothing but kindness and empathy to me before.

<hr>

The Guns N' Roses concert was in a desolate spot out of town. Miles and miles of nothingness and black highways rolled into a wasteland. When I got there, college kids and older fans who had grown up with Guns N' Roses were swarming their way into the arena. I walked to the box office, picked up a ticket Dizzy had left for me, and asked directions to the tour buses. Walking in the destitute lamp-lit field of tour buses felt eerie. I walked around for ages through icy wind, down a hill, and amid a forest of giant trucks, until I saw him standing outside a bus.

"Sorry I'm late," I said. He hugged me without a word and I started crying. He kissed me on the lips, and I pulled away. He had lost the key to the bus, so we went backstage to find Del.

Inside the tour bus, it was just me and him. The interior of the bus was exotic, with Moroccan-influenced finery and decor. The mosaics around the mirrors and the thick lull of the peach lights felt like a distant harem out of *A Thousand and One Nights*.

We sat down and Dizzy gave me a glass of Jägermeister, which I gulped down.

"Why have you been so angry at me?" I asked him. "What's going on? It's been so hard for me—you know that."

Dizzy sat across from me just staring, as if he were comatose.

"The way you've been the past couple of months: Ignoring me. First asking me to come stay with you in LA, and then cutting off all communication after the abortion. What's going on?"

"I don't remember," he stated. "I must've been drunk."

"You were so incredible to me in England and so supportive before the abortion. What's happened to you?"

He stared at me vacantly.

"I've come all the way from England to this tour bus so we could talk. You know what I've been through. Why can't you talk to me?"

I knelt in front of him, looking into his eyes. I wanted to see if he was still there, that person who'd been so adoring to me, so caring. It was like looking at a different person. Slowly we kissed. God, I loved him. I'd missed him so much: his warmth, his embrace.

"I've missed you so much." I melted into his arms, even though I knew it was a mistake. He wouldn't even talk to me, after I had flown all this way. But my heart—my heart wanted to be near him. I untied his light brown leather pants, took his dick out, and started to put it in my mouth. He drew the curtains together and pulled his pants down, pushing the back of my head down as I sucked.

"No!" I stood up suddenly and pulled away. "I can't do this. You've hurt me so much and now you won't even talk to me."

Dizzy just looked at me blankly.

"You told me over and over that you would never fuck with my head and heart. Day after day, you drummed it into me that I should trust you and not break your heart." I stood up and looked at him. He kept staring at me wordlessly. "All that time, all those things you said to me. Why are you treating me like this? Don't you like me?"

"I like all human beings. You're a human being, aren't you?" His eyes were dead, like two stones. I thought my head would explode with the shock.

"Here," I said, pulling out the picture of the scan they had given me at the clinic. "This is the reality of things. This is why it hurts so bad."

"I can't look at it," he said. "It's too hard."

I didn't know how to respond.

"I have a concert now," he said. "You should leave."

He walked me to the bus door. And then I ran. I ran so fast in my black boots that I thought my legs would come off. It was hard to breathe, as if I had cardboard in my chest. Where would I go? It was 11:30 at night. Everyone was inside at the concert. I was howling with pain and my heart would give me no comfort.

I ran inside the venue and waited until Guns N' Roses came on. I was blank. It had been so different in England. I'd been so happy then. As fat college kids hit on me, I sat frozen to my chair and watched Dizzy play the piano so beautifully.

After the concert, I left the hall, went to the VIP section, and waited for Dizzy. But only Del came to talk to me. As he planted a kiss on the top of my head, I told him everything: about Dizzy, the pregnancy, the abortion.

"There should never be any skin-on-skin contact," was all he said.

Dizzy never showed up. All I got from him was the inevitable text: "We're leaving."

I walked out into the early hours. The place was icy and deserted. There were only gray roads and bleak wilderness around me. I was in the middle of nowhere.

"Thanks for telling my road manager about the pregnancy," Dizzy texted.

"I don't know how to get back," I texted him. "Please, Diz, I know you are not like this. I am out here and I'm scared. And it's freezing."

I started sobbing. Was I nothing? *Nothing?*

I made my way out of the venue through the pitch-black night, the wind and rain slapping my made-up face raw. I walked for miles, past dark fields, along empty roads, until I finally found a taxi.

Back in the hotel room, I paced up and down, hysterical, sobbing. I felt so alone. There were just walls and Ottawa and me. Where could I go? I was going mad with grief.

I lay on the bed and degraded myself by answering the stream of abusive texts he was sending me; it was the only thing I could do to make things seem coherent and real. It felt like a terrifying jigsaw puzzle had sharded around me, and for some reason I felt like I needed him to put the pieces back together. I stared at the balcony. I wondered what would happen if I jumped. Would I get broken bones and that's it? What if I did and my life became no more than a series of hospital visits?

Pretty lingerie I'd bought especially for this trip was scattered all over the floor, a carnival of colors that now sickened me like too much candy. I cried so hard I thought I might throw up my heart.

I lay down on the floor in the half light and called my mother. It must be morning in England. I howled down the phone as soon as she picked up. "Please, help me, Mum," I said.

My mother talked me back into sanity, calming me with her soothing tone and cooing morsels of love and tenderness.

As I waited two days for my flight back home, I walked around like a zombie. Not eating, barely breathing. Every time I tried to sleep off the pain, I'd wake up with dread in my stomach. I was in a horror movie, with neither a slit of light to see with or a sliver of hope to guide me through the dark doom. I got no enjoyment from even eating a nice piece of food. I went to visit a close friend in Toronto, and even in her company I was like a dead piece of wood. I couldn't make my brain understand that Dizzy had been capable of causing me so much pain and hurt. I was going mad.

CHAPTER

53

fter recuperating at home for six weeks and soothing my nerves, I decided to go to LA. I'd been wanting to go there for a long time to see my friends and have some fun. I wanted to show myself that I was strong, still capable of loving life and being the cool girl I am. Though, maybe, on a subconscious level, I was also looking to get revenge for the way Dizzy had treated me.

"You should go there and fuck all his friends," Abigail told me with such torpedoing anger that it fired me up. "After what he's done to you, that piece of human garbage deserves it." Perhaps that *was* just what I needed. So I dragged my carcass back across the Atlantic.

The Los Angeles rock scene, I soon discovered, was an incestuous community where everyone had fucked everyone else. The Rainbow was packed nightly with Nikki Sixx clones, hot and sexy but in their late thirties, aspiring musicians with jacked-up '80s hair and tattoos. They compensated for their lack of real-world success by dating strippers, drinking abundantly, and banging as many chicks as they possibly could, so they could feel like rock stars instead of what they were—hired musicians in forgotten '80s bands, usually not even fronted by their aging original members. These musicians—famous or otherwise—were usually married to, or lived with, women who had day jobs to support them financially. It was tragic to see so many wannabe and has-been rockers depending on their women to provide food and a roof over their heads. The world was full of chicks—myself included—who lived in adoration of these musicians on the Strip. All they had to do was be in an '80s hair-metal band and chicks would jump on their dick faster than you could say "ugly wife."

On my second night in LA, I went to the Cat Club. The evening started with a promoter announcing, "From Hookers N' Blow, Scott Griffin!" A rocker stood on stage with black hair and bad boy, I'm-gonna-fuck-you-baby energy exploding from him. A *ding ding ding* lit up inside me, like a slot machine hitting the jackpot: *This is Dizzy's band.* Fucking Scott Griffin would be dirty, because he was Dizzy's friend. He even looked easy.

I stood at the front of the stage licking my lips, and he looked right back at me. He only seemed so hot because he was out-of-bounds, forbidden meat. He was slender and sinewy, dirty and rock-sleazy—the clichéd dumb musician type who would fuck me like a whore, pull my hair, and swagger onto the next girl with his cock still dripping and a beer bottle dangling from his curling lips.

Sure enough, he came right up to me after the set and started talking to me in his sleazy rocker-boy sneer. His reptilian eyes were penciled heavily with black eyeliner, his gaze and pose that of a lazy-eyed carnivore. He looked like a male whore. He drawled out his words as if he had to think about them first, but his eyes lit up when he found out about Dizzy and me—as if the prospect of doing something so taboo made him want to fuck me even more.

I could smell the testosterone oozing from him as I gave him more and more details. We went back to my hotel.

Troy Patrick Farrell was different. He was breathtaking, his beauty humbling. I adored him from the moment I saw him. His hair was a naturally thick golden lion's mane hanging lazily down his back. His eyes were languishing baby blue, with liner smudged around them that made them seem erotic and innocent. His face was boyish, yet exuded a pure, gorgeous sexuality. He seemed divine, because he was oblivious to all this about himself. Troy spoke softly, with attentive love in his voice. His milk-and-cookies-fed Chicago body was soft—not skinny, but not fat—and dressed in a lazy rock T-shirt and sweatbands. He was the drummer in White Lion.

It was New Year's Eve, 2006, and I was back at the Cat Club alone. I'd abandoned all my friends at the Key Club; I felt more at home at the Cat Club, where the matchbox intimacy and chocolate bar-size stage made me feel happy and warm. My unhappiness over Dizzy was beginning to dissolve, as if I were flying over the roofs and chimneys like Peter Pan without a care in the world. Though I was new to LA and alone on New Year's Eve, I was the happiest I had been in a long time.

Troy's face stopped my heart. I knew he was also in Hookers N' Blow and was Dizzy's friend, but I really took to him. As we talked at the bar, he realized who I was.

"Look, if it helps, it's good you didn't keep the baby," he said. "It wouldn't have been a good situation for you. He already has four kids."

Troy was so sweet; he made me feel like a blushing teenager with her first crush. My heart did cartwheels when he smiled at me. Plenty of girls in the club wanted to talk to him; I think he had sugared them all. They looked at him with the same needy, achy look in their gooey eyes, as if he were Donny Osmond in the 1970s. In contrast, girls looked at Scott Griffin with wariness, as if he were Dracula at a blood bank.

"I want to talk about Dizzy," Troy said to me as the girls stood around patiently, like hungry pets waiting for morsels of food. "Do you like spooning? We can go back to your hotel and spoon."

I smiled noncommittally. I didn't like the Dizzy part, but I felt like a teenager with Troy. I was overwhelmed with adoration and shyness. So I walked around and smoked many cigarettes in the back with all the people who were out for the New Year. Then I went back to the bar and casually bumped into Troy again. My insides were going swoosh with the glory of a ceremonial dance.

"Are you mad at me?" he asked as I walked past.

"No. Why?"

"You just walked away. Don't you want to talk to me anymore?"

I wished I could stay there and talk to him all night, but I didn't want to seem too keen. The Cat Club began to close, and people started leaving.

"Are you coming to my hotel?" I asked, gulping, as the words tumbled out of my mouth. "We can talk and have a few drinks."

"Yeah, I will. I'm just gonna help them clean up first," Troy said as he started clearing glasses from behind the bar.

I hung around for a bit. And everyone who knew about Dizzy and me could see I was waiting for Troy, Dizzy's best friend. Kenny the barman, who monitored everything in the club with the storage capacity of a robot, looked on silently. "Here's a key card," I told Troy, handing him my spare. "Come over soon."

In my room, I hurriedly retouched my makeup and slipped into a gargantuan white bathrobe so bulky that it dragged around me, the sleeves continuing past my hands and the waist gathering miles of towel material around my body.

I heard the key card click in the door. I sat on the bed and smiled. I felt like such a dork in my big robe.

"I like you in that," Troy said, and a smile slipped across my face. Here we were, alone in my big room, with me in my big robe, bathed in purring, honeyed light. He lay on his stomach on my bed. I took his shirt off so I could rub his back. He asked me for the whole story about Dizzy, and I told him as we cuddled. I felt like this kind of talk was contaminating the air, but I was happy to tell him the whole story, just as I'd told Scott. He was so sweet and such a great listener. I started to give him a massage, even though my hands had gone limp and weak from wanting to be good enough for him, pretty enough.

"You're so nice," Troy said as I continued massaging him. "Why are you so nice?" Then suddenly he brought his hand out from under him and slid it between my inner thighs.

"I'm just me," I said. He shyly stroked my body and I kissed his back and touched his hair. I arched my back so he could reach higher up my legs. We didn't speak; we only explored. He turned his head and I kissed him shyly. He was just so stunning, I had to pull away because it was too overwhelming. It felt too intimate. Moments later, he was leaning over me, his blond rugged mane smelling not of perfumes or additives but just of body smell, boy smell. He took his jeans off. His body was white and peachy. And when he kept his white tube socks on, I adored him for that. He was just so unaware, so pure. He kissed my face gently, then my chest and neck. Then he cuddled me and gazed at my face. He took my breath away. It didn't feel like fucking or anything dirty. I felt like a beginner, without sexual skills or etiquette. I was lost, just a mass of hormones and giddiness and romantic butterflies. I couldn't put on the porn-star act I did with others. I was the pure little girl me again. He could have said he wanted to do anything to me, and I would have said, "Okay, sir." The only exception was when he wanted to go down on me: He was way too gorgeous, and I was way too in awe of him to let him put his mouth where it was dirty. He looked bewildered.

"Why?" he asked, looking upset.

"I just don't like it. It's too intimate." I was being brutally honest. He must have thought I was crazy.

I felt so happy with Troy on top of me, his sweaty hair in my face, his body on mine. I wanted to be good in bed, to perform as I usually did, but I just couldn't put on an act for him. When he came on my pussy, I squeezed myself tight and absorbed it all into my labia. I came so hard that I kicked him like a pony.

This is who I'd want to be my boyfriend, I thought. In the morning, when he left the room I knew what he was thinking: that he had to be loyal to his best friend. I could feel his guilt for having slept with me, but I didn't care. I wanted to see him again.

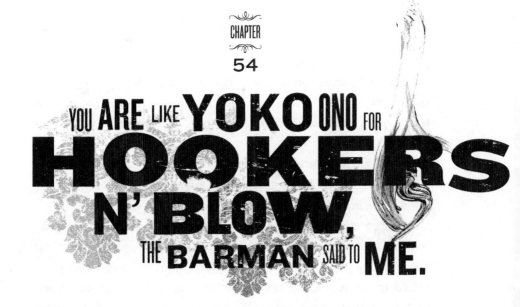

CHAPTER
54

YOU ARE LIKE YOKO ONO FOR HOOKERS N' BLOW, THE BARMAN SAID TO ME.

"This is Dizzy. Fuck off!"

Dizzy deposited his message on my voicemail the next day. It was New Year's Day, and he had called to offer me his good wishes.

"I am going to get you banned from everywhere I go," he hissed when I called back.

"Well, first of all, hello," I replied. "Second of all, it is none of your business where I go. I can go wherever I want to."

I started crying, which encouraged him even further. "I'm gonna call everywhere I can and tell them what you are," he screamed. "You won't be going anywhere in this town."

"Well I'm going to the Cat Club with Troy on Thursday," I said, trying to defend myself.

"I've already told Troy about your slutty ways," he seethed. "Who knows whose baby it even was?"

"What about *your* slutty ways? Everyone in this town knows what a whore you are. I've already been told by all the girls."

I couldn't stand it anymore. The man I'd once been in love with had become an object of terror, a boogeyman, someone I feared. I was shaking all over as I put the phone down.

Immediately, my life in LA was garroted. It seemed like he got me banned from the Cat Club, the Joint, and a few weekly rock parties I enjoyed. Even my friends got harassed if they happened to be in the same club as Dizzy. Everything about my life seemed restricted: where I went, whom I talked to, whom I slept with. I was trying, in my own way, to get Dizzy out of my system but he was trying to prevent it.

One night at a party, a couple people told me about another girl who'd also gotten pregnant by Dizzy and suffered the same treatment. I decided to find out who she was.

Sabrina was younger than me and more innocent. She was long-limbed and sleek as a gazelle, with lively, laughing eyes. She said Dizzy had gotten her pregnant about a year before; when she'd called to tell him she intended to keep their child, he had raged and insisted she terminate it. She was nearly three months pregnant when he stopped communicating with her. By then she'd decided to get an abortion, but she said Dizzy refused to help with her medical bills and isolated himself when she needed emotional support. After the abortion, Sabrina told me, she was depressed for months. Dizzy's friends actually ended up offering her the emotional support she needed. I found so much comfort in talking to Sabrina. Here, finally, was another human being who knew how I felt inside.

<hr>

Troy and Scott Griffin were in a bitter rivalry to see who could fuck more chicks. They hated each other with a competitive intensity normally reserved for Mortal Kombat. And even though they both fucked many girls, Troy was boyfriend material, more romantic and loving. With Scott, what you saw was what you got. He never tried to hide or pretend. He was just a simple old horndog in heat, prowling the streets, sniffing pussy, and ramming his cock into at least two females a night. Any female would do: crusty old pussy, young fat ugly pussy, anything he sniffed, basically. Perhaps his hunger and childlike need for acceptance stemmed from the fact that, at thirty-eight, he still hadn't made it, and was penniless and forced to beg girls for coffee, booze, and food.

The sexual double standard of our society made its ugly form known to me more and more as I remained in LA. When I saw Troy one night at the Rainbow, he interrogated me about my sexual activities and history, his voice charged with disgust and disappointment—as if my promiscuity made me a bad human being while it was heroic and awe-inspiring when he and his "bros" fucked so many chicks and then patted one another on the back. Of course they had a problem with it when females did the exact same thing.

Later that night at the Rainbow, as I cooed over Troy with my usual doe-eyed adoration, he told me he wanted to take me to Scott. My heart sank. We snuck around to the back of the now-forbidden Cat Club and saw Scott sitting by himself.

"Scott, take her back and spoon her," Troy said.

I was so fucking upset. He was clearly giving me to Scott because he was pissed off that I'd slept with Scott before him. But I was lonely and needed someone to be with. So Scott came home with me that night and stayed with me for two days.

"I'm gonna get kicked out of the band," he muttered. "And this isn't helping any."

"Then why are you seeing me?" I asked.

He looked at me with those needy puppy eyes of his. "Because I like you."

I liked this honest whore. He had balls. He was risking his livelihood for pussy. I believed he really must have liked me.

"That's insane," I said. "You're Dizzy's friend."

"He's told me I'm not allowed to see you, but I told him I really like you and want to keep seeing you." It was strange: Here he was, a guy in his late thirties, being ordered by his friend who he can fuck and who he can't.

"Dizzy is going to kill me," Scott repeated as he fucked me next to the mirror, grabbing my hips from behind and ramming himself into me. I screeched and whimpered like an animal as we watched our reflections writhe and he grabbed my hair and nipped the back of my neck.

All night, Scott's phone kept going off; it was Troy, leaving him messages that Dizzy was going to fire him. Scott went pale every time he saw a fresh text come in, as if they were death threats. I felt so bad for him.

The next morning, his phone was flooded with voicemails. "Fuck it. Fuck them," he said. "I can see whoever I want." We ate lunch at a cute little Mexican restaurant, holding hands and feeding each other. My admiration for Scott bloomed. He had guts to risk getting fired from his job just to be with me, even though being in the band was his only bread and butter.

That night, though, he failed to show up at the Rainbow, where we'd planned to meet. When I called him, his voice eked out of the phone like a pigeon. He seemed crestfallen, as if he were speaking to me from the depths of a well.

"I'm out. I'm out of the band. I don't have a job anymore. Dizzy fired me." He sounded drained of life. "I can't see you anymore. My life is fucked."

I cried. I was gutted. I felt like shit. All I wanted was to live my life, be happy, and move on.

"You're like Yoko Ono," Kenny, the barman at the Cat Club, said to me one night after I'd snuck into the club around closing time.

"And why is that?" I giggled.

"Well," he said, his bulldog features shifting with a bitter guarded vibe, "you broke up a band."

I chuckled. "Hookers N' Blow aren't exactly the Beatles, are they?"

Nonetheless, part of me got a bit of an ego high from deseaming the band the way I did. Although Scott and I kept talking on the phone, he refused to see me because he was scared of Dizzy.

After a couple weeks, Scotty couldn't take it any longer. One night around one A.M., he called, whispering like he was on a secret mission.

"I'm at the corner outside your hotel."

"Come to me," was all I needed to say.

Five minutes later, he knocked. We didn't say a word. We ripped each other's clothes off, breathed each other's smell, sucked each other's mouth. The door was still open. We tore at each other like two animals. Low yowls gushed from our throats as we fucked. My lacy nightdress was shredded in the carnage as Scott pushed me down and pump-fucked me, roaring into me as I spread my body so wide open for him to absorb his hair, his smell, his fucking. We moaned so loud I was sure someone would think I was being beaten to death. By the time we both came, I was like a rag doll. I had spread my pussy so wide for him that I ejaculated all over him.

Afterward, though, his fears returned and overwhelmed him. "You're gonna destroy my life, aren't you?" he kept saying. "You're gonna tell Dizzy, aren't you?" His voice was defeated, drained, fearful. "Don't tell anyone. Please. Dizzy will kill me if he finds out." He was trembling like a scared little boy. I wished I could take him back to England with me and protect him.

WITH SCOTT GRIFFIN OF Hookers N' Blow

pARt 5
RETURNED

WITH NIKKI SIXX

Nikon

TH THE
TEASE BOYS

SABRINA AND ME

JOE LESTE AND ME

WITH KRISTY MAJORS

KOCBOX 5100

WITH SCOTT GRIFFIN

I WAS HYSTERICAL BECAUSE I NEEDED MY VIBRATOR TO WORK PROPERLY.

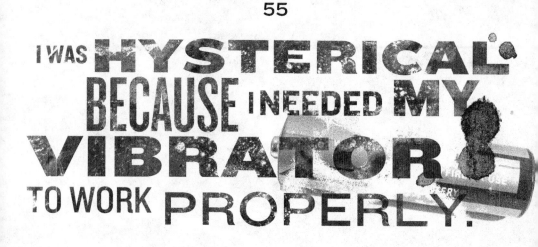

My experiences with Troy and Scott—and eventually with Alex Grossi, the fourth member of Hookers N' Blow—were like drug highs, only temporarily masking the pain I felt from Dizzy. The vitriolic texts from him that followed, on top of the months of trauma I'd endured, were the last straw. I'd felt lost since the abortion and one night it all came to a head. When I was unable to eliminate the pain any other way, I swallowed forty-five paracetamols. Fortunately, my friend Danny Demure, who played in a band called Nothing Sacred, showed up, worried by the texts I'd been sending him. As soon as he saw the empty pill containers and my blanched face, he made me vomit up the pills. I spent my last two weeks in LA with him looking after me, bringing me food, and taking me on drives through the Hollywood Hills.

When I returned home, I remained tired and ill for another month—from a combination of pills, the emotional intensity of the battle between Scott and Troy, and my own efforts to purge myself of Dizzy. My overdose hadn't helped anything and it didn't make me feel better. I cried like a lunatic, which made me mad as hell. All spring I walked around like a zombie, not caring about anything or anyone.

Then, one night, I just got out of bed, put on my makeup, and returned to the place where it had all started, the Underworld in Camden. I needed to see my friends, who were hanging out with a band called Bang Tango.

Ostara had adored Jizzy Pearl since the Adler's Appetite days; now Jizzy was back singing with Love/Hate, who were on the double bill with Bang Tango. She'd spent the day with Jizzy, walking in the park and fucking. I saw her backstage, glowing, looking like the sweet beautiful fairy doll that she was.

"How have you been?" she asked in her hushed, love-filled baby-doll voice. My attire said it all: For once I was wearing my normal student clothing to a gig instead of my usual fuck-me heels.

As Bang Tango played, I sat with a seventeen-year-old boy who was working as a roadie for Kristy Majors, the former guitarist in Pretty Boy Floyd. The only person in the room with us was Jizzy, who was warming up his voice. Jizzy scared the shit out of me. He was always pissed off, and his vibe bordered on militant and antagonistic. He scared me even more tonight, because I thought he'd probably been brainwashed against me by Dizzy.

"I hear you're doing Hookers N' Blow," he said with a sneer.

"I haven't done *all* of the members yet," I replied, trying to make a joke out of it.

He looked at me with a warmth that caught me completely off guard.

"Everything's gonna be fine," he said.

This cheered me up for a moment, so I went off to slip into the slutty clothes that I'd brought with me.

I stood on the sidelines watching Love/Hate, surrounded by my friends, and made a conscious effort to be happy. It felt like Christmas in a warm, family living room. I so wanted to find my cheerfulness again.

The crowd creamed themselves for Jizzy, chanting his name like a hypnotic mantra. The Underworld rarely went that crazy for someone like this. I had no idea Jizzy had such cult status. When he came offstage, the dressing room was filled with horny young girls, thick-booted and raucous-haired, as well as sunken-faced, older groupies, secretly optimistic.

"Only the people who are with the band, please," a roadie shouted at the crowd. "The rest of you get the fuck out."

"Oh, *she* can stay." I felt a hand grip my shoulder and looked up to see Joe Leste, the lead singer of Bang Tango. His eyes were Frisbee-round pools of sympathetic brown; his face lit up in a toothy grin with trenches of dimples dancing around it. He didn't stop staring at me the whole time we were backstage.

"You are mine! You're coming back with me—no one else!" He kept saying this, as if I were prize game. Back in LA, I'd told my friends I wanted to fuck that hot lead singer from Bang Tango, and Scott had balked with horror. Now I was about to get what I wanted.

I knew Joe's voice was powerful, as was his persona. In the '80s he'd been fairly successful riding the hair-metal wave. And tonight he wanted to act the part of rock star. He had a wide, red bandana tied around his raven hair, chains hanging from his leather trousers, and black wristbands. He also had a funny grin and a bit of a paunch. Nevertheless, the crowd of hot young girls backstage was dying to sleep with him.

He held my hand and we headed off to a late-night café by Camden Lock Hotel. The residue from the Underworld crowd trailed behind us in the form of about twelve rock chicks, their tongues hanging out as if they were stray dogs and Joe were a late-night kebab. They swarmed the streets, dragging their stilettoed heels, inebriated, smudged and eyelinered, sticky, camera-phoned, pumped with beer, and exuberant in unison. They were like a military march of the rock zombies.

Ostara had left to meet a friend, and a brunette had moved in and stuck herself to Jizzy like a stick insect. These young, gorgeous girls were cock-hungry for these middle-aged men. I wondered how many would be doing this if the men were not in a rock band. The way they lusted to lay open their young, pert, nubile bodies to these men astonished me in a most pleasant way. This was rock 'n' roll—my happiness, my soul.

Yet something in me had died. I was uniformly happy—all my friends were around me and I was gonna get fucked by an American rocker I had a crush on. And though I was happier than I had been in over a month, my spirit still dwindled. I felt exhausted, like a cardboard cutout stewardess.

Joe kept looking at me in awe. "You really are a stunning woman, aren't you?" he asked.

I didn't feel a thing.

When we got to the café, the crowd followed us in. The stick insect was still hanging onto Jizzy. There was something disturbing about it. As I walked over to talk to him, the girl looked up at me, her muted almond eyes narrowing hatefully. I thought she was going to maul me. I backed off.

"So you wanna be with Jizzy then, do you?" Joe looked mildly hurt.

"No. I was just talking to him."

"Because he's the headliner, huh?" He looked genuinely injured.

The café was still packed at three A.M., mostly with blokey local types after a night on the lash and sensible vegetarians discussing the wonders of James Blunt and organic gardening. They sipped their red wine, trying to pretend we weren't there. Joe and I crammed ourselves into the café along with the cock-hungry girls, the rest of Bang Tango, Jizzy, a dozen older groupies, emo kids, and a bunch of over-the-hill goths and junkie DJs. As a blues band played, Joe and I made out, sticking our tongues down each others' throats. A young girl pulled at Joe's arm, trying to get a kiss, but she couldn't even get a glimpse of tongue.

"God, you're so beautiful." Joe was like a tonic. Not only was he generous with his compliments, but he was also a generous dispenser of cash for everyone's drinks.

The congregation of young girls stuck around us like they were waiting for candy and cake. They all wanted to be with Joe. A weathered and prune-haired groupie who looked like Patricia Kennealy sat down and began giving me drunken advice on the pitfalls of groupiedom as if we were still in the sixties, when the optimism in the scene was rife and sunshiny dispositions were plenty. Kristy Majors' little-boy roadie offered me drugs, and I balked at the insult. Everybody was entangled in drunken group makeout sessions.

When the band launched into a Doors song, I stood up.

"You gonna dance for me, baby?" Joe was like a kind puppy.

Right there in the middle of that rancid floor, I hitched up my skirt around my ass, grabbed two chicks, and snaked and gyrated my body for the audience. As the sensible vegetarians averted their eyes, I took turns gorging on the mouths and tongues of these two young, chubby, delicious girls. I wanted to fuck them so badly, and they looked at me in awe, dripping with tender trust. I could tell Joe's cock was getting hard.

"Excuse me, I was just wondering if you could let me come with you and Joe tonight?" A dainty china-doll hand was tugging at my arm. I turned around in irritation, prickly as thorns, and I couldn't believe it: it was Steven Adler's Swedish redhead! The petite, frag-ile-boned, always-there redhead who had pissed the fuck out of me on the Adler's Appetite tour.

"Oh, hello. It's you." She giggled through her dinky cherry smile. I hadn't noticed how adorable she was. So adorable.

"Please? I really like Joe. I really want him."

You bloody lucky wanker, Joe, I thought. How many young, ten-der, perky-breasted girls would you have dying to fuck you if you weren't in an '80s hair-metal band?

"All right. You can come." I had been in similar situations, and always liked to help out little-girl groupies if they did me sexual favors. She squealed with delight and did a little victory dance, then went off with a friend to the men's toilets with Michael Thomas, Bang Tango's guitarist, to celebrate by sucking his dick.

Four girls followed us back to Joe and Michael's hotel room. One was a giraffe-tall Finnish spectacle with a Mohawk, who wailed and gnashed her teeth at the slightest sexual touch as if she were at an evangelical healing. Her theatricality was scary. Sober, and annoyed to realize that fucking young girls also meant babysitting them, I spread out my belongings on Joe's bed, and he and I started cuddling.

Immediately, though, thoughts of Scotty swathed me like tumbling sheets. I excused myself and left the room to call him.

"I'm with Bang Tango," I blabbed to him when he picked up. "I don't know why. I miss you."

"Get out of there immediately," he spat into the phone. "What are you doing there?"

He probably lost a lot of respect for me then. But at the same time, the conversation made me imagine him being with other women, and it just fucking killed me. Knowing he was surely about to go out and pick up chicks for the night himself, I went back to the room and did stuff to myself and to Joe, just to kill the fresh sting of emotion that had started budding up in my heart for Scott.

I got to work, making those girls watch as I showed them how it's done. The redhead started to join in, hands everywhere, but I kicked her away.

"I don't want you to fuck anyone else but me," I said to Joe. I wanted to try out my fantasy of monogamy.

"I won't," he promised.

So Michael got all the attention: four girls on top of him like a litter of kittens. He developed the agility of an octopus, fingering, sucking, and fucking them all at once. Suddenly, a girl who looked like the youngest stood up, clutching a can of orange Fanta. "I can't do this. I can't. It's not really me." She sobbed. "I wanna go home."

"It's okay, honey." I always had to be the fucking mommy in every situation. "I'll call you a cab," I said, calling the taxi as Joe positioned me doggy-style.

"The cab's coming, honey," I told the scared young girl as the redhead pined for Joe to penetrate her little pussy. Then I relented and disconnected myself from Joe, telling him, "You can fuck her." I wanted a bit of self-loving anyway.

The batteries in my vibrator were run down, and for a few minutes I went nuts looking for AA batteries. Then I had a bright idea.

"Where's the TV remote control?" I asked frantically as Michael and Joe swapped girls. I was almost hysterical. I needed my vibrator to work properly. I stamped my feet until Michael, exasperated, got up mid-fuck and found the fucking TV remote for me. I slid out the batteries, kicked the bewildered girls off the bed, and settled down in their place. "I'm gonna ejaculate," I soon panted as a river gushed out of me, drenching Michael's bed and leaving a massive puddle.

"Hey, my sheets are soaked," Michael exclaimed. "I have to sleep on that!"

"Sorry, Michael," I replied. "You're gonna have to sleep on the puddle. I'll put some towels underneath you."

That night, the room smelled like a Mexican brothel. Girls lay on the floor with jackets for mattresses and shoes for pillows as I cuddled up to Joe. Michael did end up sleeping on the puddle after all—and he did it like a fucking man.

I stayed with the band for the rest of the tour, but most of the time I was in a depressed haze. I missed Scotty, who had become a substitute for missing Dizzy. I'd sleep with Joe, then call Scott right away, and then cry to Joe about Dizzy. My head was a mess.

CHAPTER

56

IT FELT SO BEAUTIFUL TO GIVE MYSELF TO ONE GUY ALONE.

The problem with Scotty was that he only wanted me when he couldn't have me.

They say that sex is best with the one you love, but in the case of Scotty it was the other way around: I fell in love with him because the way he fucked and made love to me shook me to my core. There has to be a new word for what he did to me in bed. It was animal fucking, but romantic and loving at the same time. My body temperature skyrocketed when we had sex. I went limp; my knees wouldn't work. For the first time I knew what it felt like to have multiple earth-shattering orgasms. I also fell in love with his care-free spirit and gypsy soul. In my heart I knew he wasn't completely my type, emotionally or mentally. But I was desperate for love, and here was a man who had pretty much given up a band—given up everything—for me. He was my baby, my darling. Like Dizzy, Scott made me want to be monogamous. I wanted only him.

My friends thought he was the biggest loser they'd ever encountered. Not only because of the way he hurt me over and over, but because they thought he was a whiny, needy, emotionally imma-ture child who was always scrounging for beer and food. And he was the biggest whore in town. Even his own friends thought I was too good for him.

Even though he tried to fuck my best friends behind my back, I still loved him. Even though he repeatedly treated me like shit, I went back to his arms as soon as he started whimpering about his feelings for me. He was dirt poor and I would've bought him a house if I could have afforded it.

By then Scott was in the band L.A. Guns, and I was so proud of him. He kept gushing about how charismatic the band's singer Phil Lewis was and about the amazing group of musicians he jammed with. He wanted me to go with him to Vegas while he was on tour. So in April I scraped together all the money I'd made belly dancing and went back to LA.

On my first night in LA, Scott told me he wanted us to be exclusive. I was ecstatic. I hadn't realized he was even thinking that way. For days I walked around with the biggest smile on my face. When he left town for a weekend of touring, I proudly turned down calls from other rock stars, delirious that I was finally with someone who wanted only me. It felt so beautiful to give myself to one guy alone.

The day after Scott returned, I was hanging out with Carla, one of my closest friends, when we decided to do a little test. I texted Scott and we made a plan to meet. My friend Carla's boyfriend was one of Scott's closest pals, and had hooked him up with a lot of work in the past. As Carla checked her e-mails, she decided to send a message to Scott. She wanted me to see that Scott had no morals—that he would fuck a girl who was not just my friend but who was also dating his close buddy.

"Go ahead," I dared her. "Flirt with him."

A naughty glimmer skimmed across her eyes as she threw a bunch of sexual innuendos on the screen.

"I really want to fuck you," Scott typed in response. "Come over to my place. I'll go get some beers." Then he gave her his address.

I felt sick.

Scott knew how close Carla and I were. He knew I was only in LA for two weeks. I was so hurt and humiliated.

Minutes later, he texted me: "I actually can't see you tonight. I'm just gonna go hang out with my buddies and chill out at their place."

In the meantime, on the screen, another message from him appeared for Carla: "What time are you coming over? I'm just going to get those drinks."

"I told you so." Carla looked at me sympathetically.

All night, as I sat at her place wishing I still drank, Scott kept texting her, asking what was taking her so long. I felt sick.

"Cut him out of your life," Carla said.

I didn't listen.

At six A.M., I was still going fucking crazy. I called Scott and left a message. A couple hours later, he called me back. I was hysterical, calling him every name under the sun.

"How could you do this to me?" I screamed. "She's my friend. My fucking friend. And her boyfriend is your buddy who's helped you so many times. How could you?"

An hour later we met outside a nearby café. My face was puffy, and my voice hoarse. He fell all over himself apologizing.

"I'm so sorry," he begged. "Will you forgive me, Roxana? Please. I was so drunk and stupid. I never meant to hurt you."

I cried quietly as he drove to Venice Beach. It was a beautiful sunny day and we walked along the beach holding hands. He sat me down in the sand, bought me lunch, and started kissing my feet and hands. As his face came close to mine to kiss my lips, I smelled something.

"Your mouth stinks of pussy!" I pulled away in disgust. "Were you fucking someone last night? Be fucking honest."

"I went to the 'bow last night and picked up this chick. She came back to my place." He smiled like he was proud.

"So let me get this straight," I said. "You couldn't fuck Carla, one of my closest friends. So you went out and picked up some whore at the 'bow?"

"Yeah. Look," he said in his puppy-dog voice, "I also told your friend, Jenna, that I really liked her."

I still don't know why I didn't cut him out of my life then. Maybe I liked pain. Maybe I felt I deserved to be treated like a piece of shit.

Instead, I just sat on the beach and shook. He couldn't let his wet cock rest, even for just the two weeks I was there. I listened to him apologize and I let him hold me, as though that would make it all right.

That night, Scott tried hard to be romantic. He kissed me, held my hand, massaged me. I slept at his place, the sheets reeking of perfume and crusty pussy. It was hard for me, but I really liked him. In the morning, while we were still asleep, there was a thunderous bang at his door.

"Scotty, please. Open the door. I really need you. Please!" A teary-voiced girl was banging on his door. Scott's face went white.

"Do *not* say anything!" he whispered to me. "If you do, you're out of my life!"

"Who is she?" I whispered back.

"Shut up! Stay quiet!" He put his finger to his mouth.

We sat there while this girl screamed and banged on the door, yelling, "Scotty, I know you're in there. Please open the door! I need you today. I have an interview!"

Eventually, she left. Scott waited two minutes, until she was out of sight, and then went after her. He left me alone for over an hour while he did what he had to do with her. And I still adored him— though he was nothing compared to Dizzy. Nothing.

CHAPTER

57

went back to London feeling like I had been kicked in the teeth. It all felt so familiar. I wasn't getting love when I desperately needed it, and so I found myself back in my comfort zone.

Twelve worn-out rockers and one girl—me—in the belly of a hotel with three '80s hair-metal bands: Faster Pussycat, BulletBoys, and Enuff Z'nuff. I was wearing my new flowery prom dress, and I was horny. My insides danced a ceremonial frenzy. I was holding the hand of Faster Pussycat bassist Eric Stacy, the most authentic old-school rocker there. He was the rawest male animal, squalid in his appeal—a gravelly, multiple-rehab visitor with heavily black-linered eyes and tattooed, needle-tracked arms. He gazed at me with the adoring look of a pining cat, as if I were his savior that night, giving him momentary relief from the status quo and pulling him into the realm of rock stars again. My body seared with the thrill.

Eric took me to his room, which he shared with Todd, their new Canadian guitarist. Todd had been wanting to take pornographic photos of me for weeks, but he seemed shy now. I found his little country-boy naïveté nauseating—like looking at a gorgeous piece of cake and then discovering it's been marinated in animal fat.

Eric and I sat on the bed. A tiny, doll-size merch girl called Miss Fifi, a fixture on the scene whenever an American band was in town, got the message and vacated the room. I lap-danced slowly for him, grinding my naked crotch on his studded leather trousers, which were drenched in chains. Potholes decorated Eric's arms— remnants of years of drug use. To someone else it might have been putrid flesh, but to me it was rock 'n' roll. His eyes were coagulated with liner and his abundant jet-black hair was tied with a red bandana. I was starting to unzip his pants when a heavy pounding on the door interrupted us.

"Eric, open up. You have to open up now!"

It was Brett, the fucking drummer.

"I need to speak to Eric," he said. Shaking like a lamb, Eric pulled up his zipper and left the room. I heard whispers punctuated by raised voices outside. Moments later, Brett marched in like a headmaster.

"Eric loves his wife," he explained. "You are too tempting for him. Please leave."

"I just wanna get laid. Please!" I stamped my feet. "Tell him to come here and say it to me himself."

Brett left and I wondered what had happened to rock 'n' roll.

Eric shuffled in with his head hung low, weeping like a child. I held him and let him cry into my back. "Please, I love my wife—and you are hot," he sobbed with his face in his hands.

"Okay, sweetie," I said in my best mommy-is-here kind of voice. "We don't have to do anything. I promise I'll keep my hands to myself."

"Okay then." Eric nodded and wiped his eyes.

"Don't cry. Let's go out for something to eat. You'd like that, wouldn't you, huh?" I took his hand. Of course, he was even sexier now that he was crying. I found it incredibly hot.

We went into the room next door to get the rest of the band. As we did, I cursed loudly that I'd probably been in every single room in the Camden fucking Lock Hotel. Eric shot me a look, worried. But I was actually laughing at the absurdity of it all. Todd and Brett were surprised to see me smile, as if they'd been priming themselves for a monumental fit. Eric took my hand, and Brett chaperoned us to the late night café around the corner from the hotel to make sure we didn't suddenly forget our deal and start having sex in the middle of the kebab-hungry crowds.

We ate junk food at a table surrounded by brickies and Chavs, with Eric holding fast to my hand. I felt like we were on a 1950s high school date, accompanied by a sanctimonious parent.

When Brett went for a bathroom break, Eric asked me to score him some heroin from the street dealers lurking outside.

"No! Bad!" I slapped his arm. "I will not allow you to do that."

Later, Brent Muscat, the guitarist for Faster Pussycat, invited me to stay at his and Brett the cockblocker's room as Eric trotted off to bed. I started off in Brett's bed, but soon slipped over onto Brent's. In the dense darkness of the room, he and I started making out. I slowly moved down on his body to get him nice and stiff to penetrate me. At last, I was gonna get laid. I shook with happiness.

"No, no, no!" Brett suddenly screamed. "He's not allowed. Brent is married, too!" Brett had become the fuck police.

"But I'm horny!" I kicked my feet, as Brent lay next to me quietly, blue-balled. "Please!"

"Oh, we can just cuddle. That'd be good, wouldn't it?" Brent tried to be helpful.

"No, it would not, for fuck's sake! I just want cock. Go and find me a guy from one of the bands," I ordered them both. "I'm horny and I need to get fucked."

"What about one of the crew?" Brett said. "I can go find one."

"Do I look like I fuck roadies?" I was livid. "You're the one stopping me from getting laid. Go find me an American rocker."

He left the room then returned a few minutes later. "Everyone is asleep," he said sheepishly.

"Right. That's it. I'll go take care of this myself."

Walking around half naked in the corridors of the Camden Lock Hotel was as familiar to me as brushing my teeth. I knocked on door after door until an amazingly leggy dude with a gruff voice opened the door to room 112.

"Oh my God. I can't believe a goddess like you would want to come to my room." It was Chip from Enuff Z'nuff.

I weighed my options. Chip wasn't hot, but he'd been sweet and lovely to me on the tour so far, and made me warm with his paternal manner. I went in.

I took off my clothes and lay on the bed. We got cozy under the sheets and cuddled. Immediately, Chip started going down on me, which was my most reviled sexual activity. But I was tired and horny, and since I didn't really want to have sex with him, I lay there and let him get on with it.

As he was eating me out, suddenly an earthquake rumbled under the sheets. His mouth, his tongue, were Godlike—better than any vibrator I had, better than any porn I had jerked off to. I shuddered and exploded my cum into his mouth. He kept making me come, as if I were a slot machine. He was a magnificent artist.

"You're so beautiful—and so nice, too," he said in his rough, gangstery Chicago voice.

I let him cuddle me safely in his sweeping, warm eyes. Chicago. I *love* Chicago.

In the morning, I got up and, like a bitch, went back to Eric.

Having fun with bands was the playground I needed to live in to stay in one piece. But it was also a quicksand marsh full of land mines, and I never knew which one could end up being love, the one that destroyed me. When I stepped on a mine and triggered that love, I needed to go back to the playground of rock 'n' roll to cleanse myself. It was a vicious circle.

HAVE YOU GUYS EVER DOUBLE-PENETRATED A GIRL? I ASKED, GENTLY. I DIDN'T WANT TO SHOCK THEM.

Soon after I got my master's, I started thinking about going for a PhD so I could teach at university. The idea made my mother ecstatic. After my experience with Dizzy, she was petrified by the thought of me going anywhere near "garbage, low-class psychopaths that are not worth your intelligence," as she put it. She also hated my belly dancing, which she considered beneath me. She didn't understand that rock 'n' roll was my plaything, my outlet, full of fun and volcanic orgasms—and that my sexual appetite could only be sated by American rockers. It had consumed my life.

I was especially horny that summer, and dying for some real rock 'n' roll. I needed a real man, one who knew how to fuck me like a rock star. Thankfully, Tracii Guns came to town.

Tracii Guns had been the original guitarist in L.A. Guns. After parting ways with Phil Lewis, the band's singer, he now led his own version of the band. With him was Jeremy Guns, as the posters always billed him; the promoters liked the idea that Jeremy (who'd also been with Tracii in Brides of Destruction) was Tracii's son, though they weren't actually related. Everyone knew Tracii wasn't Jeremy's dad, but the elaborate charade gave the band a father-son trademark. To me, Jeremy was just a cutesy little hedgehog-haired kid I'd cock-teased a year or so ago on the Brides of Destruction tour when I'd been with Scot Coogan.

I had never paid much attention to Tracii, except to acknowledge his presence on the Brides tour briefly when he kept teasing Scot and I about our intimacies. But after the tour, my friend Abigail had salivated to me about his sexual prowess—and she hardly talked like that about anyone.

The L.A. Guns gig was in Crewe, another northern shit hole. So I packed up my dildo, condoms, KY Jelly, and high heels and got on the train. Across the aisle from me, a young Pakistani boy looked at me with hope, and I smiled. He clearly had a quivering wish of getting his penis in the vicinity of my vagina. I could see the sheer need in his lamb eyes. In my bag, nestling among my warm silk clothes, my dildo suddenly made a buzzing noise and the Pakistani boy jumped.

It was pitch-black in Crewe. The venue was surprisingly roomy, with the charm of a working men's pub. Several layers of flooring, like layer cake, twisted into dark, cryptic corners. The Red Star Rebels, who were opening for L.A. Guns, greeted me as they always did: with japes and piratey smirks and a bottle of port, which was an extension of their lead singer Blacky's hand.

I went down to the basement, where hordes of fat, depressed biker types watched old-fashioned movie clips on a flimsy screen. I wore slutty clothes—clothes to get me fucked to orgasm—and stood at the front of the room, getting disgusted looks from the females in attendance. In particular, a fat goth girl, who kept telling anyone who would listen about being on tour with L.A. Guns and meeting Buckcherry, was shooting vitriol my way. She was moon pale, raven-haired, and rotund as a barrel. She talked loudly so I'd be sure to hear how many bands she had hung out with.

"I've been on the whole tour. I got to hang out with Tracii." I could actually see her chest puffing up with pride.

"That's nice." I smiled at her.

"I'm really close to them now," she continued. "Maybe, if I have time, I'll introduce you to them later."

"I'm gonna be busy," I said. "Getting fucked by them."

A roadie with a horse face had been eyeing me all night. He had long straggly hair and bony features. The Red Star Rebel boys kept whispering to me that he had a huge dick, as if that would magically beef up his roadie status. Eventually, he got up the nerve to approach me.

"I want you up there on the stage when L.A. Guns come on," he said in a hoarse voice. "There's a song I want you to dance to."

ONSTAGE WITH L.A. GUNS

Joining me onstage was a balloon-like blonde with Miss Piggy hair and trotters to match, who was sweating plentifully at her escalating status there onstage with an American rock band. I like soft girls—young, innocent soft girls in particular—so I grabbed her crotch and sucked her mouth, eating her tender teenage face, which smelled of home hair-dye kit and cheap perfume. There was a brunette, too, skinny and Bambi-like, hopping around in glitter jeans. I kept my tongue out of her throat.

When we came offstage, the horse-faced, allegedly horse-cocked roadie put his head to one side, as if he were expecting a lump of sugar.

"Gimme whatcha got!" he sneered. I sneered back as I walked past him to go to the toilets.

When I returned, he was still standing there waiting for me, his mouth split in a smoky-toothed grin. I ran over to Tracii.

"Hello, Daddy."

"Hello, sweet pea." He gave me a hug. Then Jeremy wandered over. It was weird seeing them without Scot Coogan. I ruffled Jeremy's hair. I wanted to spend the night with both of them.

On the way back to the hotel, I sat at the front of the bus, my legs closed tight for fear of the roadie. He was still sneering at me. White bits of spit had caked in the corner of his mouth, as if I were a prime rib he was preparing to devour. I could practically smell the sperm, straining to fountain out from his trousers and splash in my lap.

In Tracii's room, Bambi girl and her companion, a dowdy introvert, smoked Marlboro Lights with Paul Black, the lead singer. I was stuck with the roadie. I dreaded the prospect of becoming his reward, of being subjected to some sort of groupie-etiquette fine print just because he'd gotten me on the bus.

So I ran over to Tracii, and the two of us started getting high. He was a stoner—loved smoking the herb. Tonight he was smoking out of an empty Coke can. We stumbled and giggled for a while, until Paul and his two companions got the hint and left. The roadie stuck around for what seemed like forever, staring at us. When I buried my head deep in Tracii's neck, the roadie huffed and puffed, stamped his foot, and slammed the door behind him.

Jeremy, the "son," was sitting on the corner of his bed, fiddling on his mobile phone, trying not to look at Tracii and me, who by now were in a state of undress and in a semi-sixty-nine position.

Poor young lamb. "Watch me, Jeremy," I purred to him with urgency. "Watch us." I spread my legs in front of him as I let Tracii fuck me. Jeremy watched from the safety of his bed as my tits pumped up and down with Tracii's every masterful thrust.

"Come here, come to me," I whispered, my voice cracking with moans. Jeremy came closer. He touched my arm shyly, and then all along my breasts. He started massaging them and putting my nipples in his mouth to suck on them. I could see the outline of his erection in his jeans.

"Jeremy, get your cock out and join in," Tracii encouraged his "son."

Oh, this is so cool, I thought. As Tracii pounded me, I sucked Jeremy's cock and within a couple of minutes he came in my mouth. I let the cum dribble down my chin. It made a gurgling sound.

"Did ya come already?" Tracii chided him, as any father would.

"Yeah," Jeremy said, staring meekly at the ground. He fell back on his bed, eyes rolled up. I pulled Tracii out of me, walked over to Jeremy, and kissed him all over his mouth, letting his own cum stick to his face.

"I'll be with you in a minute," I said to Tracii as he stood there, apple-green-condom erection in his hand. "Hold on."

My body was seething—hot and raw. I was so turned on my cheeks burned. I wanted both of them inside me at once. I so wanted to get pumped hard with double penetration: one of them in my butt and the other in my vagina.

"Have you guys ever double-penetrated a girl?" I asked them, gently. I didn't want to shock them.

"No, never. Why—do you want to do it?" Tracii smiled, and I felt relieved.

"Come on, I'll show you how," I replied lovingly. They both giggled; they were such willing participants that I gained a new respect for them that night. If two guys were so comfortable with their masculinity and sexuality that they were willing to try such an intimate sexual position together, then in my eyes they were real rock stars. That's how rock stars should be.

I lay Jeremy down and sat on his dick. Then I got Tracii to go behind me and fuck me anally. They were now both inside me. I kept still as they fucked me simultaneously. It was heaven, like a delicious double milkshake. As I remained still, all my sensitive points were scrubbed and rubbed hard in one big raw bang. I tried so hard not to come—not yet. Tracii grabbed my hips and pounded my ass as Jeremy thrust his dick in my pussy, fucking me hard as I kissed him. Tracii was skillful at not hurting my ass, and Jeremy's eyes were wide as a meerkat as he rammed himself into me, not giving a shit that his balls were slapping Tracii's.

"Don't come," I moaned, begging them both. "Please don't come." I wanted the feeling to go on forever—this feeling of help- lessness, getting fucked doubly like I was in seventh heaven. It was so good I thought I'd faint if I came. I had been doubly, even tri- ply penetrated before, but with Tracii and Jeremy it felt like I was being reborn. I felt stunningly beautiful, helpless, brand new.

Afterward, I couldn't walk. They both kissed me, and we all fell asleep in a heap. It was time for bed.

CHAPTER

59

y high with Tracii and Jeremy floated me in the direction of my beautiful boys, Buckcherry. I joined them for every show on their UK tour, drifting with them like a stray flower.

One night in Cheltenham, as I stood with my two friends Mia and Kate, screaming the words of songs that pumped us with testosterone and hallelujahs, I decided to do the whole band together. I watched them onstage, watching me as if they knew the immensity of my adoration and respect for them. They knew me inside out: my sexuality, my pains, my crashes, my studies, even my reading preferences.

When I'd last seen them, our group love had been in the semi-haze of my post-abortion yearning to be rescued from hell. One by one I had gone through the band, with plenty of blood and pain thrown in. Now I was ready to do it in a happier state of mind.

Mia and Kate followed me back to the tour bus. Tonight I was wearing a white cotton summer dress with daisies in my hair and beige sandals. The moon was full that night over the miniature conservative English town of tea and biscuits, full of sanitized literature and arts.

"Are you feeling horny?" Josh Todd asked when he saw the smile on my face.

"Can you round up the boys?" I urged him.

Keith Nelson, the lead guitarist, was first on the bus—followed by Stevie, the rhythm guitarist; Xavier, the drummer; and then a cute young boy who was a friend of the band. I left Mia and Kate with Josh and made my way to the lounge at the back of the bus.

Keith was the first to enter. I lay on my back on the tiny table as he put his beer on the counter. He pulled down his jeans and then his boxer shorts, with his massive arms, his face and brawny jaw looking down at me. I remembered his huge cockring and grimaced, fearing its choking discomfort. But as he kissed me and touched my body, I mentally prepared myself for the ring and urged him to slide his cock into me.

"Hey, girl, I heard you were horny tonight," Keith said, looking down at me kindly. "How many of us are you gonna be able to handle?"

He was tender and sweet, his quiet, broad features in heavy concentration. I adored this band; they always fulfilled my every need. I drew my legs up to his shoulders, and we rocked in that tiny little space in the back of the bus. After Keith finished and left, it was Stevie's turn to come in. Locking the door behind him, he pulled down his pants and fucked me from behind. He was shirtless and tattooed, his body lithe like a tiger's. My dress was still on, scrunched up to my waist. The daisies in my hair tumbled off and were trampled under our knees.

"You are a wildcat, aren't you?" Stevie drawled in a rock-star mellow voice, which made me shy and little-girly. I cocooned in my nest of tour-bus sex as Stevie's guitar fingers played me nonstop.

"I want more!" I yelled, so Stevie sent for Xavier. Xavier had long hair and a ravaged soul; he grunted as he fucked me to the cheers of the others listening on the bus. This time I tasted his cum, sweet and low and abundant like milk. He kissed me and smiled, leaning over me with his long hair.

The boy was next—a young, wide-eyed teen with spiky black hair and nervous attitude. I made him watch me until he couldn't take it anymore, then let him rip me apart. Inside I was laughing. But I still needed more. I tumbled out of the area and stumbled over to Josh.

"Don't tell me you're still horny." Josh looked at me in disbelief. "I can't believe you. You're something else!"

"I wanna be with you again," I wanted to say. "You were amazing the last time." Instead, I walked back to the tiny room at the end of the bus as Mia and Kate yawned and looked at their watches, waiting for me to hurry the fuck up and get satisfied. It was a full moon in Cheltenham that night.

AS I LEFT MATT SORUM'S ROOM, MY WHITE DRESS AND STOCKINGS WERE RUNNING WITH BLOOD.

ou girls are old-school!" Matt Sorum smooched into my neck. Abi moaned a low animal sound as Matt fingered her while sucking my mouth.

It was summer and I was happy again. Scotty's residue had finally been rinsed away and I felt free. Abigail and I were in Milan for the Gods of Metal Festival with Mötley Crüe, Velvet Revolver, and dozens of other bands. That Friday we'd gone to a nightclub to meet Matt Sorum of Velvet Revolver, who had just flown in from Switzerland.

We were being driven to the Four Seasons Hotel. It was midnight or maybe one A.M. The cobbled streets were steeped in dignified silence and decadently Renaissance. The Italian driver stole intermittent glances in his mirror at our bodies as we writhed like alley cats in heat.

Matt's assistant turned to look at us. "You girls really *are* old-school, aren't you?" He repeated what Matt had said as if he knew he'd get a double Christmas bonus for finding us for him.

I wore my white virgin-whore dress—tight, trimmed with shredded cotton and a white rose pinned on the breast. I hadn't worn panties, just dressed my legs with sheer white lace stockings.

"Don't finger me too much. I have my period," I told Matt as his palm turned blood orange.

"I don't mind if you don't," he said and rubbed my clit harder.

Matt's little-boy drunkenness was naughty, joyous, and giggly. He wasn't my usual type, but I had a feeling he might be the only man who could match my wild spirit, my abandon, my sexuality. I wondered if I'd be here with him if he wasn't in Velvet Revolver or an ex-member of Guns N' Roses, because he didn't look like a rock star—more like a techno DJ.

I put on my cowboy hat and entered the hotel. The lobby was sweetly lit, delicate and baroque. Kindly Italian guards were posted in every corner. My white dress, virginal and whorish, was a canvas speckled with daisy droplets of period stain.

"Hey, cowgirl!" a guy at the other end of the lobby waved at us. My lack of contact lenses clouded my judgment. To me, he was a blur, a nobody. "Why don't you come over?" His voice drawled a deep-clipped purr.

"No thanks, roadie," I muttered under my breath as we walked to the elevator. Couldn't he see that I was with a rock star?

The elevator doors shut a clean, gold thwack.

"That was Scott," Matt smirked.

"Scott?" I felt a deep freeze grip my throat. Fuck, don't say it motherfucker. Don't say it was Scott . . .

"Scott Weiland."

Fuuucccckk motherfucker fucking shit. I felt like I was going to shrivel up with stupidity. I wanted to stop the elevator and run back to Scott, but that would have been rude to Matt.

"Oh," I grinned through my teeth at Matt. "I thought he was a roadie." Matt looked overjoyed at that.

Matt's room was eggshell white, a careful execution of hostile gentility, and stripped of all alcohol to help Matt stay good.

Matt's assistant pulled me aside. "Don't give him drugs," he said.

"I promise. I know about his past history." I spit on my palm and shook his hand. But I couldn't help thinking that keeping Matt away from cocaine would be like keeping a kid away from candy. "Please. If the rest of the band finds out, he'll be in trouble," the sweaty assistant pled, crumpling.

Matt's body was strong—pure rippling muscle. He was also blond, clean-cut, exfoliated, moisturized, his skin decorated with more lotions and potions than tattoos. But I liked dirty. I liked long black hair, eyeliner, a non-gym-enhanced body covered in ink, and the aroma of stage sweat and unwashed skin. I liked the imperfect bulk gained from drinking, fighting, and fucking.

But I realized, despite his appearance, that Matt was dirty as hell when he threw me down on the bed and punched me in the jaw.

I moaned with the pleasure of defeat and helplessness. Matt held my face and, in between light kisses and licks, ripped my legs wide open. "You wanna be fucked so bad, don't ya?" He spat the words in my face as he held me down. Unzipping his trousers furiously with one hand, he held my arm down so hard with the other that I thought it was gonna snap off. At the same time, he placed little kisses like parcels of sugar on my lips. Then he let go and we cuddled. I wanted more of him—more, more, more.

Abigail spread her legs next to me and started to finger herself as she watched me getting rammed. Matt's cock was big and it hurt. Blood flowed down onto the sheets—lovely light, puffy Italian cotton.

I was getting fucked so hard that my body felt flawless—like one big pulsating sex organ. Matt slapped my face and I punched him hard. His drummer's arms were giant, packed chunks of rock. I felt like a feather compared to him. But I didn't wanna give in. I wouldn't. I bit him, and he pinned me down with his knees. The pain was excruciating. Then he moved on to Abigail. I tugged at his arm as he fucked her, so he turned me around and fucked me doggy style as he fingered Abigail in synchronized motion. Then he decided to eat me, to lick up my menstruating vagina. He lapped at my pussy like a hyena. As he came up, his face looked like he'd been gorging on game. There was blood everywhere. Then he lined up Abigail and me side by side, doggy style.

"Show me your assholes," he ordered both of us. He wiped his face while deciding which ass to take. His cock was giant; I was a little alarmed at the thought of anal sex with someone so big, and Abi seemed to feel the same. But then we both learned a very important lesson: If you're turned on enough, anal sex with someone that huge doesn't hurt. In fact, it's like a double orgasm.

After a while, I let Matt sit and watch Abigail and me. I hadn't fucked her in so long. I took her breasts like two heavenly pillows, and sucked her nipples. We kissed so deeply that I fell in love with her skin. I wanted to fuck her so badly. I wished I had a penis.

"Eat me on my period," I ordered her, my eyes blazing like a wolf. I pushed her face into my pussy. She was reluctant but dived in deep like a good girl, messing up her makeup. I was close to coming. I lay on my back and told Matt to watch me, then spread my legs and rubbed a buzzing egg sex toy along my labia until I exploded, gushing out all over the bed. My vagina contracted.

"Give your cock to me now!" I shouted, my voice breaking, and Matt started fucking me just as I had my second orgasm, wetting and staining his balls.

Matt got in the bed, and I massaged him. "Sweetie, you have to rest," I said. "You have a big show tomorrow."

"No, I can go all night. Not bad for a forty-six-year-old, right?" he grinned expectantly.

"Wow! You're forty-six?" Abi and I looked at him in disbelief.

"Look—I can do push-ups. With one hand! Look!" He jumped out of the bed and did a few fast, furious one-handed push-ups.

"Oh, you don't have to do that, honey, you'll hurt your back!" Abi and I tried to get him up, barely able to contain our smirks.

"But I can do it! I have a personal trainer. Look at all those protein shakes over there." Matt got up, took a bunch of protein powder containers from a leather bag, and then got back on the ground for more push-ups.

"*Very* impressive!" Abi and I clapped in praise.

"You should get some rest," I said. "Seriously, it's six o'clock."

"Can you get any blow?" Matt asked.

"Oh, honey, no!" I said. "You can't do that. I'm not gonna let you." I felt like the mean babysitter.

"Oh, I just want a little bit. Not too much."

"I know your past. I can't let you do drugs." I felt genuinely upset. But Abigail couldn't resist him. She called an Italian dealer she knew named Emmanuel, and he was at the hotel in ten minutes.

As I passed the array of quiet rooms on the way to the lobby, I contemplated knocking on Slash's door. But Matt was waiting upstairs for his drugs. I met the dealer, who had brought a skinny, bug-eyed teenage girl along. I felt a pang of guilt for going back on my word to Matt's assistant, but Matt was so excited and I wanted to experience Matt in his natural habitat: drugs 'n' sex, rock 'n' roll.

Back upstairs, I ate a bit of mango and apricot as Matt and Abigail snorted their drugs. I fucking hated drugs. I watched porn and played with myself while waiting for them to finish. I wanted to go to sleep, but Matt wouldn't let us. He wanted to keep fucking.

"Dude, it's fucking daylight," I protested. "I wanna go to bed."

"But there's still time to fuck some more." Matt grinned mechanically, like some kind of sex android.

"Dude, go to bed," I said as Abigail cuddled up to him. "You have a show in a few hours."

It had been six hours now. Matt had fucked Abigail and me in every possible position, style, and color; in every length, corner, and elevation of the room. And he hadn't come once. The bed was a blood-and-girl cum bath. Stains of my blood patterned the sheets like a Renoir painting.

"Matt, we're leaving. Sorry." I dragged Abigail away.

"You're gonna fuck Tommy Lee at the festival, aren't you?" Matt shouted after us. "I know it!"

In the lobby, the hotel guards were still kind, smiling though we looked like we'd been in bloody battle. We stumbled into daylight. The weekend had begun. The warm buzz of coffee and cake brewed in homes around us. My white cotton dress was stained red and slimy white, and my white stockings were running with blood. I looked like a virgin bride who'd been gang-raped. Abi looked like a rag doll.

We fell into the first taxi we saw, tumbling into the backseat. The taxi driver looked about eighty. He did a double-take and crossed himself. I stared at the big picture of the Pope hanging by his rearview mirror. The Pope stared back.

IN ROCK 'N' ROLL, LOVE IS A DIRTY, DIRTY WORD.

When I returned to LA in September to see my friends, Scott bombarded my phone with messages. I'd been on a roller-coaster ride of debauchery, trying to forget about him and remember why I'd originally been seduced by rock 'n' roll. I'd been on tour with Ratt, Whitesnake, and Def Leppard, and seduced younger bands like Aiden and Black Stone Cherry.

And I had been with a member of Papa Roach at the Download Festival. Tiger eyes blazing on a mischievous face, rippling muscles roaring on his chest, and unrelenting slices of ink tattooed all over his G.I. Joe arms. "All-American soldier you are," I had muttered to him as my two vixen vampy girlfriends and I had pulled him into our hotel room at Download. There the Papa Roach soldier had fucked me and two of my friends all night, taking turns, blowing his load over and over again until I wondered whether he was on Viagra or just a natural scientific marvel. His tattooed arms were giant bulks as he held me down again and again, then Tasha, then Vanna until my friends and me got out of breath and exhausted, and told him to leave our room.

But none of these experiences gave me the feeling of liberation, recklessness, degeneracy, and depravity I'd thought rock 'n' roll embodied. At most, they were amusing diversions. I couldn't let my heart get taken back to a place where it would be trampled on again, so I ignored Scott's messages and tried to get on with my life.

Eventually, he pulled me back in—taking me out on proper dates, showing me off to his friends, and being considerate and romantic. Soon I found myself telling him I loved him—that I wanted to cook for him, buy him gifts, bring him women to have threesomes with, and give him all my love.

But once again I paid the price for breaking the rules of groupie-dom. One night, two days before a show he was playing with L.A. Guns at the Whisky, he told me he'd be bringing another girl to the gig.

"You're very pretty, but you can't just have sex," he said. "You get emotionally involved. You want to be special. But you're not."

I felt my heart just cave in.

"There's so many guys out here tonight—go have fun with them," he said.

"But I just want one guy," I said, feeling the lump rising in my throat.

So while Scott played the Whisky, I walked up and down the Sunset Strip like a zombie. I must have looked destitute. When Taime Downe of Faster Pussycat saw me standing outside the Roxy, he took one look and gave me a massive hug. I just stood there, frozen, staring into space. I couldn't believe I'd allowed myself to get here again.

That was the moment when I understood it all at last.

I was full of heart, full of beautiful love, full of the sunshine my mother and grandmother had fed me every morning, noon, and night in Iran. I wasn't the simple, stagnant, sexless, meek, subservient accessory these rockers seemed to want as girlfriends. I had tried my best to be, but my mind had kept getting in the way. I had too much passion, sexuality, and wild spirit for them.

I was coming to terms with the fact that I was made up of two very strong, conflicting sides. One was the academic, whose home was the university library and whose passion was absorbing books on gender theory and postmodernism. The other was the nymphomaniac in love with rock 'n' roll, who only felt at home sidestage at a concert watching her favorite bands and lovers performing.

Living these two separate lives had exhausted me. It had split me in half.

But that moment of self-knowledge wasn't enough to heal me. When I went back to England a few nights later, I began to get panic attacks. A weird feeling of fear would come over me, and I wouldn't be able to breathe. Then I started feeling disconnected from reality, as if my senses were underwater. This scared me even more, which only increased my panic attacks. And then came the horrific nightmares. I felt drained. I would sleep all day, and wake up with my left hand shaking. I felt like I was losing my sanity.

Around April of that year, my doctor finally checked me into a psychiatric ward. The psychiatrist there diagnosed me with posttraumatic stress disorder. I was given Valium and antidepressants, and put in the ward for a month.

It was a hellish existence. Patients wandered the corridors in a zombie-like state. Some had Parkinson's disease; others had posttraumatic symptoms like I did. We had to have the lights out by eleven P.M. and were awakened at seven A.M. Even so, I had no desire to leave, although I could have checked myself out whenever I wanted. I couldn't understand why I was so ill—why the panic attacks and nightmares, so horrific they seemed sent from Satan, had engulfed my existence. I wondered if my shredded heart had made my brain give up on me. I had been so in love, and suffered one crushing letdown after another in the space of fourteen months at the hands of two men I had absolutely adored. I think I was experiencing a nervous breakdown. But the antidepressants eventually helped numb my heart to the pain of Dizzy and Scott.

I had once thought of the world of rock 'n' roll as a wondrous place, full of free love and free spirits. But it wasn't. It wasn't the sex that had led me to this place—it was the love. And in rock 'n' roll, love is a dirty, dirty word. Perhaps the backstage world was actually too conservative and limiting for my wild spirit. Rock 'n' roll had sold itself as a utopian playground, but as a groupie I wasn't allowed to be as wild as I wanted to be. What was required of me was just a mere fraction of who I was. I wanted free love, creativity, an abundance of sex and poetry, broken taboos; I wanted to be taken places I'd never gone before. I wanted that thrill I'd felt climbing down into my grandmother's cellar all those years ago.

This is why my encounter with the embodiment of rock 'n' roll, Nikki Sixx, for dinner, was the final nail in the coffin. The god of depraved sex and degenerate acts, the epitome of excess and free-spiritedness, the human whose quest for experience knew no boundaries turned out to be nothing more than a businessman, committed to marketing, gardening, and early nights. That night took the color out of that world for me. Having moments of fun here and there with rock stars had splattered me with fleeting orgasms but no continuity. They were nothing more than a series of little snapshots, like the fleeting images spliced together in the moving-picture box from my childhood in Tehran.

The week after my dinner with Nikki Sixx, I agreed to a date with another kind of man: a well-known politician who had been working tirelessly on environmental issues. Finally, here was someone honorable, intellectual, and compassionate I could sit down with for an intellectual conversation. It was about time I left the world of rock 'n' roll and went forward in life with a respectable man.

My mother was ecstatic when I told her about the date. "Finally!" she said, beaming. "He is educated, dignified, and a decent man. I am so glad you're finally getting away from low-class, disrespectful men."

CHAPTER

62

"Your place or mine?" was the first thing Mr. Politician asked me. We had met outside the Leeds train station, where he was picking me up for what I had assumed was a dinner date.

"Ermm." I swallowed nervously. My hands were clammy. I still couldn't quite believe I was going to spend time with such a huge personality, whom I'd seen only on the news. But I had imagined we'd be spending it at a public café, not his place or mine.

It was summer, yet he was wearing a heavy coat. In his mouth, a foul-smelling canoe-shaped pipe chimneyed away with pomp and ceremony, the plume of a man who defended the environment.

The politician and I had met briefly at a fund-raising party the previous year and swapped e-mails so I could send him some of the politically themed essays I was planning to deliver at American and European universities. It was only now, a year later, that we were finally meeting again to discuss politics.

The interior of this respected politician's vintage Jaguar was a fairground of candy wrappers, empty soft drink bottles, and papers. As I tried to keep up with his political chatter, wondering if my university education was too flimsy for his rants about the prime minister and the lunacy of war, the foul fumes of the pipe he perpetually puffed on made me want to vomit.

We pulled into his driveway. Willowy and dusky, his house loomed like a shadow from the distant past. Persian carpets swooned the floors inside like seductresses, curvy and come-hither. Beautiful Arabic paintings and rugs roared from the walls and exotic lanterns hung from every face of the ceiling. Rich cushions with Middle Eastern motifs, curling in deep blushes and tawny yellows, writhed on the settee.

In the sooty black, he didn't turn on any overhead lights—just a small lamp and candles. The flicker of the TV lit up the murky corners of the living room.

"Champagne?" he asked from the kitchen. "I kept it chilled for you."

"I don't drink, sorry." I felt bad. So he came back to join me, and soon he was off on a rant about Tony Blair.

I was enthralled by his knowledge of the world: the Iraq War, Parliament, the well-known politicians he worked with, Islamic fundamentalists. He seemed to know it all. He was very charismatic, his savage alpha-male fighter's spirit and rebel's tongue crowned by a genius political brain. His monologues in support of the downtrodden were inspirational. But his love of the limelight and hero-worship gave him away as the frustrated wannabe rock star he was.

If he couldn't be a genuine rock star, he seemed content to act like a Spinal Tap version of one. "When was the last time you were fucked?" he blurted, interrupting our talk about Hugo Chavez.

"Huh?" I was too shocked to answer.

"I fucked a nineteen-year-old Somalian girl on that couch last night. Just where you're sitting."

I glanced down, looking for stains.

"Met her on Facebook. It's a great place for getting pussy, let me tell you."

I nearly choked on my cranberry juice.

"I took her to quite a few sex parties. Have you ever been to one? There's a beautiful sex club in Paris. No one knows me there."

"Yes, I like sex, too," I stammered. "It's nice."

I checked my choice of attire: Long skirt? Check. No revealing bosom? Check. Sensible shoes? Check. Nothing that revealed any skin. I hadn't been this dumbstruck for a long time.

With a flick of the remote control, he hopped through the TV channels. The room was dark and cold. My drink was gone.

"Aha! There!" he stopped at the movie *Braveheart*. Mel Gibson's Scottish accent hacked at the screen. He left the movie on, with the Scottish fighting the English in bloody battle, and moved on to me. Pulling up my skirt, he dove down between my legs to suddenly lap at my pussy with little bobs of the head like a terrier.

"I'm gonna pick a fight!" Mel Gibson snarled from the TV.

"Ooh. Ahhh," I fake-moaned, trying hard not to laugh. I was frozen to the couch, wondering what the fuck was going on.

"Oh, yeah!" the politician snarled like Mel as he lapped ferociously at my pussy. I wanted to be kind to him—he was trying so hard to do a fantastic job—but he was nothing more than a barrel-shaped old man trying to be sexy.

"Let's go upstairs," he said when he came up for air. And I agreed, because I was curious.

The staircase was lined with photo after photo of famous politicians; his bedroom was enveloped in darkness. He switched on a tiny lantern by the bed and we were off. I lay there and stared into the faces of Fidel Castro and Che Guevara as he humped me, crushing me with his dead weight until I couldn't breathe. After a few minutes, he stopped, wheezing and gasping for breath. He had come. Rolling over, he re-lit his clunky pipe, talked a bit about Bill Clinton, and thrust a book about the Amazon rainforest into my hand. And that was that.

A few days later, the politician called to say he was speaking at a rally and was having a tough day. He asked if he could see me afterward, but I had plans with my family.

"One day soon you'll be at my side when I'm campaigning," he said proudly. "Would you like that?"

"Yes, that would be very interesting." I swooned with genuine excitement.

The next time I saw him, he took me to an actual restaurant. It was an Iranian place where a weepy Persian singer curdled out grievings about love and roses. I ordered *chelo kabab* and rice with *mast-o-moosir* (yogurt with shallots) and various other dips, pickles, and fresh herbs, because I wasn't worried about having garlic breath. I really hoped this time we could talk about literature and politics, and not about how many young Somalian and Middle Eastern girls he was fucking every night.

Velvety compliments dribbled from his purring tongue. His almond-brown eyes narrowed in a catlike slant. "I want you to be my girlfriend," he announced. And before I had a chance to respond, he continued: "And I want you to come on holiday with me to Portugal."

It was a lovely gesture, and I was touched. I swallowed divine apple juice and blushed apple blossom. "Thank you," I stammered, shyly. "That's very sweet."

But there were other things about the way he carried himself that made me queasy—like the way he tossed off stories of how he fucked a different young Somali or Middle Eastern girl every night. Then he told me he wanted to take me to sex parties. "I wanna watch you get fucked by ten guys," he said, bringing his face close to mine. "Ten big black guys with huge cocks. Would you like that?"

He spoke as if he were giving me the gift of a lifetime. The kabab was oozing grease in my stomach. Be his girlfriend? Was part of the deal going to sex clubs so he could watch me get fucked by ten big black guys?

By the time we got back to his house, I felt uncomfortable. Here was a man worshipped by untold thousands of people who voted for him because of the respectful, ethical image he projected—but who spent his free time trawling the Internet for young Somali and Middle Eastern girls to fuck.

"I'm going to New York next week for a conference," he said as we lay in bed. "I'd ask you to come with me, but I'm meeting an Iranian girl there. We've been having phone sex. She's got big tits."

"So why exactly do you want me to be your girlfriend?" I asked.

"Oh, I would want you to be free also. Free to fuck as many guys as you want. In fact, I insist on it."

My stomach began to turn. Looking up at the Fidel Castro portrait was a comfort in comparison. Still, I followed him upstairs again.

"I want you to come," he panted, handing me a dildo from his bedside table.

I felt nauseated that he wanted me to use some unknown girl's dildo. "It's okay. I've got my fingers." As he fumbled his way around my tits, crushing me until the pain made me squeak, I touched myself, looking over at a portrait of Stalin and wondering why he had insisted on such a bushy mustache—and why Che Guevara was such a fucking horndog.

I was bored, but he couldn't tell. As he humped away, wheezing and squeezing his eyes shut, I reached for the remote control. Flicking through the channels, I froze on just the video I needed: one with Axl Rose.

I concentrated hard on Axl, never taking my eyes off him. As Fidel and Che swirled in my head like cake mix, I sighed and juddered and yowled, bringing my Axl-fueled orgasm to a shudder.

The politician came up, pleased with himself.

"Well done! Well done!" He patted my back.

"Thank you very much," I said.

He switched off the TV, clicked off the table lamp, and went to sleep. I decided never to see him again. At least rock stars weren't hypocrites. They were what they embodied. And so was I.

EPILOGUE

Somewhere over Iran
May 1

I don't like flying. Something as big and heavy as an airplane isn't supposed to be up in the air. It's unnatural. That's what gravity is there to prevent. When the plane rattles and shakes and drops like a roller coaster, my heart pounds with fear. People around me sleep like babies, but I just squeeze the metal armrests of my seat and pray.

I pray that the sun's power will penetrate through the clouds. I pray that the plane will keep still and on an even keel. I pray that my final resting place won't be in the sea below. I pray I don't explode in midair and become meat for the fat clouds. I don't want a permanent vacation.

I'm going where the sun is shining. I'm going where the political weather doesn't suit my slutty clothes. I'm going back to my childhood home. I'm going to a place that will love me and where I can love. And I'm going to stay there until I am fed full and all the synthetic layers I have lacquered on start molting.

I will walk the sleeping sunshine alleys of my childhood in plastic slippers. I will walk past the fruit trees and the gardens. I will walk into my grandmother's derelict house and try to be me. I will sleep on the rooftop of my cousin's home under the sharp blaze of the stars so I can shed this skin and hatch the real yolk of me. I will go to the ancient cities of Esfahān and Shiraz to see the splendor of my country's epic history. I can't wait to go to family parties, eat a banquet of Persian foods, and dance like the Iranian girl that I am.

When I was ten years old, I found myself uprooted from the loving nestle of my culture, my community, and my kinship, and thrust into a deserted zone. When I went searching for a new place to belong, rock 'n' roll swept me up and took me into its cradle of family. It slathered me in its culture, smudged and daubed me with its emulsion of colors.

But I have seen the utopian playground of rock 'n' roll up close—I have lived there for years—and I've learned that it's a place of both euphoria and degradation. A place where the sexual double standards are no different from those in an Islamic fundamentalist country. A place where a female's active pursuit of sexual adventure, experimentation, and variety dooms her. It's an extremely limiting place for a so-called wild and free-spirited movement. My view of it was highly, dangerously romanticized.

As the plane descends, past ancient Persian mountains, chalky and restless secret nomads, it jolts and I'm thrown forward. I cling to my Guns N' Roses and Doors songs. Rock 'n' roll is still my love, and I listen to it while my eyes see my other love, beautiful Iran.

I think of my life in rock 'n' roll. I think of the fucking, the passion, and the pain. I wonder what would have happened if I hadn't been sent to England. I might have married my childhood sweetheart, endured the war, and suffered the massive restrictions imposed upon women. But I probably wouldn't have lost my childhood joy and spirit, and I would have been surrounded by family, friends, and possibly some stability.

My heart swells with love. And I want to give it to the whole world. As the plane lands, I am so happy. From top to toe, I am fully covered in black Islamic garb.

But underneath I'm wearing no panties. Just in case.

ACKNOWLEDGMENTS

I wrote most of this book when I was at university, where my soul was fed by Foucault, Baudrillard, Butler, and Woolf. To my university and my tutors: a big humble hug of adoration for giving me a lifeline by letting me immerse myself in the other love of my life, academia. Especially to Jonathan Neale, who taught me to be really brave inside and to never censor myself.

My eternal love and gratitude goes to my editor, Neil Strauss, who has believed in my writing from the beginning and has tirelessly championed my book. Thank you for dedicating so much of your time to get my book out there and for having so much faith in me. Ever since I read *The Dirt*, I knew Mötley Crüe was Mary Poppins compared to me!

Anthony Bozza: Thank you for your understanding and generosity . . . and for being so nice and making me laugh during the tough times. I appreciate everything you have done.

Cal Morgan: Thank you so much for your kindness and your amazing support and guidance. Your words of encouragement and wisdom mean the world to me, and I am so grateful. To Karen Louth and Kristine Miller for your time and patience. And a big thanks to Todd Gallopo.

Monique Mayes: Giant thank yous and even bigger hugs for all the fucking hard work you have done day and night. Your unbelievable patience and tender loving voice have been beyond amazing in the process of this book.

Gottfried and Renate Helnwein: I am honored to have been given the chance to use your images in this little book of mine. I have been in awe of your watercolors and photography for as long as I can remember; the images of abused children have resonated in my being since I was a child myself.

To my guardian angel D—for all that you have done for me. You are not human; you are a pure saint. You should always know that.

Mummy—Ma, *ghorboonet beram*. You have sacrificed so much for me and your family. You have given your life to us selflessly. The strength that you have in your heart and your guts is beyond anyone's comprehension.

My darling brother, one of the most beautiful, funny, warm, pure-hearted generous souls I have the honor of knowing. Your creative genius and heart-breaking documentaries inspire me.

To my rock-and-roll family: Lori—my soul sister who went through everything with me. Sidestage is never the same without you. I love you so much. Rock 'n' roll would never have happened without you. Em—my poet, my Keef Richards lover—I can't believe all the things we have been through together. I love you. Ostara, my fairy angel. You are dirty as hell and I love it! A combination of Princess Diana and Marquis de Sade. My ideal girl! Unending thank yous for being so kind and generous to me. You truly are one of a kind. Paul Brannigan—I love you even though you love emos. You are sexier than any rock star and you should know that! Thank you for all your support and time. Stephen T—a thousand thank yous. Danny Demure—the king of Sunset Strip and my LA brother—how could I have survived without you? Sabrina, you were the only one who knew what I was going through during "that" time. Eternal love for being there for me. How can I thank you enough? I am so happy for you and your baby boy. Laura, thank you for your huge support and endless chats and patience. We have so many more backstage adventures to come! JB—you started it. And to all the rock stars who have given me some of the most beautifully deranged and exhilarating times of my life! Thank you for your kindness, your love, and making me feel like family. Your crazy exterior has a very protective and loving humanity underneath it.

Thank you to the Buckcherry boys who came up with the alternative title for my book: *Are You Fucking Man Enough? The Legend of Roxana.*

To my beautiful country Iran . . . you majestic dusky seductress, you. You are the most beautiful country my eyes have ever seen. I will be buried in you; I know it.

And, finally, to all the men and women who work tirelessly against the suffering and horrific cruelty to animals that goes on in our world. Especially to those who try so hard to stop the medieval torture and skinning alive of over one billion cats and dogs annually, just for their fur so that the masses can buy it and wear it. I still haven't been able to watch an entire video of those acts. To the people who fight this bloodcurdling cruelty, you truly are my idols.

PHOTO CREDITS

COLOR INSERT CREDITS

ABOUT THE AUTHOR

ROXANA SHIRAZI WAS BORN IN TEHRAN, IRAN, AND WAS SENT TO ENGLAND AT AGE TEN. SHE HOLDS A MASTERS IN ENGLISH FROM BATH SPA UNIVERSITY, AND SPEAKS AT INTERNATIONAL WOMEN'S CONFERENCES ON THE SUBJECT OF GENDER AND IDENTITY. SHE CURRENTLY LIVES, LOVES, AND WRITES IN LONDON.

★★★★★★★★★★★★★★★★★★★★★★★★★★★★★★★★★★★

COMING SOON FROM IGNITER

★★★★★★★★★★★★★★★★★★★★★★★★★★★★★★★★★★★

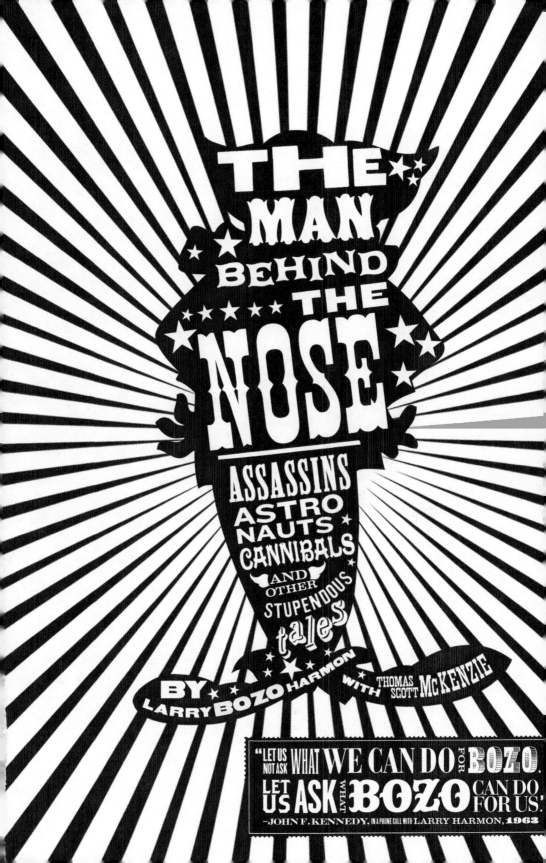